HOLMES, M. The labour government
1974-79

1717918

HF   5/88   £ 8.95

330.941

Please renew/return this item by the last date shown.

So that your telephone call is charged at local rate, please call the numbers as set out below:

	From Area codes 01923 or 0208:	From the rest of Herts:
Renewals:	01923 471373	01438 737373
Enquiries:	01923 471333	01438 737333
Minicom:	01923 471599	01438 737599

L32b

23 FEB 2002

15 March

4\12

2 6 APR 2002

16 DEC 2005

25 MAY 2006

' 33

By the same author

POLITICAL PRESSURE AND ECONOMIC POLICY:
BRITISH GOVERNMENT, 1970–4

THE LABOUR GOVERNMENT, 1974–79

Political Aims and Economic Reality

Martin Holmes

Lecturer in Politics
Lady Margaret Hall, Oxford

MACMILLAN
PRESS

© Dr. Martin Holmes 1985

First edition 1985
Reprinted 1987

Published by
THE MACMILLAN PRESS LTD
Houndmills, Basingstoke, Hampshire RG21 2XS
and London
Companies and representatives
throughout the world

Printed in Hong Kong

British Library Cataloguing in Publication Data
Holmes Martin, 1954–
The Labour government, 1974–79.
1. Great Britain–Economic policy–1945–
I. Title
330.941′0857   HC256.6
ISBN 0–333–36735–9
ISBN 0–333–42820–X Pbk

CONTENTS

ACKNOWLEDGEMENTS

The author and publishers wish to thank the following who have kindly given permission for the use of copyright material:

Andre Deutsch Limited for an extract from *Inside the Treasury* by Joel Barnett.
David Higham Associates Limited on behalf of Barbara Castle, and Holmes & Meier Publishers Inc. for an extract from *The Castle Diaries, 1974–6*.
David Higham Associates Limited on behalf of Lord Wilson of Rievaulx for an extract from *Final Term*.
William Keegan and Rupert Pennant-Rae for extracts from *Who Runs the Economy?*
Times Newspapers Limited for an extract from the article 'The Day the £ Nearly Died' by Stephen Fay and Hugo Young, in *The Sunday Times* (1978).

My thanks are also due to the many Labour cabinet ministers, junior ministers, MPs, trade-union leaders and civil servants, who gave their time to be interviewed in the course of writing this book.

Special thanks are also due to Gillian Peele for her constant encouragement and wise advice, and to Sam Brittan who shared with me his economic knowledge and expertise.

My secretarial assistants, ably orchestrated by Alison Clarke, also deserve praise and thanks.

I am also grateful to Mr T. M. Farmiloe of Macmillan for the speed, efficiency and courtesy with which he handled the typescript.

Needless to say, any faults or errors in the following pages are my responsibility alone.

Martin Holmes
Lady Margaret Hall
Oxford

CHAPTER I

The Short Parliament

WILSON'S DUAL INHERITANCE

It is not an exaggeration to claim that no post-war Prime Minister took office in more difficult circumstances than Harold Wilson on 4 March 1974. Apart from heading the first minority Labour Government since 1931 – with the consequent necessity of another general election in a short period of time – Wilson's inheritance was a dual one. Firstly, he inherited an appalling economic situation partly created by the policies of the 1970–4[1] Heath Government and partly inflicted externally by the world oil crisis. Secondly he inherited a Labour Party which in opposition had moved further leftwards than Wilson had hoped, and which, now in office, expected immediate radical socialist solutions. Put bluntly Wilson had to keep his party together as party leader as well as attending to prime ministerial policy determination in relation to the economic situation.

Wilson's Cabinet reflected his task of balancing left and right in the party. Michael Foot, whose career had seemed destined to end as a backbench voice of conscience on the left, was made Employment Minister. Tony Benn was appointed Industry Secretary, a crucial portfolio for the left, though in Mr Benn's case his move leftwards in the party had been comparatively recent and at a late stage in his ministerial career. Barbara Castle, who had retained her left-wing credentials after the *In Place of Strife* debacle of the late 1960s, was the Social Services Secretary. The left was therefore well represented in comparison to previous Labour Cabinets and had the added advantage of greatly increased support in the party and trade union movement as a whole. Thus Wilson later recalled that 'Foot was good Cabinet material, and he did a great job with the unions. When I told the union leaders Michael Foot was Secretary of State for Employment, Jack Jones had a broad grin on his face.'[2]

1

However many of the figures of stature and considerable ministerial experience in the Cabinet were on the right. Roy Jenkins returned to the Home Office, Tony Crosland was made Environment Secretary, Denis Healey became Chancellor, despite being an unimpressive Shadow Chancellor, and Reg Prentice was appointed Education Secretary. The rest of the Cabinet, including Foreign Secretary James Callaghan, were considered to be in the centre, though with hindsight, centre–right would be more accurate.

Wilson's task in moulding a collective will – in accordance with the traditional doctrine of collective Cabinet responsibility – was therefore made more difficult simply because he had to include a left–right balance. Whilst this arrangement was a strength in terms of internal Labour Party politics it was arguably a weakness in policy formation.

One cabinet minister recalled that:

Wilson's main purpose was to keep the Labour Party together. The Cabinet reflected the divisions in the party and Wilson would give us lectures on the need to speak with one voice.

74–6 was a strong Cabinet of individual talents but it didn't pull together. It reflected the contradictions within the party. You could divide the Cabinet into three. The right – Jenkins, Lever, myself, sometimes Mason and Shepherd; the left – Benn, Foot, Barbara [Castle], Shore on some issues, and later Booth and Silkin. The soggy centre did what the PM decided, waiting to see which way the wind was blowing.[3]

Both aspects of Wilson's dual inheritance fed upon each other. For whilst the economic inheritance demanded tough measures, as was the case in all Western economies, the party's move leftwards reflected in the February 1974 election manifesto commitments, was essentially geared to economic circumstances intrinsically more favourable in terms of economic growth. The Cabinet battles and party disputes described by Harold Wilson[4] and Barbara Castle[5] could not escape from this central dichotomy.

In March 1974 the most immediate aspects of Wilson's dual legacy were dominated by the economic situation. The country was still on the three-day week imposed by Mr Heath; inflation was accelerating with wage rate rises up to 20 per cent;

unemployment was the highest since 1940; public expenditure was out of control and the balance of payments in chronic deficit. Mr Wilson could be blamed for none of these figures. Indeed Wilson is right to stress the serious balance of payments crises which had confronted him on both occasions he took office from the Conservatives. In mentioning the dimension of the balance of payments inheritance Wilson has argued, rightly, that:

> It seems to be almost a law of British politics that when Labour becomes the Government, we inherit a record balance-of-payments deficit, and, equally, that we bequeath a record surplus when we go out of office.
>
> In 1964 the out-turn for the year was a deficit of £356 million, the fourth quarter running at a rate close to £600 million. When we left office in 1970, we left a surplus for the year of £695 million which rose to £1,058 million in 1971, an all-time record. In the concluding months of 1973 the worsening of the overseas trade and payments figures had already led to emergency measures by the Conservative Chancellor of the Exchequer. The final figure for the year was a deficit of £909 million, which rose to £3·537 million in 1974. But the underlying trend, influenced of course by monetary movements, some of them speculative, was already disastrous before the end of 1973. Calculations by the Treasury showed that in the fourth quarter of 1973 the deficit was running at a rate of £4,000 million: of this only £90 million were accounted for by payments on high-priced oil. Thus the basic figures, disregarding oil, were by far the worst since trade and payments figures were first officially collected in 1822.[6]

This balance of payments legacy and the consequent problems of financing the external deficit were to bedevil the whole 1974–9 period of Labour administration. What made the problem worse was that the left was initially oblivious to it and it was not until 1976 that an 'alternative strategy' emerged with which the left could establish alternative policies that recognised the external constraints on the British economy.

The Wilson Government's first priority in dealing with the economic legacy was to solve the dispute with the miners and return the country to a full working week. Wilson later recalled that 'I came in with a State of Emergency – it was almost illegal to

4 *The Labour Government, 1974–79*

put a kettle on in a factory.'[7] Within two days of taking office the dispute was settled conceding the miners 29 per cent, more than they had expected when in July 1973 they put in for a 25 per cent increase.[8] Similarly the State of Emergency, which had lasted almost three months was ended and the three-day week abandoned. However Barbara Castle noted that even at the first real Cabinet meeting of the new government Michael Foot warned that the miners' settlement didn't mean that 'we had abandoned Stage III of Heath's incomes policy. That must stay until he had negotiated the basis of a voluntary agreement with the T.U.C., otherwise the flood-gates would be opened.'[9] Like the external payments problem, that of pay policy was to dominate the life of the government from the first Cabinet to the last. Similarly the party's leftward drift made an acceptable pay policy most difficult to procure.

If the economic crisis was Wilson's first part of the dual inheritance, the party's move to the left, and considerable manifesto commitments to radical change, was the second part. During its opposition years 1970–4 the left made significant advances.[10] Leaving aside the contentious issue of the EEC, the right was on the defensive throughout the 1970–4 period. A number of factors contributed to this development. There was a sense of disappointment that 1966–70 had been a wasted opportunity in that socialist policies had been sacrificed at the balance of payments and devaluation altars. There was the natural reaction to what was often regarded as a right-wing confrontationist Heath Government whose incomes policy restraints and Industrial Relations Act were to some on the left different not in principle but in degree from the Wilson incomes policy and *In Place of Strife* proposals. There was the growing march of the left in constituency parties where party activists tended to be more middle-class, intellectual, younger socialists rather than Labour's traditional working-class, trade-union stalwarts. Not that the unions themselves, and particularly national leadership, had been immune from a shift to the left. Hodgson rightly notes that:

> This radical shift in policy can only be explained by the leftward shift in the Party as a whole and the increased power and confidence of the trade unions. The latter, now nominally committed to the Labour Party's proposals for industrial

re-generation, did not want to repeat the disillusioning experience of 1964–70. By 1974, most of the major trade unions had Left or moderate-Left leaderships and an ideological commitment to the main planks of Labour Party policy. This was the counterweight to the veiled opposition to public ownership within the Labour Cabinet.[11]

All these factors made policy formation a most acute process of right/left disagreement, which given the importance of the National Executive Committee, elected by party conference, in policy-making meant that the left made considerable progress. There was no attempt to resurrect the spirit of *In Place of Strife*. Indeed, repeal of the Industrial Relations Act and further measures to strengthen trade union powers were promised. Unemployment, which had passed the dreaded politically-sensitive 1 million mark under Heath, aroused great passion in the labour movement and many regarded full employment as attainable as long as a Labour Government was determined to attain it. The rebuilding of the bridges between the party and the unions, exemplified by the joint TUC/Labour Party Liaison Committee, led to a commitment to return to free collective bargaining especially as compulsory and statutory wage control was an evil then associated with the Heath Government's incomes policy. Furthermore the impetus for radical programmes for British industry based not on the 1964 encouragement of the 'white heat of the technological revolution' but on extension of public ownership and control, was accelerated by the Heath Government's extension of the public sector in industry through the nationalisation of Rolls Royce, the Upper Clyde Shipbuilders rescue and the 1972 Industry Act.[12]

In this way in February 1973 a joint TUC/Labour Party Liaison Committee 'Statement on Economic Policy and the Cost of Living' envisaged a Labour Government committed to

(a) what it termed 'a wide ranging and permanent system of price controls', particularly on food;
(b) a new approach to housing and rent that would include the repeal of the 1972 Housing Finance Act, the long-run municipalisation of private rented property, the public ownership of required building land, and the building of at least 400,000 houses a year;

(c) the strengthening of public transport, and experiments with free public transport in major conurbations;

(d) a large-scale redistribution of income and wealth, by wealth taxes, gift taxes, and steeply progressive direct taxation;

(e) the end of prescription charges, and an immediate rise in pensions, with pensions thereafter to be annually updated in line with average earnings;

(f) the expansion of investment and the control of capital by further public ownership, by the extension of state supervision of private investment, and by new measures of control to prevent excessive investment overseas;

(g) the extension of industrial democracy, by bringing investment policy and closure policy into the scope of collective bargaining.[13]

Consequently at the 1973 Labour Party Conference the document 'Labour's Programme for Britain' outlined a future Labour Government's policy based on the extension of public ownership, a system of planning agreements with major companies, and the passing of a new Industry Act. These and other measures relating to social welfare, housing and pensions, formed the basis of what became known as the Social Contract whereby the government would carry out its stated – and agreed – programme of radical socialist reforms in return for voluntary wage restraint from the trade unions.

The Social Contract was thus born out of the turmoils of the Labour Party in opposition between 1970 and 1974. One junior minister at the time recalled that: 'The Social Contract flowered in the setting of the Heath Government. We could no longer assume a relationship between the government and the unions, so we had to do a deal.'[14] It represented a significant move to the left, away from Labour's 'managerialism', 'efficiency' and 'technology' of 1964–70 and was Wilson's inheritance from his party in March 1974. Although it was not clear at the time in the Labour Party that the Social Contract conflicted directly with Wilson's inheritance from the Conservatives and from the world oil crisis, it was not surprising that, for the time being, the government should seek to get the best of both worlds.

THE SOCIAL CONTRACT

Working closely with the trade unions, and particularly with Jack Jones of the T & GWU and Hugh Scanlon of the AUEW, the government was able to carry out many Social Contract obligations in a short space of time. Obviously the radical restructuring of industry envisaged under the Social Contract, and a return to full employment, were not amenable to fulfilment before the next election but a number of other measures were within the government's immediate powers to confer. Indeed the extent of the measures did not lend credibility to the view that minority governments must be hamstrung and impotent.

Following the settlement with the miners the Pay Board was abolished and the policy of compulsory wage restraint jettisoned in July. The Price Code and Price Commission were retained and a rent freeze imposed. Museum charges, introduced by the Conservatives, were abandoned as were the wasteful plans for a third London airport and a Channel tunnel. A new Ministry of Prices, Consumer Protection and Fair Trading was established with Shirley Williams, as Secretary of State, sitting in the Cabinet. Food subsidies were subsequently introduced in Denis Healey's first budget. The much hated Industrial Relations Act was repealed, itself a central, rather than a peripheral, part of the Social Contract.

The Act was supplanted by the Trade Union and Labour Relations Act 1974, which abolished the NIRC and repealed the Industrial Relations Act though retaining the provisions on unfair dismissal, provisions for industrial tribunals and conciliation. The legal powers of the unions in relation to trade disputes were also strengthened. Barbara Castle noted in her diary in April 1974 that Harold Wilson was acting as 'custodian of the Manifesto . . . playing it straight down the line of party policy. After being crucified for four years for his determination to keep the party together at all costs, he now was determined to justify himself by sticking firmly to the policy we had thrashed out between the Shadow Cabinet and the NEC.'[15] In view of the range of measures taken in the Short Parliament such an analysis was perfectly rational at the time.

Important though such measures were in political terms, attention rightly focused on Chancellor Healey's attempts to improve the economy. Healey's first two budgets in March and

July 1974 were presented not only to the background of the Social Contract obligations and the near certainty of an imminent general election but to the background of an economy seriously out of equilibrium. Difficult or unpopular decisions were therefore harder to take in political terms than is normally the case for a Chancellor presenting his first budget. It may be argued that the government was not prepared to face the economic realities in 1974. As one senior Treasury official put it, though not in a disparaging way, 'when the rest of the world was deflating in 1974–5 we were not'.[16] Similarly Keegan and Pennant-Rae noted that:

While the Government was trying to avoid unpleasant policy decisions, two things were taking their toll. The rest of the world was not reacting to the oil crisis in the manner prescribed by Whitehall Keynesians; instead there was a huge cutback in demand, with countries like Germany and, especially, Japan throwing all their efforts into balancing their payments, come what may. The world found itself in the midst of the worst recession since the war, and the UK – through lack of demand for exports – was dragged into this whether it liked it or not. Meanwhile business confidence at home was shattered by inflation and the problems it posed for making future plans for investment in new factories and plant. The UK went into recession anyway, but after most other countries.[17]

Ironically, of Denis Healey's two pre-October election budgets the first in March seemed more aware of the seriousness of the economic situation than the second in July. In general Joel Barnett is right to claim that 'the first months of the new government were characterised by our spending money which in the event we did not have'.[18] One minister recalled that 'Public expenditure in a sense was similar to 1964 when we assumed we could be successful and obtain benefits before it was shown they were there. Both governments started without full majorities and so couldn't take a long view.'[19] The March budget may be described as mildly deflationary.

Pensions were substantially increased, in accordance with the Social Contract and following Jack Jones's prolonged campaigning for higher pensions in real terms, as were unemployment, sickness and other short-term benefits. Food subsidies were raised to £500 million and housing subsidies were raised by £70 million, increases which, falling equally on those with low and high incomes, are not necessarily defensible on socialist grounds. However, as Harold Wilson put it, 'the need to cut the public sector borrowing requirement, particularly after the previous increase, inevitably meant a massive increase in taxation'.[20] VAT was therefore extended to confectionery and similar goods and to petrol and other road funds. Together with traditional, ritualistic increases in taxes on drink and tobacco, indirect taxation was raised by £680 million.

Among the changes in direct taxation personal allowances were increased at a cost to the Exchequer of £684 million and the basic rate of income tax was raised by 3p in the £ along with what the Conservatives regarded as draconian increases in the tax of higher earned income and investment income. These changes were to yield £954 million and with increased social expenditure by £700 million offset by a £1400 million tax yield the Chancellor could reduce the PSBR by £1500 million from the 1973–4 figure of £4250 million. However it may still be argued, with hindsight, that the PSBR remained too high given the economic situation of a vast balance of payments deficit and rising inflation. When, later, the PSBR turned out to have been £4 billion short of the real figure, Joel Barnett was right to note that the 'whole course of the next five years might have been changed had we decided we could not plan for such a high PSBR and therefore not increased public expenditure to the extent we did'.[21] If Mr Barnett is right, which the evidence suggests, the IMF crisis, with the political agony of spending cuts for a Labour Government, could have been avoided. It is a truism in British politics that increasing public expenditure is easier than reducing it when departmental ministers and other vested interests seek to preserve their domain. The whole tone of Barbara Castle's diaries are testimony to this fact.

This truism was demonstrated in Mr Healey's July 'mini-budget'. The best thing that can be said about the 'mini-budget' is that it had inevitably to be an election budget. However its economic effects were, and still are, less defensible. Partly because of the wage threshold increases[22] still operating from the Heath incomes policy, for which Mr Healey was not, of course, culpable, the Chancellor decided to cut the VAT rate from 10 per cent to 8 per cent in the hope of reducing the price-inflationary threshold increases. Similarly food subsidies were extended by £50 million in the hope of bringing down the retail price index. These measures, along with the doubling of the regional employment premium at a cost of £118 million simply provided an added inflationary boost to the economy which, given the balance of payments situation and the quadrupling of oil prices required an opposite solution. Harold Wilson has rightly argued that 'inflation is father to unemployment'[23] and defends his government's action over the July 'mini-budget'. But the real effects were to make both inflation and unemployment worse. As Samuel Brittan has analysed with particular clarity:

> Mr. Healey has deliberately tried to maintain employment at a time of accelerating inflation by raising home demand. His pre-election cut in consumer taxes in July [1974] never received the critical censure it deserved. He may have succeeded for a time in keeping the British unemployment percentage below that of other countries, but at the expense of greater and more prolonged unemployment in the period still ahead of us. A fiscal stimulus can sometimes act for a short time to sustain demand, although it will eventually peter out if not backed by a corresponding expansion of the money supply.[24]

Similarly Joel Barnett admits that as a consequence of the July measures 'there can be little doubt we planned for too high a level of public expenditure in the expectations of levels of growth that, in the event, never materialized'.[25] The July measures, with the centrepiece of holding down unemployment to below 800 000, were a classic example of the government fulfilling its side of the Social Contract and indeed justifying its action in terms of the *success* (my emphasis) of the Social Contract. Significantly Barbara Castle reveals in her diaries that before the March budget Denis Healey had stated that he would look again at restoring public expenditure cuts if unemployment started to rise.[26] The government was therefore prepared to react in the entirely conventional Keynesian way to rising unemployment irrespective of the causes of unemployment and other overriding economic commitments. That other Western industrialised countries were taking an opposite path was irrelevant to those like Harold Lever who commented that 'when I look at what other countries are doing I congratulate the Chancellor on his courage'.[27] One cabinet minister recalled that 'there was enormous sensitivity to unemployment after Heath's 1 million, and this led to a feeling we had to protect jobs at any cost. Benn was attracted to concepts like Meriden and Jones and Scanlon also wanted job protection. We fell over ourselves carrying out the Social Contract obligations – very rapid increases in public expenditure, pensions, rent control and food subsidies – without getting wage restraint in return.'[28]

One cabinet minister, recalling the ease with which public expenditure was rising, noted with surprise that 'when I went to the Treasury for £60 million for the Belfast Harland & Wolff Shipyard I got it'.[29] In general the Social Contract period was an Indian summer for spending ministers until the realisation dawned that the unions were unable, or unwilling, to deliver their side of the bargain. However when the £6 pay policy eventually emerged in July 1975 it may be argued that the early Social Contract phase had at least accustomed union leaders to the philosophy of a *quid pro quo* with the government. Thus one minister argued that 'the Social Contract did one useful thing in that it involved the unions and made them feel responsible which made subsequent deals later possible'.[30]

However in July 1974 when Phase III of the Heath policy elapsed, the Social Contract obligations on wages were firmly in the unions' hands. The political will, however, both on the government's side and, more naturally, from the TUC was lacking to make inflation control a priority if such necessary measures could prove damaging in an election run-up. The electoral restraint in the summer of 1974 was a significant factor. But it would be wrong to claim it was the only factor.

An equally important consideration was that the Labour Party in opposition had not developed a coherent anti-inflationary strategy beyond criticising the Heath incomes policy as unfair and calling for stricter prices and rent controls. A prices policy in accordance with the reformist spirit of the Social Contract did exist but – and this is the key point – both compulsory wage control and deflationary measures were strictly ruled out. Wage control and cutting public expenditure were heretical to the Social Contract. The emphasis was on voluntary restraint under free collective bargaining (itself arguably a contradictory concept) together with expansionist policies to reduce unemployment. Inflation control was simply not a political priority under the

Social Contract that emerged in the Short Parliament. One left-wing backbench MP recalled that 'the left didn't have a policy line on inflation. We had a negative reaction to it.'[31]

Furthermore the reliance on voluntary restraint was thought to be sufficient almost irrespective of whether the government was inflating or deflating and it is arguable that, given continuing expansionary Keynesian policies in 1974-5 no amount of artificial holding down of wages, either voluntary or statutory, could prevent inflation. Because it failed to face economic reality the whole Social Contract strategy on inflation was fatally flawed.

Although the government had denounced the Heath incomes policy and envisaged the Social Contract succeeding under free collective bargaining, both government and unions were still talking in the language of incomes policy. As one prominent economic commentator argued:

> The Labour election victory did not lead to any large change of economic philosophy. Denis Healey, who became Chancellor in March 1974, took over in all essentials Mr. Heath's corporatist and incomes policy approach. There were personal similarities between the two men in their abrasiveness and intolerance of criticism. But there was also a great deal in common in their vision of society. Both favoured a form of state-managed capitalism with taxpayers' money available on concessionary terms to approved firms.[32]

Thus, apart from the miners, the nurses, teachers and postmen were regarded as 'special cases' before Stage III expired and in June 1974 the TUC General Council produced 'guidelines' for pay published as 'Collective Bargaining and the Social Contract'.

Like much of the language of incomes policy the guidelines sounded reasonable and painless. Their chief task would be not to reduce the rate of inflation but to 'maintain real incomes' by claiming 'compensation' for rises in the cost of living. A twelve-month interval between increases was recommended and a low pay target of a basic minimum wage of £30 a week was suggested, without any hint that this would increase unemployment among the low paid themselves or distort relativities. The June 'Collective Bargaining and the Social Contract' contribution from the unions to the Social Contract was the high water mark of incomes policy philosophy even if it did not involve statutory or compulsory powers.

However well intentioned, like the Heath incomes policy before it, the Social Contract's reliance on voluntary restraint was essentially irrelevant as long as the government was expanding the economy despite the oil crisis and accelerating inflation. Between October 1973 and October 1974 wages rose 22 per cent and the RPI 17 per cent, a twelve-month period covered by a statutory incomes policy and a subsequent voluntary policy of restraint. Given the oil price increases, the deficit-financed inflation of the Heath period and Healey's continued Keynesian expansion, especially the lack of control over public expenditure, such figures were not surprising. The language and trappings of incomes policy could affect the political climate of the forthcoming election campaign but could not affect the economic reality – the pound, for example, had depreciated by 20 per cent between 1972 and 1974.

As Barnes and Reid rightly note, 'the Trades Union Congress at the beginning of September was a pre-election rally, the main purpose of which was to secure endorsement of "Collective Bargaining and the Social Contract" as evidence of the unity of the labour movement'.[33] Harold Wilson noted that in his speech to the TUC 'there were a series of anything but oblique references to "the coming General Election". Few who heard it or read it were in any doubt that, in parliamentary terms, there was an odour of dissolution about.'[34]

Nevertheless, Hugh Scanlon's AUEW only backed the TUC's line on voluntary wage restraint after stronger proposals on price controls and wealth redistribution were accepted into TUC policy. Nor was the unanimous acceptance of 'Collective Bargaining and the Social Contract' as monolithic a view as might be supposed. Coates is right to claim that the most radical trade union leaders were unhappy with wage restraint of any sort.[35]

Of the senior trade union leaders Jack Jones was the most enthusiastic for the success of the Social Contract both in terms of the government's obligations and in terms of wage restraint. Jones feared that the return of a Conservative Government would be disastrous for the trade union movement and the whole period of the Short Parliament bears his mark. An illuminating account of Jones's commitment to the Labour Government can be found in

Barbara Castle's description of his support for both sides of the Social Contract when the Labour Party/TUC Liaison Committee met in June 1974 to discuss 'Collective Bargaining and the Social Contract'. Mrs Castle noted that:

> Liaison Committee with TUC met in sombre mood, only deepened by that sombre panelling at Congress House. H.W. sent apologies. So did Hughie Scanlon, Willie Simpson and George Smith. Also Alex Kitson. But Jack was there, brooding with his usual stern intensity. Our business was to discuss the TUC document 'Collective Bargaining and the Social Contract'. It was already approved by their Economic Committee and due to go to the General Committee this week. As Alf Allen pointed out from the chair, the document was not brought to us for endorsement. At first we hesitated to comment, till Ron Hayward blundered in to say that, with an election imminent, he wished there would be more speeches from the trade union side about their contribution to the Social Contract. They looked hurt: they had obviously expected a warmer welcome than this. David Basnett and others pointed out that helpful speeches never received any publicity, though plenty were being made. Jack retorted huffily that we are bound to have 'exaggerated' wage claims – e.g., the miners' and engineers'. Many speeches, he said, were being made from the trade union side but, by and large, 'the press and TV don't want to know'. He thought the document was a 'pretty good trade union response'. It wasn't just a question of the size of wage claims but, even more important from an inflation point of view, 'how far we can reduce the number of disputes'. And he added earnestly, 'We are genuinely trying to make a contribution to the reduction of tension.'[36]

Albert Booth, then only a junior minister but who later joined the Cabinet, thought Jones to have undergone the same changes that had affected the T & GWU. Mr Booth put it that:

> I only came to know Jones when I became a minister and he was a man who changed with his union. He was an instrument and a product of that change. He had seen the dominance of the TUC barons and was old enough to remember Bevin so that he knew what absolute authority was. He wanted change to

involve the unions 'lay' members but by then he was enmeshed in the baron's seat.[37]

Another cabinet minister recalled that: 'Jones was forceful and the peacemaker for the TUC. What Jones wanted he usually got. He had a close relationship with Foot and it was as if a Jones/Foot axis was governing the country.'[38] A backbench MP commented that 'Len Murray never wanted to fight the big union bosses'[39] which helps to explain why in the autumn of 1974 Murray was as keen to support voluntary pay restraint under the Social Contract as he had been keen to oppose pay restraint under the Conservatives. What was concentrating the minds of the TUC was the general election which it was announced on 18 September would take place on 10 October.

THE OCTOBER 1974 ELECTION

The success and continuing prospect of the Social Contract was central to Labour's campaign. It held out the hope of conciliation between the government and the unions to an electorate whose memories were still fresh with the 'confrontation' of the Heath era and the circumstances of the February election. Mr Wilson, as ever the shrewd tactician in an election campaign, cleverly exploited this fact and Mr Heath and the Conservatives never had a satisfactory reply that would convince the voters otherwise. Indeed the Conservatives seemed unable to convince the electorate of very much and Mr Heath's campaign performance can be described at best as uninspiring and at worst as disastrous. Even holding out the prospect of a coalition government – itself an admission of the Conservative loss of self-confidence – failed to inspire the electorate.

Certainly compared to the trauma of February the October election was, as Harold Wilson put it, 'relatively quiet and uneventful'.[40] Labour made the running from the start and opinion polls – now regarded with greater suspicion after doubts on their accuracy cast both in the 1970 and the February 1974 elections – gave Labour the lead. The mood in the Labour Party was far more confident than in February and Harold Wilson's jaunty self-confidence was reminiscent of 1966. One minister recalled that 'I expected victory in October 1974, Wilson was a superb tactician'.[41] Apart from the feebler Conservative campaign which included advocacy of voluntary incomes policy, non-reintroduction of the Industrial Relations Act, food subsidies and higher pensions, all of which Labour could already claim to have achieved, the Liberals sought to maintain the impetus they had achieved in February. The Liberal leader, Jeremy Thorpe, an effective and energetic election campaigner but with little command of policy issues or priorities, hoped to increase the Liberal vote from the six million of February to up to ten million. Unlike the Conservative campaign, the Liberal campaign made the best of what it had and the major parties had to take the Liberals seriously given the possibility of another hung Parliament.

But for Labour there were good reasons to fear the decline of the Liberal vote. Harold Wilson has succinctly argued that:

I was worried about the Liberal vote.

The Liberals in the main do very well under a Conservative Government. Any Government, Conservative or Labour, becomes unpopular over a period of time, particularly if it is trying to follow a long-term strategy in the short term. So in by-elections, and to a lesser extent in a General Election, people who had voted for the Government party tend to stay at home or to switch their vote. In by-elections, particularly but also in General Elections, there are many Conservatives who would rather be found dead than vote Labour, but who have a sense of duty that they must vote, and who therefore find themselves in the Liberal camp. This certainly happened in the first election of 1974; the political consequence was not so much the number of Liberals elected, fourteen, but the number of seats where Labour came in on a minority vote, through Conservative votes going Liberal. But when Labour is in power many Conservatives return to the fold.[42]

In the end Labour's fears were unfounded, as irrespective of the total percentage vote for the Liberals, the key marginals were Labour versus Conservative battles, such as Bolton West, Bury and Radcliffe, Oxford, Peterborough and Hemel Hempstead where Liberal strength was less marked than in safe Conservative seats, where in February tactical voting had pushed the Liberals into second place with Labour third.

One particular interesting aspect of the campaign which Joel Barnett accurately describes[43] was Denis Healey's claim that inflation was down to 8·4 per cent. Because of the temporary effects of the July cut in VAT to 8 per cent Denis Healey could claim that the then three-month rate, if annualised, would be 8·4 per cent, which, if the economy was dependent on no other factors, would have been correct. In fact the 8·4 per cent claim was an electoral tactic of a statistical sleight of hand but it enabled the Conservatives later to accuse Labour of being solely responsible for the increase in inflation which occurred in 1975.

Mr Barnett, rightly, argues that:

> The more intelligent Conservatives knew, of course, that this was never more than a debating point. Indeed, the transparently honest Keith Joseph, having made the whole-hearted conversion from a big-spending Minister of Health to a 101 per cent monetarist, could always be relied upon to concede, to the embarrassment of Ted Heath – his former Prime Minister – and many of his current colleagues, that the high rates of inflation in the early years of the Labour Government were primarily caused by the profligate money supply policy of the previous Conservative one.[44]

However, an irony remained that, assuming Mr Healey's 8·4 per cent claim gained Labour votes, the Social Contract had dealt with virtually every matter except reducing inflation which appeared as the *caveat* of voluntary wage control. Mr Healey's skill as a politician, not his ability as a Chancellor, allowed him to make, and get away with, the 8·4 per cent claim.

The general election result confirmed the polls' predictions. Labour gained 18 seats from the Conservatives giving them a majority over the Conservatives of 43. But Labour's overall majority was only 4 given the SNP's gain of 4 seats, Plaid Cymru's gain of 1 extra seat giving them 3 and the Liberals retention of 13 seats compared to 14 in February. Labour's majority therefore was clearly vulnerable should by-election defeats follow, which indeed they did. As Harold Wilson argued:

> It was for this reason that I pressed the Cabinet at our first post-election meeting to push on fast with our declared legislative programme, particularly with Bills likely to prove controversial, and/or complicated and lengthy. The strategy was to get on with the major legislation in the first two sessions,

and after that to pursue a policy – good for the Government and certainly good for the country – of concentration on governing.[45]

In electoral terms the reliance on the Social Contract had succeeded. It remained to be seen, as Harold Wilson formed his fourth administration, whether it would succeed in economic and political terms as well.

CHAPTER II

The Fall of the Social Contract

THE INFLATIONARY PROBLEM

The period between Labour's October 1974 election victory and July 1975 when the £6 pay restraint policy was adopted is usually regarded as the ending of the Social Contract. However a definitional problem does arise if the Social Contract is seen as existing right through the 1974–9 period. Hugh Scanlon recalled that the 'Social Contract enabled us to bring down inflation to 7·9 per cent *in 1978* [emphasis added] although at a cost of a reduction in living standards. I don't want to apologise for the Social Contract.'[1] Similarly referring to pay restraint one MP remarked that 'the unions delivered their side of the Social Contract but the government didn't deliver theirs'.[2]

For the purpose of this account – and arguably in the way the Social Contract was seen at the time – the Social Contract period is deemed to have ended with the introduction of the compulsory (though not statutory) £6 pay limit. Thus because a strictly voluntary arrangement on the unions' behalf characterised the Social Contract in 1974 the abandonment of this voluntary aspect, in effect a *de facto* suspension of free collective bargaining, may be regarded as too decisive a policy reversal for the Social Contract to survive. Indeed the language of the Social Contract and protestations at its success diminish rapidly with the return of conventional wage restraint.

There is no mystery as to what killed the Social Contract – inflation, at a rate never previously seen in Britain. By the spring of 1975 inflation was running at 25 per cent, just a few months after Mr Healey's 8·4 per cent claim. This is not to argue that both Mr Wilson and Mr Healey did not realise the nature and extent of the problem – their difficulty lay in extricating themselves from the Social Contract so that effective remedies could be applied. The Queen's speech in October 1974 contained more radical

Social Contract inspired measures but also a strong warning about the threat posed by inflation to the economy. The speech contained proposals to introduce a wealth tax, a capital transfer tax, an Employment Protection Bill, further trade union and labour relations legislation, nationalisation of the shipbuilding and aircraft industries and North Sea oil, and plans to introduce 'planning agreements' on private industry. However the speech saw the Social Contract as an essential element in curbing inflation as well as 'promoting social and economic justice'. By and large while the legislative proposals of the Queen's speech were enacted, the unions were reluctant to make voluntary pay restraint a reality. At the end of October the TUC General Council expressed its concern that the guidelines of 'Collective Bargaining and the Social Contract' were not proving effective. With many settlements running at 20 per cent and upwards at the end of the year the question of inflation, which had been largely forgotten during the Short Parliament, was beginning to concentrate minds both in the government and in the General Council. Barbara Castle notes that in November 1974 the survival of the Social Contract was clearly linked to the problem of inflation by a number of cabinet members; Roy Jenkins argued that:

'. . . we need a contingency plan, though not a siege economy. We must face the danger that the Social Contract may fail and include this in our contingency plans.' (The danger of this is, of course, that once Cabinet is willing even to contemplate a return to statutory controls the news seeps out through the very bricks of No. 10 and a run of wage increases starts overnight.) Shirley was equally gloomy. We faced, she said, a rate of inflation of 26–30 per cent next year. 'Can we shore up the Social Contract through a tax on inflationary settlements? Otherwise we may face a terrible choice between the Social Contract and unemployment.' We must eliminate waste and move faster on English devolution. We must follow the devolution of power by the devolution of responsibility.[3]

However, at this stage, as Barnes and Reid note, there was little the government could do on the wages front but exhortation once the TUC had rejected proposals of penalties against employers giving increases beyond the guidelines of 'Collective Bargaining and the Social Contract'.[4] Similarly it may be argued that the government's general control over the economy was bound by the spirit of the Social Contract and that moves towards either wage control or public expenditure cuts had to be made by stealth. One cabinet minister recalled that: 'We took office in the disturbing circumstances, wittingly or willingly, by benefiting from industrial action. This inflated people's expectations and we acquiesced in an inflationary spasm, rather than making wages march with reality.'[5]

In November 1974 Denis Healey produced his third budget with the hope of checking the rise in unemployment by injecting £1500 million of extra liquidity into the company sector by easing price controls, encouraging bank lending to favour manufacturing industry and reducing subsidies to state industries. Coates comments that the 'government's need of trade union support in the establishment of effective wage control prevented any further easing of the price code at the time but the drift of policy was set'.[6] Joel Barnett noted that the government intended 'to establish firm control over the demand on resources of the public sector as a whole so as to make sure that the programmes do not increase in demand terms by more than $2\frac{3}{4}$% on average over the next four years' which gives an indication of the extent of the government's public expenditure commitment. As Mr Barnett points out, even with public expenditure 9·5 per cent higher in 1974–5 than in 1973–4, the pressure from spending ministers was for still further increases.[7] As one treasury official put it, 'most of the Cabinet were hell-bent on more not less public expenditure'.[8] Thus moving by stealth was the government's only option given the existing rhetoric of the Social Contract.

This was soon to be demonstrated in relation to public expenditure which in 1975 dealt with 1976–7 and which occasioned an actual 3·8 per cent fall in real terms. Given the scale of the PSBR this was a small amount but in the Social Contract context almost a bold move. Even still before the 1975 April budget cut public expenditure by £901 million there was a January Public Expenditure White Paper which outlined additional government spending and a February jobs subsidy package worth £215 million. So the government's move by stealth was by its nature tentative coming so soon after the generation of high expectations of public expenditure increases.

There is no reason to question the accuracy of both Barbara Castle's and Joel Barnett's accounts of the Cabinet battle over the

1975 cuts. Of the key Cabinet meeting on 25 March Mrs Castle
noted that:

> In the afternoon we at last turned to Denis's public expenditure
> proposals. His determination to cut £1 billion off the pro-
> grammes for 1976–7 has come as a traumatic blow so soon after
> the January White Paper and I am furious at the lack of
> planning and proper forecasting it reveals . . . The discussion
> then took its predictable course: most of the Cabinet resigned to
> the inevitable and all of us conscious that something had to be
> done to stop the inflationary drift. Tony C. complained again
> that we didn't know what the overall strategy was. Peter said
> that the package must contain both public expenditure cuts
> and tax increases. 'The composition of the package is a matter
> for Cabinet' (We all keep saying this, but we are no nearer
> getting Cabinet control of tax policy.) Peter then proceeded to
> echo my thoughts: 'If we just have a deflationary package, we
> won't be in a better position at the end of the year to seize our
> opportunities. There is a missing component in Denis's pro-
> posals: an effective element for increasing exports or reducing
> imports this year.' Wedgie fumed: 'These cuts mean we are
> abandoning the Social Contract. They constitute a massive
> deflationary package which will cut productive capacity and
> investment. As Cabinet knows, I have put forward a paper with
> proposals of my own, but we are not even allowed to look at the
> alternative.' I declared this was 1966 all over again. The moral
> appeared to be: 'A Labour Government can never increase the
> social wage.' We must have a socio-economic strategy worked
> out with the trade unions. Why didn't we put the alternatives to
> them? Once again we had fallen back on cuts: no import
> controls or social objectives. . . . Denis gave his usual wordy
> piece of self-justification at the end. 'The things we counted on
> haven't happened: the Social Contract and reflation by other
> countries.' He had been in continuous discussion with the
> TUC: 'It won't come to them as a surprise.' Our trouble was
> that we had no industrial strategy and were pouring out money
> on everything from fruit juice to BB indiscriminately. As a
> result of the cuts unemployment would only be seventy
> thousand higher by the beginning of 1977. Of course, he got his
> way and those wretched bilateral talks with the Treasury are to
> begin.[9]

Joel Barnett, who was on the opposite side of the argument to Mrs Castle, recalled of the 25 March Cabinet meeting:

> On this occasion we were seeking approval in principle for public expenditure cuts of over £1 billion. For some colleagues, it was the worst crisis since 1931 – that traumatic date in Labour Party history when Ramsay MacDonald nearly destroyed the Party by forming a coalition when most of his Labour Cabinet colleagues could not stomach, among other things, 'expenditure cuts' that seem pretty paltry by comparison with what we were now envisaging. The Cabinet meeting gave rise to strong attacks on 'the siege economy', the derogatory and emotive way of describing QRs. Even so, most of those who agreed with us, which was a substantial majority, did so with great reluctance. One or two, like Shirley Williams, while basically recognizing that there was no real alternative, feared we were using 'traditional Treasury deflation' (that criticism was not entirely a prerogative of the left). Shirley, as she often did, suggested a middle way. She felt we should give a choice to the people – in practice the TUC – by making the toughness of the expenditure cuts package depend on the level of pay settlements.
>
> The more traditional opposition came from Tony Benn. For him it killed the 'Social Contract'. It had of course already been killed by the pay explosion, despite everything the Government had done to meet its side of the Contract. Michael Foot too thought it would make our relationship with the TUC impossible. In fact, despite the cuts, the next two pay rounds were the best we were able to obtain from the TUC. As ever, the most powerful criticism came from Tony Crosland. But even Tony, much as I admired him, had no coherent alternative strategy. He just didn't like public expenditure cuts – but who did? So Tony Crosland could only argue that our paper was inadequate and ask for a prolonged debate to consider an alternative Budget strategy. I felt he basically knew there was no alternative, but he had to go through the motions.[10]

Another minister recalled that 'the trouble was that we were living hand to mouth. There were no priorities and in the first year or so departments just got what they wanted. In the end though we got to a point of saying "no" to everything.'[11]

In the event Denis Healey, to whom the serious consequences of continued inflation were clearly apparent, got £901 million of £1 billion worth of cuts he had requested and on 15 April presented his budget. Personal consumption was cut, the price code eased, £100 million made available for firms starting new capital projects, taxation increased by £1250 in a full year, nationalised industry subsidies reduced, food subsidies cut by £150 million and housing subsidies by £65 million. The budget marked the government's reassertion of control, in an albeit limited way, over the economy and a diminution of reliance on the Social Contract. The Conservatives, with new leader Margaret Thatcher committed to a more monetarist approach, made great political capital out of attacking the budget but in their hearts knew that it moved the economy in the right direction and that the free-spending early Healey budgets were unlikely to be repeated.

In his speech Mr Healey declared his own determination to bring down the rate of inflation and made an effective side-swipe at the TUC guidelines on voluntary pay restraint. He noted that the 'general rate of pay increases has been well above the increase in the cost of living and much further still above the level in countries which compete with us . . . As a result, by February the retail price index stood 19·9% over a year and the wage rate index was 28·9% . . . pay has been running about 8% or 9% ahead of prices. I do not believe that anyone would claim that the TUC guidelines ever intended to permit this result.' That Harold Wilson took the same line, in contrast arguably to his 'custodian of the manifesto' line of a year earlier, is inferred from his quoting of Mr Healey in his memoirs.[12]

Nor was Mr Healey oblivious to the real alternative policy if the TUC could not deliver pay restraint. Barbara Castle reported Mr Healey's comments at the Liaison Committee as 'our flicker of warning to the trade unions':

> I've appealed to the unions not to try and make good the increase in the cost of living from the Budget. If they do, the only way I shall be able to deal with the situation is by cutting public expenditure. The level of settlements has been well above the spirit of the guidelines and I hope we can discuss how we can prevent this from happening again.[13]

Following the April budget the government actually sought a

traditional incomes policy alternative to the Social Contract's voluntary guidelines. Although in his tougher April budget Mr Healey had already taken some measures to reduce the excess demand in the economy, which led ultimately to a fall in inflation, the political concentration was on pay policy in the belief that this was crucial to reducing inflation. The question of rising unemployment was also involved as Denis Healey took the view that high wage settlements could lead to higher unemployment – in later monetarist terminology workers pricing themselves out of jobs. Barnes and Reid put it that:

At the beginning of 1975, with wages rising at an annual rate of about 37 per cent, Denis Healey entered the debate on inflation and the operation of the social contract. With the rapid rise in unemployment, the TUC Economic Committee had emphasised the need to protect jobs as part of the social contract and Murray had argued that the maintenance of living standards and the maintenance of full employment were mutually reinforcing. Healey now openly disagreed: 'It is far better that more people should be in work, even if that means accepting lower wages on average, than that those lucky enough to keep their jobs should scoop the pool while millions are living on the dole.'[14]

However the unions did not share the same view even though the weight of evidence was moving clearly with Mr Healey's arguments. Other cabinet ministers were also restive, particularly following a 33 per cent wage deal for the miners and both Tony Crosland and Reg Prentice, who stated that the union must not 'welsh' on the Social Contract, questioned the high level of settlements. Michael Foot, the Employment Secretary, despite his veteran left-wing credentials, was known to favour a strong line on wage restraint. Barbara Castle noted in her diary for March 1975 that:

As I listen to him I can't help smiling to myself. Here he is now: the most determined advocate of wage restraint and damn the ideological consequences. I remember how in the 1966–70 Labour Government he helped to pillory me from the backbenches when I was having to face the realities as he is now.[15]

Thus by the time Mr Healey presented his April budget 'Collective Bargaining and the Social Contract' had proved incapable of providing economic or political success for the government. Indeed more than half of the key wage agreements had sanctioned increases 10 per cent or more than the rise in prices for the previous year with little evidence that the low paid, who lacked union muscle, had received pay priority. From the government's point of view the unions just had not kept their side of the Social Contract bargain. Rather than moving by stealth the search now began in earnest for a traditional incomes policy.

THE £6 PAY POLICY

It is widely believed, and rightly, that the key man in the return to incomes policy in the summer of 1975 was Jack Jones. The majority of the Cabinet needed no persuasion but to many union leaders the preservation of free collective bargaining was a matter of faith. Jones, however, was completely devoted to the maintenance of a Labour Government and the prospect of a Thatcher administration appalled him as a convinced socialist. Barbara Castle's pen-picture of him at a TUC/Labour Party Liaison meeting in January 1975 paints an accurate portrait of his influence at the time in the labour movement:

And as soon as Jack took the chair I realized how important it was for us to meet. Here is the Government, beset by so many economic difficulties it would have sunk us in 1964–70. Here was the trade union movement which had contributed so much to our 1970 defeat. And here was Jack Jones in the chair, who had always been considered by my officials, when I was at Employment and Productivity, as the archetypal trade union villain and who had in fact been arid and negative then. But today Jack sat in the chair as an almost gentle and certainly benign influence. I believe he is the greatest voice in the trade union movement today in favour of what I have always wanted to see: the trade union movement being made socialist. And what is more, he is someone who realizes that politicians have to operate in the real world as much as trade unionists do: in the world of the possible.[16]

In that real world of the possible Jack Jones saw, in colossal wage claims, a threat to the Labour Government and in May 1975 floated the idea of a small, flat-rate wage increase across the board as a practical proposal. Jones recalled that 'there was a fever about pay claims which were often pitched in anticipation by some officials. I put forward the flate rate approach to calm things and help the lower paid. I put forward the idea of £8 originally but it was modified to £6 in discussions.'[17] One senior Treasury official recalled that 'Jones felt that inflation on the scale of 30 per cent would kill the Labour Government and bring in a right-wing, anti-union government. His views were political not economic.'[18]

One junior minister at the time summarised the situation by arguing that 'We had to have a period of free collective bargaining before we could get round the table and it needed an emergency response for us to do so.'[19] To Joel Barnett, 'Jack recognised that high wage inflation was damaging to his members and that there was a simple equation that higher wages led to less employment.'[20] Harold Wilson recalled that 'Jack had a grip on his union and influence in the movement. He was really anxious to make a success of it and was a great idealist.'[21]

Barnes and Reid correctly note that political consequences were crucial to Jones's attitude:

Equally persuasive were the political consequences. Unless the rate of inflation could be reduced there was little prospect that the government could implement policies to which Jones and the trade union movement were committed – and, indeed, it might not remain in office. The social contract was very much Jones's creation; he did not want to risk its destruction.[22]

However external factors came to Jones's and the government's aid. The left suffered a defeat over the Common Market referendum and as there was a considerable overlap between anti-marketeers and opponents of compulsory incomes policy (Jones himself being a notable exception) the government's authority was enhanced by a public display of support. This enabled Mr Wilson to demote Tony Benn from Industry to Energy without creating a left-wing rebellion.[23]

Far more significantly as far as the Jones initiative was concerned was the position of the pound. In Cabinet, according to Mrs Castle, Denis Healey assessed the situation with considerable pessimism:

Denis came next, more sombre than I have seen him for a long time, but still sticking firmly to voluntary policy. The problem, he said, was more urgent than any of us realized. On the balance of payments deficit we had done better than anticipated but output would still be falling to the end of the year and inflation was 'terrifying'. Borrowing could stop 'overnight'. Anything could trigger off a disastrous run on the pound and force us into £1 billion's worth of public expenditure cuts this year. There was not a minute to waste. 'We must have a credible policy by the end of July.'[24]

With the added threat that the Treasury was known to be pressing for statutory controls, the pound fell 5 cents on 30 June against the dollar and it was rumoured that the governments of Kuwait and Saudi Arabia were seeking to withdraw larger sums of sterling from London. Mr Healey's assessment of the perils faced by the economy had proved to be correct. As the pound fell foreign holders of sterling began to react to the inflationary situation and funds began to be withdrawn. For a Labour Government, especially a Wilson Government, this brought back painful memories of the 1960s and added urgency to restoring confidence by reducing inflation, or at that stage bringing it under control. A 30 per cent settlement of the NUR's claim was even considered a victory by the government, so serious had the problem become.

Harold Wilson recalled that:

The Treasury was utterly depressed, and when depressed it tends to go fetishist. Their fetish on this occasion, not for the first time, and not unnaturally, reflected international market demands for statutory controls over pay. The Treasury of course, can hardly ignore market prejudice. No matter that all experience − including that of Mr. Heath's final months − taught us that statutory sanctions would not dig coal . . . Without a legal framework, indeed one backed by criminal sanctions, we were told, sterling would go. At 1.00 a.m. ministers emerging from the Cabinet room were so advised. In this respect Mr. Joe Haines's book reproducing his note to me on the midnight Treasury demarche is accurate.

On the Tuesday sterling fell from the overnight depreciation of 28·9 per cent to 29·2 per cent, picking up slightly on the dollar. Denis Healey made an announcement which we had authorized the previous evening. He and other ministers had been conducting talks with the TUC. He said that the TUC would be given another week to produce 'results' or the Government would take action on its own. By results he meant the setting of a 10 per cent limit on pay increases, effective in each case for a year. That week would cover the opening of the mineworkers' conference, which we had recognized all along would prove decisive.[25]

The urgency of the situation led to a quickening of the pace of events with the Jones formula the obvious solution not least because of its simplicity. Keegan and Pennant-Rae argued that a concentration of minds led to the need for tougher action.

It had been remarkable how the oil money kept flowing to London during a period – first half of 1975 – when increasingly apocalyptic diagnoses were being made about British inflation trends and the threat they posed for democracy. Among other people, these warnings were reaching the ultimate guarantor of the British economy – the American Government. The dry-run for the sterling crisis of 1976 took place in June/July 1975. This concentrated minds sufficiently for ministers and the biggest union leaders to accept that the manifesto commitment to free collective bargaining had been a bad mistake, and the £6 limit on incomes was introduced, to back up an earlier move towards tighter monetary policies.[26]

The government made clear that its declared aim of working towards a 10 per cent rate of inflation by the end of 1976 was no bluff and ministers painted a grim picture of public expenditure cuts if a TUC agreement for positive action was not forthcoming. At a series of NEDC meetings the trade union representatives, Jack Jones, Hugh Scanlon, David Basnett, Lord Allen and Daniel McGarvey accompanied by Len Murray and David Lea discussed the exact nature of a wage restraint policy with ministers led by Denis Healey and including Michael Foot, Eric Varley and Shirley Williams.

What finally emerged was the £6 wage rise limit with a zero increase for those on £8500 or above, operable from 1 August 1975. The Jones formula, originally floated in May, had emerged as the most mutually agreeable to all sides. Furthermore the

government promised that its powers under the price code would
be used to prevent excessive rises being passed on in the form of
high prices, no assistance would be given to compensate nationalised industries who exceeded the £6 limit and, similarly, local
authorities which exceeded the limit would not be reimbursed
through the rate support grant. The TUC General Council
accepted the policy by 19 votes to 13 and a Reserve Bill for
statutory control was consequently dropped by the government.

On 9 July the TUC's formal version of the £6 policy, 'The
Development of the Social Contract', was published but in reality
the language of the Social Contract had been made redundant,
and could not disguise the fact that this was incomes policy on the
traditional lines of restricting wages to reduce inflation. One
backbench MP, who favoured incomes policy for socialist reasons
of redistribution and economic planning recalled that 'the
weakness of incomes policies from the late 1940s, through the
1960s and 1970s was that all governments at the outset were not
committed to it and then when it was introduced was for deflation
and not as production related or equity distribution'.[27] While
such a comment is factually correct, the £6 policy in being
applicable in flat rate terms helped the lower paid and as such,
may be regarded as more socialist than a percentage rise policy,
which would have preserved differentials. As one minister put it:
'The £6 policy was a socialist policy in that it had to take care of
the serious problem of low pay. We had to get an agreement
quickly and one which was simple – or rather ostensibly simple –
and fair.'[28]

Another minister, who supported help to the low paid, but who
was sceptical of a long-term incomes policy thought that:

> The £6 was OK initially, but if you set out to help the lower paid
> the question is that about differentials. I remember Hughie
> Scanlon, and Joan Maynard arguing and Hughie said 'tell me
> the last time the agricultural workers got £6?' £6 was a big
> increase for the lower paid.[29]

On 22 July the government received a majority of 58 for its
policy even though the government no longer could count on an
overall majority. On the second reading Conservatives abstained
and the Bill to give back-up legislation effect to the policy received
Royal Assent on 1 August. The £6 policy, however, did not mean

the end of the government's problems and dilemmas with pay policy but rather it necessitated a shift in direction. It did solve the political, as opposed to economic, crisis which had developed in the summer of 1975 but it opened up, as all compulsory policies had done before it, a Pandora's box of economic difficulties. The language of the Social Contract gave way to the familiar language of incomes policy control – 'norms', 'arbitration', 'relativities', 'flat-rate increases', 'special cases', 'tribunals', 'flexibility', 'fairness' and so on. Hugh Scanlon recalled that 'the £6 was not an ideal – it was rough justice. For certain people on £18 per week or so £6 meant a lot, something they could not have got in negotiation.'[30] One backbench MP remarked that 'the £6 policy was a good norm for the lower paid but incomes policy became an accumulation of nonsenses'.[31]

THE PHILOSOPHY OF WAGE CONTROL

If the £6 pay policy helped the government to conquer the political anxieties of mid-1975 and brought to an end the Social Contract as a political panacea, it also helped to postpone vital and painful decisions on the direction of Britain's economy.

As has already been argued, the Social Contract contained within it the seeds of its own destruction because controlling inflation was regarded as a matter of (voluntary) wage restraint and once this had been seen to have failed the next logical step, in the absence of an alternative theory for the high level of inflation, was compulsory wage control. Strong evidence however existed, and still exists, that a causal link between the rate of inflation in 1974/5 and the rate of wage increases was conspicuous by its absence.

First, a rising inflation rate was part of Mr Wilson's 'dual inheritance' from Mr Heath's ill-considered 'dash for growth' policy in 1972/3 resulting from a desire to reduce unemployment from one million in February 1972.[32] Incomes policy restraints themselves initiated by Mr Heath made the situation worse in that they then broke down following the miners' crisis of 1974. The subsequent explosion was largely in the nature of catching up on the artificial restraints of Heath's stages I–III. This point is made pertinent, rather than merely circumstantial, by the fact that Heath was inflating the economy with the money supply out of control and public expenditure rapidly accelerating. Joel

Barnett was right to claim that Conservative criticism of Mr Healey's 8·4 per cent in October 1974 was a debating point and right also that the more intelligent Conservatives realised it. Mr Wilson, therefore, was not guilty of creating the inflation of 1974/5 merely of not taking appropriate action until the April 1975 budget by reducing excess demand, and only then by not very much in view of the Social Contract commitments on public expenditure in 1974.

Secondly, evidence exists to suggest that inflation was starting to fall in 1975 and would have done so irrespective of the £6 pay policy. As Brittan and Lilley argue, the widely-held view that the £6 policy was a 'turning back from the abyss just in time'[33] is not supported by evidence, particularly that relating to the money supply. Brittan and Lilley noted that:

> Market economists predicted that the rate of inflation would stop increasing and eventually start to decline. Some did so on the basis of the money supply. The expansion of the broadly based money supply fell back from 28 per cent in 1973 to 12 per cent in 1974 and 8 per cent in 1975. This was largely due to the ease in financing the Budget deficit, first from the deposits of the oil producers and official overseas borrowings and later, during the depths of the recession, from domestic savings. Others predicted a slowdown in inflation more directly from the turn-round in the labour market and the rise in unemployment, which became very severe in the course of 1975. A more international approach focused on the world recession and the turn-down in commodity prices. Although all these approaches may be consistent with each other they do not come to quite the same thing, as the time lags and short-term relationships are not known, and are not the same in each cycle.[34]

Thirdly, the actual movement of prices and wages when reviewed in more detail does not lend weight to the argument that the £6 limit alone brought inflation to an end. Wholesale prices were declining throughout 1975 from 29 per cent in the first quarter to $12\frac{1}{2}$ per cent in the last quarter and notifications of price increases to the Price Commission showed a similar decline well before the £6 policy and the summer economic crisis. Wages similarly reached their peak compared with a year before early in 1975 not during the summer crisis. However, preemptive wage claims were made as the government's resolve to introduce tougher pay controls became known at first in veiled private reference and then openly following Denis Healey's April 1975 budget comments. Thus Brittan and Lilley rightly argue that:

> The opponents of incomes policy claim that there was a rush to make settlements in the late spring and early summer of 1975, as it was known that the government was anxious to negotiate a wage limit. The unpublished index of settlements which gave cause for alarm, as in 1972, might have been recording a rush to beat the pay ceiling or a rush to get in claims before the guillotine fell. There was also statistical argument on whether wages were increasing more slowly in the private sector, which felt the influence of market forces more directly.[35]

In fact, rather than marking a return to 'realism' in the government's and the unions' approach to the economy and particularly inflation control, the £6 policy marked a postponement of 'realism'. In this sense the £6 policy may be seen as an extension of the Social Contract philosophy in that the £6 limit, like voluntary restraint before it, was an alternative to necessary measures such as public expenditure cuts and a reduction of aggregate demand. The £6 policy in postponing the necessary painful medicine only made it more painful when its application, 18 months later at the hands of the IMF, could not be postponed. However well intentioned, the £6 policy was not the economic answer – that was to come later – but instead was a political answer to the crisis of summer 1975.

Of course it may be argued that such necessary measures as public expenditure cuts to restore reality to public spending expectations would have been politically unacceptable to the unions and the left of the Labour Party in 1975. This argument is perfectly rational in that for a Labour Government to deflate would have been to repudiate 1974–5 too swiftly to be politically credible. Deflation in 1975 on the scale actually required was politically too great a retreat from the Social Contract; the £6 pay policy was not. Thus political expediency in July 1975 stored up or postponed deflationary measures for a time when they would be either politically acceptable or as it turned out politically and economically unavoidable.

The philosophy of compulsory wage restraint enabled the

government to postpone economically painful measures and enabled the unions to believe they were playing their part in sensible, realistic economic management. Moreover the resort to incomes policy and the peculiar language of incomes control, stored up problems with relativities, fairness, equity and industrial muscle, which were ultimately to explode in 1978–9. The £6 pay policy marked the closing of the Social Contract chapter of 1974–9 but it was barely beginning the chapter which was to prove an intractable source of conflict. For once the government was committed to the philosophy of compulsory wage control, the commitment was long term. One minister thought that 'it's easy to get agreement at the top – that I call elite Fabianism – but the problem is ignoring the people you represent. You can only carry on an incomes policy for a limited period.'[36] The £6 policy which began life as Jack Jones's short-term expedient for the crisis of summer 1975 thus projected immense problems for the government as incomes policy became a permanent feature of the 1974–9 administration.

CHAPTER III

Labour's Industrial Strategy

THE IDEOLOGICAL BACKGROUND

During the Labour Party's move to the left between 1970 and 1974 industry policy became a key battleground between left and right as, arguably, it has always been, given the great debates about Clause iv of the party's constitution. The left's success, however, meant that an industrial strategy emerged which, by the time of the February 1974 election, committed a Labour Government to increasing state intervention in industry way beyond the scale of expectations, let alone performance, of 1964–70.

It is not difficult to ascertain the fascination and often obsession in the Labour Party for industrial matters. Industry policy is to the Labour Party a shibboleth, as defence policy is to the Conservatives. The gigantic costs of industrial aid are often as irrelevant to the Labour faithful as the gigantic costs of NATO, or Trident missiles, are to the Conservative faithful. Many on the left of the Labour Party have a romanticised view of the working class and talk in neo-Marxist language of transferring power to the working class as if the working class were a monolithic entity rather than a diverse collection of individuals loosely bound by socioeconomic customs. Consequently many on the far left of the Labour Party regard the working class as superior to other social classes as if class membership *per se* is a matter of self-congratulation rather than an accident of birth. To advocate the view that the working class has no preordained right to political power, or that social class is not a matter of merit, or that matters of good and evil cut across class divisions, is to put forward an unpopular view in the Labour Party which draws disapproval.[1]

Thus as the left increased its strength in the Labour Party during its years in opposition the answer to the question of transferring wealth and power in favour of the working class came to be seen in terms of an industrial strategy to regenerate manufacturing industry. Manufacturing industry, and those who worked in it, therefore came to be regarded as more deserving of government aid than other sectors of the economy, in the belief, arguably quite erroneous, that Britain is a nation which over-whelmingly depends for its livelihood on manufacturing industry in the form of an 'industrial base'.

In opposition the left's schemes for an industrial strategy knew no limitations, an understandable reaction given Mr Heath's acts of nationalisation and the interventionist 1972 Industry Act. The Labour Party conference and NEC led the way forward in preparing a radical industrial policy to make 'a clear political commitment to industrial intervention and to economic planning which must include an expansion of the public sector'.[2] The left argued that the previous Labour Government had been beset with economic problems which only radical policies, such as control of the 'commanding heights' of the economy could have tackled. They were determined that a future Labour Government would take office with an industrial strategy based not on managerialism and technocracy but a socialist fundamental of shifting economic, and hence class, power.[3]

Central to the left's strategy was the National Enterprise Board which according to an Opposition Green Paper in 1972, would coordinate economic planning to 'introduce public ownership into the stronghold of private industry'. *Labour's Programme 1973* went further, aiming at 'a massive shift . . . in the social and regional distribution of growth' which could 'only be achieved by a conscious effort to *plan* the economy'. To achieve successful economic planning three specific areas of industrial intervention were detailed. First was the creation of a new public enterprise and state holding company to establish 'a major stake in manufacturing industry'. Secondly a 'planning agreements' system was envisaged to 'place all our dealing with the major companies on a systematic and coherent basis'. Thirdly, not to be outdone by Mr Heath's 1972 Industry Act, a new Industry Act was proposed to provide a future Labour Government with 'all the industrial powers it will need to meet its economic objectives'. Given such commitments it was not surprising that Harold Wilson had to use all his political acumen, and knowledge of the labour movement, successfully to resist a demand to nationalise the leading twenty-five companies, as advocated during 1973 by the NEC. Wilson knew, not least from experience at successive general elections, that nationalisation was not popular with the public at large, including ordinary Labour voters. Wilson also knew that the industrial strategy, given the oil crisis and miners' strike which devastated the economy, was light years away from a practical solution to actual and immediate economic needs. However Wilson was forced to bide his time and defer to the strength of left-wing opinion in the party. The February 1974 election manifesto thus committed the next Labour Government to a far-reaching programme to implement the industrial strategy. It advocated that Labour would:

Sustain and expand industrial development and exports and bring about the re-equipment necessary for this purpose through the powers we shall take in a new Industry Act and through the Planning Agreement system which will allow Government to plan with industry more effectively.

Wherever we give direct aid to a company out of public funds we shall in return reserve the right to take a share of the ownership of the company.

In addition to our plans set out . . . above for taking into common ownership land required for development, we shall substantially extend PUBLIC ENTERPRISE by taking mineral rights. We shall also take shipbuilding, ship-repairing and marine engineering, ports, the manufacture of airframes and aeroengines into public ownership and control. But we shall not confine the extension of the public sector to loss-making and subsidised industries. We shall also take over profitable sections or individual firms in those industries where a public holding is essential to enable the Government to control prices, stimulate investment, encourage exports, create employment, protect workers and customers from the activities of irresponsible multi-national companies, and to plan the national economy in the national interest. We shall therefore include in this operation, sections of pharmaceuticals, road haulage, construction, machine tools, in addition to our proposals for North Sea and Celtic Sea oil and gas. Our decision in the field of banking, insurance and building societies is still under consideration. We shall return to public ownership assets and licences hived-off by the present government, and we shall create a powerful National Enterprise Board with the structure and functions set out in Labour's Programme 1973.

We intend to socialise existing nationalised industries. In consultation with the unions, we shall take steps to make the management of existing nationalised industries more responsible to the workers in the industry and more responsive to their consumers' needs.

Regional development will be further encouraged by new public enterprise, assistance to private industry on a selective basis, and new REGIONAL PLANNING MACHINERY, along the lines set out in Labour's Programme 1973. We will retain and improve the Regional Employment Premium. Revenues from North Sea oil will be used wherever possible to improve employment conditions in Scotland and the regions elsewhere in need of development.

Nor was Wilson, yet, in a position to resist the left by appointing an Industry Minister who was not completely committed to the industrial strategy. Consequently Tony Benn, with Eric Heffer as his deputy, took over the Department of Trade and Industry when Labour gained power in 1974.

THE SCOPE OF INTERVENTION

Tony Benn's personal commitment to the industrial strategy was a strong one. Ideologically Benn had moved left late in his political, and indeed ministerial, career. In the 1960s as the Postmaster-General he had been regarded as the epitome of Wilson's managerial technocracy and during the Clause IV battles of the late 1950s and early 1960s he had been a peacemaker and in the centre of the party rather than a committed protagonist. However during the Short Parliament few observers were in any doubt that Mr Benn meant exactly what he said about a radical shift in industrial policy on the lines advocated by the left in opposition.

As legislation in the Short Parliament on the industrial strategy was ruled out because of lack of time and lack of a majority the Department of Industry brought out a White Paper in July 1974, *The Regeneration of British Industry*. The White Paper was the cause of left–right acrimony even before it appeared and marked the beginning of the right's fight back on industrial policy. Harold Wilson recalled that:

> It was not until late July that the Department of Industry's draft White Paper emerged. As I had feared, it proved to be a sloppy and half-baked document, polemical, indeed menacing, in tone, redolent more of an NEC Home Policy Committee document than a Command Paper. One basic weakness was that it appeared to place more emphasis on the somewhat amorphous proposals for planning agreements than on the NEB.
>
> A special committee of senior ministers was set up under my chairmanship to mastermind its re-drafting, which quickly decided that the document should be re-written. The final draft owed a great deal to Michael Foot, writing within the parameters we laid down. The section on planning agreements was cut down to size: in the event, at the time of writing, four years later, only one planning agreement with a public company has come into force. The role and powers of the NEB were strictly defined; above all it was to have no marauding role. It should act specifically within guidelines announced by the Secretary of State, which were to be made public. These provided, inter alia, that it could not go secretly into the market, whether directly or through nominees, buying the shares of a company with a view to acquiring control, but had to follow normal Stock Exchange procedures.[4]

However, even if the language and priorities of the industrial strategy envisaged by Mr Benn were toned down, *The Regeneration of British Industry* still went a long way in extending state intervention in the economy. Coates describes the White Paper as a defeat for the left:

> The Regeneration of British Industry is a classic example of the process of gradual retreat. It was presented to a Party in which all sections were agreed on the need for economic growth, and for a new kind of government intervention in industry to get it. But it was also presented to a Party whose left wing saw this intervention as one important route to the achievement of radical changes in industrial power and social justice. The White Paper promised new interventionist agencies, while

remaining absolutely silent on the degree to which they would be used for radical industrial and social ends. That silence was already a defeat for the Left, and constituted the start of that retreat from the industrial objectives of the 1972 and 1973 Programmes which would accelerate and become more obvious later.[5]

In terms of the context of Labour's ideological divide such an analysis is accurate. But it fails to make the distinction between the experience of 1964–70 and the extent of state intervention in 1974–9. The left's victories in 1970–5 made sure that even a toned down industrial strategy would go further than the experience of 1964–70 or the expectations of the left on Labour leaving office in 1970. The ultimate test of the industrial strategy was not on Labour's ideological purity but on the British economy and in this regard *The Regeneration of British Industry* did represent a significant move leftwards even allowing for the increased state involvement of the Heath years. The dispute between Labour left and right was a matter of degree – both were united on the need to expand the public sector – and following the October 1974 election victory, legislative enactment of the industrial strategy proposals became a reality.

Legislation on the creation of the NEB was painfully slow. The second reading was in February 1975 and the Bill did not receive Royal Assent until December following a series of Lords' amendments. All the time the British Leyland crisis fore-shadowed events which the NEB was being set up to influence.[6] The 1975 Industry Act, while not satisfying the left, did go further than any previous legislation in increasing the state's role in industry. A sum of £1000 million was allocated to the Industry Department to provide industrial assistance to specific industries; a system of voluntary (the left would have preferred compulsory) planning agreements could be set up within a legal framework; the NEB was created with an initial budget of £700 million and a further £300 million depending on parliamentary approval; the powers of the NEB included buying shares on the open market to extend public ownership into profitable private industry and the power to invest £10 million in any one firm or to take up to 30 per cent of its voting shares, irrespective of the blessing of the Industry Minister. Furthermore extra financial assistance was available to the NEB from the government in rescue cases approved by the

Department of Industry. As Coates rightly points out 'the government's hope was the NEB would be a catalyst to generalised investment and effective management in the private sector, rather than a source of the bulk of that investment itself.[7] To the left the NEB was a disappointment. Grant, in an authoritative study of the industrial policy which covered the 1974–9 government, rightly noted that the NEB 'as it developed was very different from the original conception of Labour's left-wingers of an organisation which would spearhead the transformation of Britain's industrial economy from capitalism to socialism'.[8] The NEC criticised the Act for making planning agreements only voluntary and for not including proposals to ensure the compulsory purchase of companies (except in the case of a foreign takeover). Furthermore the NEB funds were regarded as insufficient by the left. One left-wing MP commented that the NEB was 'a catchall for left and right. We were frightened to take over the commanding heights.'[9]

The government's choice of Sir Don Ryder as the Board's first chairman also disappointed the left. Ryder was a businessman with no interest in the socialist ideology of shifting class wealth and power. It may be argued that his enthusiasm for the NEB's interventionist role may have been considerably less had he himself not been chosen as its chairman. He saw the NEB's role as largely resurrecting industrial lame ducks which was entirely rational as lame ducks were in abundance after years of nurturing by the Industrial Reorganisation Corporation in the 1960s and then by Heath's 1972 Industry Act.

More disappointing still for the left was Tony Benn's demotion in June 1975 to Energy Secretary. One MP commented that 'Wilson had a hatred of Benn. Wilson killed off the Industrial Strategy.'[10] The removal of Mr Benn deserves further scrutiny. Mr Wilson never had his heart in the industrial strategy originally worked out by the NEC in opposition and backed to the hilt by Tony Benn. Furthermore Benn's habit of attacking private industry seemed to Wilson behaviour ill-fitted to the Industry Secretary. Following the left's defeat in the EEC referendum in June 1975, in which Mr Benn had campaigned as an ardent anti-marketeer, Mr Wilson was in a strong political position to reshuffle. Wilson's weakness as party leader in opposition now contrasted with his prime ministerial powers of appointment, dismissal and patronage.

Harold Wilson's own description of the circumstances of Benn's demotion is a paragon of tactful discretion. Benn was moved 'sideways' not demoted:

> On the Monday evening after the referendum result I began my reshuffle, telling Tony I was moving him to Energy. He took it extremely hard, and it looked virtually certain that he would choose to retire to the back-benches, the last place where I wanted to see him. Late that evening Michael Foot came to intercede on his behalf, but I made it clear that my mind was made up, and told Michael – as I had emphasized to Tony – that Energy would be a wonderful field in which to deploy his energy. Eric Varley, to whom I had offered the job of Industry Secretary – saying that I was prepared to move Gerald Kaufman over to help him – was very chary, and when he heard through the grapevine of Tony's reaction came to tell me that he would not accept if Tony resigned, as appeared highly probable. However, the next day Tony came to see me again, and when I asked him straight out whether he was refusing it, he said – not with his usual charm – of course he'd have to accept it, Eric then came into line.[11]

Other accounts describe the left's agony. One MP recalled that 'Benn bought the move to Energy. All he could do was to visit oil rigs. It was a walk-over for the Prime Minister.'[12] Barbara Castle reflected in her diary that:

> Tony Benn was sitting at his desk, a figure of tragedy, surrounded by a cortege of political advisers: Michael Meacher, Joe Ashton and other figures I could barely make out, because the curtains were drawn against the brilliant sun. The heat was stifling. 'Have you heard anything?' I asked. 'Yes,' he replied, 'I am being moved to Energy.' I was staggered, my first feeling being that it was the cleverest move Harold could make. Wedgie said he had talked to Eric [Varley], who has been offered Industry. Eric had written to Harold saying he would not take the job if Wedgie were to resign, as he seemed to be contemplating. It must be a straight swap or nothing. Wedgie was clearly hesitant. Harold had demanded an instant reply and Wedgie had been 'very rude' to him. He thought he was at least entitled to twenty-four hours to think it over. We all

supported him on this. Apparently Michael [Foot] has been in and was ready to act as go-between . . . I consoled Wedgie: 'At least Harold has moved you to another power point in the Manifesto.' 'Yes,' he replied gloomily, 'but I shall have no part in the negotiations with the oil companies. Harold has made it clear that that will remain with Harold Lever's committee.' 'But as Secretary of State they can't keep you out of the picture,' I replied. 'And if things are going the wrong way, you can bring it to Cabinet. It gives you a better resigning position.' I think he had already made up his mind to accept, however reluctantly.[13]

Tony Benn's move to Energy was a considerable defeat for the left. Unlike his successor Eric Varley, a man with no political imagination or intellectual flair, Benn was an energetic minister, who completely believed in the Industrial Strategy and, despite the limitations in the NEB's powers, would have been able to have pushed state intervention much further had he not moved from Industry. As a politician and a minister Benn was a success – the problem was that, on industrial matters, he was simply wrong. Benn knew nothing of the practicalities of industry whether those of a capitalist economy, a mixed economy like Britain's or a soviet-style economy. One cabinet minister recalled that 'Benn and workers' control – that was very small beer',[14] while an MP not unsympathetic to radical economic solutions commented that the 'industrial economic policy put forward by Benn was half-baked and conspiratorial'.[15] Benn's enthusiasm for worker cooperatives bore no relevance to economic reality. Joel Barnett noted that:

The issue at stake – which, in one form or another, took up much ministerial time, though only comparatively small sums of money – was worker cooperatives, sometimes known as 'Benn's Follies'. There was Meriden Motor-cycles, a subsidiary of Norton Villiers Triumph (NVT); Kirkby Manufacturing and Engineering, a small company with a troubled history, which made radiators, orange juice and parts for British Leyland; and the *Scottish Daily Express*, later the *Scottish Daily News*.[16]

Similarly on another occasion Mr Barnett recalled that:

Industrial rescue cases continued to be a source of great irritation. Invariably, much as I would have liked to be convinced, the cases that came up were just not viable. Bear Brand stockings, yet another Merseyside case, once again brought me into direct conflict with my old friend Eric Heffer. The dispute with Tony Benn over Concorde also continued to simmer, as did the worker cooperatives, Meriden Motorcycles and Kirkby Manufacturing and Engineering ... At one meeting in March 1975, when I had again opposed aid to Triang and Bear Brand, Tony Benn delivered a strong attack on me and 'the Treasury' for opposing all his schemes. I replied that the fault was his for insisting on bringing forward cases that did not have a cat in hell's chance of succeeding.[17]

Such indiscriminate use of public money by Mr Benn in supporting workers' cooperatives cannot be criticised in isolation. Much government money was discriminately apportioned in far greater sums in pursuit of the industrial strategy. British Leyland and Chrysler are the best two examples.

BRITISH LEYLAND AND CHRYSLER

The British Leyland crisis, which to the general public is as long running as Coronation Street (though possibly less popular), effectively broke in important political terms in December 1974. The crisis was tailor-made for what the government envisaged would be the NEB's role – only the legislation establishing the NEB had not yet passed through Parliament. British Leyland, formed in 1968 by the merger of Leyland Trucks and British Motor Holdings – the Austin Morris group – faced a liquidity crisis by the end of 1974 and appealed for government aid in view of the unwillingness, which was quite justified, of the private sector to make further injections of private capital. For Harold Wilson's Government, committed to an interventionist industrial strategy, the question was not whether or not to rescue British Leyland but how, and at what expense, the rescue would take place.

On 4 December 1974, therefore, Wilson asked Don Ryder, who was to become the NEB's first chairman, to head an inquiry into the company's future prospects, which, given its huge size, its export contribution and its position as Britain's largest single employer, were still considered vital to the 'regeneration' of industry itself. To the government such aspects of the crisis were more political than economic and the pattern of the 1970s of political expediency overriding economic necessity was enthusiastically inaugurated.

Mr Heath's 1972 Industry Act provided Mr Wilson with the instant source of public money that was required to offset the immediate liquidity crisis, in the form of an interim £50 million. The government then passed the British Leyland Act giving it a large measure of control over the company but not, as yet, full public ownership. However the British Leyland Board was so restricted from December 1974 onwards in relation to investment, borrowing, the sale of assets and wage negotiations, in return for public money, that the difference between full and partial public ownership was from the start academic. The atmosphere of crisis in December 1974 and the sense of urgency should not be underestimated as it set the precedent for later rescues. Harold Wilson noted in his memoirs that:

> The commitments we were entering into were prodigious, and there could be no certainty that the cost of saving Leyland might not be even more than the working party had estimated. But we could ignore neither the cost to the balance of payments nor the effect on employment if Leyland were suffered to go under. Leyland's direct exports from Britain in 1974 had reached almost £500 million. Moreover,
>
> > The company employs over 170,000 people directly in this country, and the livelihood of several hundred thousand more is dependent upon it. I must tell the House that in this decision a million jobs are at stake.
>
> There was no doubt about the gravity with which this announcement was received by all parties in the House. The Conservative Front Bench fairly asked for time to reflect on it. When however I emphasized the measure of the crisis, by saying that while the company was not bankrupt, failure of the Government to act on the lines I announced would have meant Leyland going into liquidation or a receivership, some Conservatives shouted 'No' to my suggestion that such action would have been the last thing MPs would wish.

As more Conservative back-benchers criticized the decision, I warned again about the loss of a million jobs, if the action on which we had decided were not taken. The announcement was warmly received on the Labour side, but it became clear that the debate to give Parliamentary approval to the expenditure could be very controversial.

When the British Leyland Bill came before the House for Second Reading it was strongly attacked by both Conservatives and Liberals. The vote was 282 in favour, 261 against. The vote on the Money Resolution authorizing the necessary expenditure was carried by a majority of 19. A further Financial Resolution to increase the December vote for interim aid was carried at midnight by 226 to 58.[18]

The Ryder Report, although drawn up in considerable haste given the political importance of its deliberations, was published in March 1975 and can only be described as inadequate. It told the truth about British Leyland but not the whole truth. It looked at the company too much in macroeconomic rather than microeconomic terms and seemed to miss the fact that investment in itself has no particular merit, if that investment is wrongly channelled into a poor product. The report did show many of the known problems of British Leyland; plant and equipment were outdated, productivity was very poor, greater investment was required, industrial relations practices were less than satisfactory and the company's organisational structure was inefficient. The report in its recommendations ducked the question of gross overmanning by not envisaging large-scale closures and redundancies and urged the organisation of British Leyland into four separate businesses dealing with cars, trucks and buses, special products and international activities. It envisaged British Leyland continuing as a major volume car producer but had very little to say about what sort of volume cars should be produced. Essentially the report was overambitious and overoptimistic, relying on huge injections of public money, rather than improving the product range, for long-term revival. Thus the report estimated that the investment programme would cost £1500 million over seven years, equivalent to £2800 million with inflation taken into consideration with up to £1400 million generated from outside the company. The Ryder Report was well-intentioned and, in macroeconomic terms, quite rational, but it did not deal with the crucial question of the existing product range and how it had gone so seriously wrong. Barbara Castle's account of the Cabinet's reaction to the report illuminates this point:

> Ryder's report was ruthlessly thorough. What was wrong with Leyland was poor management (Stokes would have to go), grotty machinery and bad industrial relations. What Ryder proposed was the only way of putting it right. The alternative was to accept the unemployment of nearly one million people and the abandonment of a comprehensive motor industry. Harry Urwin had been an invaluable member of the Ryder Committee, accepting that there had been bad overmanning and that industrial relations had been partly responsible for the whole mess. And so, with very little opposition, it was agreed. Even Wedgie warned that we must be cautious and monitor each stage of the development carefully. That would be done by the NEB (i.e. by Ryder himself). Harold Wilson said that we might get some Arab funds involved: not directly through Leyland, but through the NEB. And he added wistfully that Donald Stokes had been a long-standing friend. This would hurt him terribly and he hoped that he might be used in the sort of job he excelled at: as a travelling export promotor for the company. Only Harold Lever really let fly: we were rushing into a 'grandiose folly', he said; it was like a 'bad Pharoah's dream' in which we weren't even promised seven fat years after the seven lean ones. But he didn't cut much ice.[19]

It is tedious to list the inadequacies of the product range but necessary given that this aspect of British Leyland's failure is so often ignored by the policy-makers. For politicians there are no votes in the minutiae of the product range. In 1974 when the British Leyland crisis became a major political issue the product range deficiency was well advanced. The Mini, introduced in 1958, had never been properly priced to yield profits for reinvestment. The successful Morris 1000 range had been phased out in 1972 just before the oil crisis and rocketing petrol prices made the Morris 1000 an even more viable volume car. The 1100 and 1300 range had been replaced by the Allegros which were infinitely inferior and attracted a 'Panorama' investigation into their lack of safety. In 1978 a report by the British Safety Council detailed the Allegro's deficiencies after a High Court action for damages relating to the Allegro's wheel faults. The British Safety Council recounted how in March 1977, after direct pressure from the Council, 290 000 Allegros were recalled at a cost of £1·5 million to rectify defects in the suspension and braking systems. The BSC report stated that: 'The specific defects have come to light and were known about by both British Leyland and the Department of Transport as long ago as September 1975 when the police reported a number of their Allegros faulty. Repairs were carried out immediately – but only on police vehicles.'[20]

The 'replacements' for the Morris 1000 range, the Marinas, were another chapter of woe. Introduced in 1973 the Marina was available only with 1300 cc or 1800 cc engines, thus failing to compete with Ford, Vauxhall and other manufacturers' successful 1600 cc fleet company cars or family saloon ranges. Unlike the Allegro, the Marina was safe enough to drive – except when it was raining, as the windscreen wipers, inexcusably set for a left-hand drive model, failed to cover the driver's field of vision. As a result any right turn made in the rain was positively dangerous as the driver would strain to look underneath a huge uncovered area of the windscreen.[21]

Similar design inadequacies plagued other British Leyland cars. The popular Triumph Herald range was never adequately replaced and the Triumph 1300, 1500 and 1750 models failed to capture the car-buying public's imagination largely because of their dreary and unsophisticated appearance. The MG range of sports cars lived almost entirely on nostalgia and one motoring correspondent was correct to describe the MG as a 'Marina in drag'. The fact that the MG plant at Abingdon was strike free is a further condemnation of the product range as MG's problems could not be blamed on industrial militancy. The 1800 range was replaced by the Princess, again with the Princesses showing little or no improvement. Indeed the sluggish performance of both the Princess and the Maxi indicated they were seriously under-powered. The Maxi, while arguably a 'hatchback', could not compete with the small-car 'hatchback' range developed by virtually all British Leyland's rivals in the 1970s. It was not until the 1980s that the Metro appeared to plug this gap but by then the opportunities of the 1970s had been lost. Even the new Rover range introduced in the late 1970s attracted considerable criticism and it was not until 1982 that Rover thought of installing a rear wash/wipe on a car that was, after all, at the luxury end of the market. Even in 1982 BL still had no 'hatchback' 1600 cc model, unlike for example Ford, Fiat and Volkswagen, and were still producing 'updated' Marinas (called Itals), Allegros and Maxis, the latter barely improved since their launch in 1968. In short, only in the Land Rover, Range Rover and the bus/truck categories were British Leyland in the 1970s properly competitive.

Even in December 1974, when British Leyland effectively slipped into the public sector, if productivity had been improved, strikes eliminated, investment guaranteed, marketing rationalised and overmanning reduced, the problem would still have remained while the product range remained so inadequate. Investment was not the main problem in the 1970s – the NEB saw to that with public injections on a vast scale – but the rate of return on investment was. The problem was that the rate of return on the mid-1970s product range would never prove sufficient to ensure the company's viability.

However during the 1970s the arguments about British Leyland's future were never discussed, at the political level, in microeconomic terms. The political answer was simply to pour more public money into the company in the hope that such investment would prove adequate. Thus it was natural that British Leyland would eventually come completely under the aegis of the NEB, which by perpetually guaranteeing public financing did nothing to bring a greater sense of realism to a workforce which had grown accustomed to industrial militancy and low productivity. Ironically in view of the amount of public money authorised by the Labour Government for British Leyland, an unofficial strike at Longbridge in February 1979 contributed to the 'winter of discontent' which made the Labour Government so unpopular with the general public. Referring to the management's refusal to make parity payments Mr Derek Robinson, the Longbridge convenor, told the workers they should reply to Leyland 'in the only language the management know – the language of force'.[22] Indeed throughout the whole period of the 1974–9 Labour Government the threat of industrial action was an ever-present worry to management attempts to rationalise and restructure the company.

Thus when the NEB bailed out British Leyland with a £50 million loan in September 1977 it did so to a background of the toolmakers' strike which cost 120 000 vehicles in lost production earlier in the year, and differences between the T & GWU and AUEW over the company's proposals for a rationalised pay structure. The then NEB chairman, Leslie Murphy, explained that releasing further money would depend on the view taken of Leyland's future plans. He commented that 'I must stress that the future size of Leyland will definitely depend on how successful it is and whether the management and workforce of the company can perform satisfactorily'.[23] In November 1977 the new British Leyland chairman, Michael Edwardes, was equally platitudinous in explaining his decision to accept the chair:

> 'If British Leyland fails to succeed it will have the most dire effect on jobs and investment prospects not to mention the reputation of Britain and British goods overseas'. The question you will ask is, 'Can you really hope to influence such a situation?' I don't know. The task is enormous; some people could even say impossible.
>
> But I am going to try because I believe that British Leyland does have a future. It is a company which has talent at all levels, talent that can and must be fully utilised. Given the right support from all in the company and the Government it is still possible to restore its growth and realise its full potential.[24]

The problem of the product range was not deemed worthy of public comment. Nor was it when in April 1978 the Industry Secretary, Eric Varley, promised a further £450 million of aid as part of the government's support for Michael Edwardes's restructured corporate plan. Joel Barnett, referring to British Leyland, candidly noted in his memoirs that:

> Once we had hived it off into the ownership of the National Enterprise Board (NEB), provided hundreds of millions of new capital, and appointed Michael Edwardes to run it, we were able to let them get on with it. Even so, the reports we got left us with no illusions – it would be back as a massive problem before too long.[25]

Mr Barnett's judgement proved correct.

As well as the perpetual problem of British Leyland, Labour's industrial strategy, being by definition interventionist, had to deal with the problem of another ailing car company, Chrysler. The same arguments that were used to justify the British Leyland rescue were paraded – loss of jobs and the threat of deindustrialisation. Chrysler had taken over the old Rootes Group in the mid-1960s and experienced strikes and bad industrial relations with 30 per cent production lost through stoppages. The product range, while better than British Leyland's, was poor in comparison to other competitors. Harold Lever, however, recalled that during the negotiations over the future of Chrysler: 'The Department of Industry never raised the question of the type of car. It was not raised once and was something they never brought up. I don't understand car making but I understand employment.'[26] Such a failing by the Department of Industry – not by Lever, whose brief was essentially political – underlay and undermined the whole Chrysler rescue strategy. One Treasury minister commented that 'the civil servants in the Department of Industry were ill-equipped to make investment decisions. They had no background in industry and no experience.'[27] In the view of one cabinet minister 'the civil servants at the DTI didn't understand the trade union dimension. The DTI briefs to ministers were management briefs from high up in industry.'[28]

In November 1975 Chrysler warned that unless the British Government covered the £75 million loss and funded another £80 million Chrysler UK would be closed down. Perhaps the American parent company was bluffing, but if not the spectre of increased unemployment at places like Linwood, where unemployment was already high, was politically too potent a threat for a Labour Government to ignore. Furthermore, as Grant rightly points out, the Cabinet's decision to bail out Chrysler 'was influenced by the fear of giving a propaganda boost to the Scottish Nationalists'.[29] Barbara Castle recalled the arguments which Industry Secretary Eric Varley put to the Cabinet in November 1975:

He thought that Chrysler's share of the UK market had probably gone completely and we should concentrate on making British Leyland a success. But 25,000 jobs were at immediate risk. The CPRS report had shown how we were suffering from overcapacity in the motor car industry and he was going over the report with the trade unions that afternoon. There was no clear view coming from local MPs. The press were wrong in saying that Chrysler was asking for money. Chrysler were saying 'It's your worry; take it over.' He concluded by saying he thought we might try offering Chrysler some money in return for a phased run-down. Harold said that the banks were not willing to put any more money into Chrysler US unless it shed Chrysler UK . . . Willie then stormed away about the effect of closure on Scotland. Linwood was the only part of the motor industry Scotland had, he declared. 'This will be politically disastrous.'[30]

Joel Barnett noted that both Edmund Dell and Eric Varley thought that:

it would be crazy to pour millions of pounds down the drain, when the facts showed the position to be irredeemable. But it was not long before the bogus argument of de-industrialization, and the even more bogus argument that somehow you save real jobs by spending huge sums in a lost cause, came up again. Harold Wilson, having originally stood firm, now asked Harold Lever to put his financial mind to devising a scheme to persuade the main Chrysler board in the United States to keep its UK subsidiary going.[31]

The government thus became committed to Chrysler UK, a competitor of British Leyland, for the same reasons that it was committed to British Leyland. As well as the unemployment constraint on the Cabinet's action the Iranian Government applied diplomatic pressure as Chrysler UK manufactured Hillman Hunter kits which were supplied for assembly in Iran. Harold Lever, who negotiated the Chrysler agreement, recalled that 'Chrysler was a very skilful rescue to save employment. We kept 5 years of employment at Linwood and the exports to Persia. I brought to Cabinet a telegram from our ambassador in Teheran which stated that Hoveyda (the Iranian Prime Minister) at the Shah's request had asked to make it clear that if we didn't maintain the Iranian contract it would affect every aspect – economic, trading, diplomatic – of our relations.'[32]

One of Lever's cabinet colleagues, who was less enthusiastic, thought that 'Lever was overidentified with Chrysler – he had too much responsibility and later was over-defensive'.[33] The decision to maintain employment ultimately prevailed and the government duly sanctioned a £162 million rescue operation. The government committed itself to covering £72·5 million of Chrysler's losses over a four-year period in return for a promise that Chrysler would not withdraw from Britain and would sign a 'planning agreement' with the government. The 'planning agreement' itself was a charade and was the only one forthcoming during 1974–9 despite the left's strong advocacy of planning agreements as a part of the industrial strategy.

This was conclusively demonstrated in July 1978 when Chrysler UK was sold by the parent company to Peugeot–Citroen without informing the government until the agreement was signed. Again it appeared that the government had, in Harold Wilson's words, 'been presented with a pistol at its head'. However this was really a pistol of the government's own making in that it refused for political, not economic, reasons to sanction an end to state financial aid. Thus, despite protestations at the way Chrysler's American Chairman John Riccardo had conducted business, the government felt they had no option but to comply. (One trade union leader commented that 'Chrysler's American businessmen looked like gangsters and behaved like them.'[34])

Political considerations were paramount for the government. As the *Observer* commented in August 1978: 'The Government considers a good deal for the Scottish workforce to be essential politically. If Mr. Callaghan declared an October election with Linwood at obvious risk, the Scottish Nationalists would be given just the electoral help they need. Labour psephologists reckon the Party must hold all or nearly all, its 41 Scottish seats (out of 71) to have a chance of an overall majority.'[35]

Although in the event there was no October election the *Observer*'s analysis was accurate in political terms. Finally, to the inauspicious background of a Chrysler strike over pay, the government agreed in September 1978 to approve the Peugeot–Citroen takeover of Chrysler's debt. Eric Varley stoically declared that the prospects for Chrysler UK under Peugeot–Citroen 'will be at least as good as under the present arrangements'.[36]

Ultimately the government got the worst of all worlds with both British Leyland and Chrysler ending up as a bottomless pit of public money whether through the aegis of the NEB or the guarantees of foreign motor manufacturers. One backbench MP commented that 'the NEB guidelines were pathetic. We should have nationalised both Chrysler and BL and then had small plant loyalty',[37] a solution which may have avoided the political embarrassment the government suffered with Chrysler but which held out little prospect of an economic solution. A junior minister arguing with the benefit of hindsight put it that 'as far as Chrysler was concerned we had our hands full with BL. We couldn't support them both',[38] which is again an argument relating to the degree of industrial interventionism rather than the principle.

However tempting and rational to a Labour Government such interventionism is, which it was under the industrial strategy, the evidence suggests that the principle itself is flawed, producing the opposite result of industrial regeneration – industrial fossilisation. Both British Leyland and Chrysler demonstrated this, not once, but repeatedly throughout the lifetime of the 1974–9 Labour Government.

THE INEFFECTIVENESS OF THE INDUSTRIAL STRATEGY

To the left of the Labour Party the industrial strategy did not go far enough and the plans carefully nurtured in Opposition, 1970–4, were simply not translated into political reality. The NEB was not interventionist enough, it was a toothless bulldog, which could not frighten, let alone take over, the commanding heights of the economy. For those who believe in a planned socialist economy of whatever model, rather than a mixed economy, such a view is rational and accurate. It is not the purpose of this book to put forward a critique of socialist economics; rather it is the aim to examine in detail how the economic and industrial policies pursued between 1974 and 1979 affected the British economy and the Labour Party. In this context it is necessary to argue that more socialism, rather than less, would have made the economy worse and the Labour Party's political prospects less electorally viable. The evidence for this lies to a considerable degree in the failure of the limited socialism that the industrial strategy represented to improve British industry in particular or the economy in general.

The failures of government intervention regarding British Leyland and Chrysler have already been mentioned. Planning agreements were never properly tried, not just because of the out-manoeuvring of the left by Labour ministers but because such agreements offered no prospect of tangible industrial benefits. By the end of 1977 Victor Keegan noted that in any case, planning

agreements had been replaced by a looser system of industry/
government cooperation, aimed at mutual benefit:

> In August 1974 the Government published a White Paper,
> 'The Regeneration of British Industry' which explained how
> the revival of manufacturing industry was to be achieved
> through the establishment of a National Enterprise Board and
> the negotiation of 'planning agreements' with large companies.
>
> Now, 40 months on, the NEB is in business albeit on a
> modest scale, but not a single voluntary planning agreement
> has been signed with a large private corporation. The only one
> that exists in the private sector was forced on Chrysler UK,
> when it had its hands tied behind its back and was facing the
> firing squad – and that has hardly proved a model of its kind.
>
> The Government is hoping shortly to announce its first
> 'clean' planning agreement devoid of coercion and a few others
> may follow once the present stalemate – caused by the
> reluctance of companies to be the first to break the CBI's
> intransigent opposition to such agreements – has been broken.
> But as a major instrument of industrial policy they have quietly
> bitten the dust.
>
> Planning agreements may be dead but planning discussions
> (sic) between Government and companies are increasing at a
> sharp pace. The Department of Industry has been talking to
> 100 companies in the past nine months about such matters as
> their Corporate plans, investment proposals and manpower
> needs. These have apparently been friendly and mutually
> beneficial. Most of them will probably not end up with a formal
> 'planning agreement' since most companies appear to have
> deep-rooted objections to signing a piece of paper called an
> 'agreement' which has legalistic overtones despite its essen-
> tially voluntary nature.
>
> Such agreements provoke among companies almost Pavlo-
> vian fears about Bennite intervention long since discarded by
> the Department of Industry.[39]

One cabinet minister who thought that voluntarism was no
effective substitute for compulsory planning agreements, recalled
that the 'Industrial Strategy was a curate's egg. We got some
superb results with the foundry industry but our basic problem

was that we were doing it on a voluntary *ad hoc* basis and never seized the chance of making investment grants conditional on a planning agreement.'[40]

However, although the left's view – that what was wrong with planning agreements was that they were never tried – is consistent in political terms, it is far less certain that greater use of planning agreements would have avoided the sort of problems that arise in the normal routine of state intervention in private industry. It is arguable that compulsory planning agreements would have come to resemble little more than the job support system of industrial fossilisation that emerged with British Leyland.

The NEB hardly presents a picture of success, especially given the enthusiasm for it, in one form or another, at the outset of the industrial strategy. Its role came largely to be that of a rescuer of lame ducks, so that by the end of 1978 BL was the NEB's biggest single customer with £450 million already committed in aid as opposed to the £150 million granted to Rolls Royce to develop a new aero engine. Moreover the government's allocation of an extra £3000 million to the NEB in 1979, with increased aid specified for the Scottish and Welsh Development Agencies, may be seen as electioneering rather than shrewd economic investment. The NEB's record of entrepreneurial successes was very limited, with microtechnology perhaps being the best case.

Other government industrial aid also had little economic success. One particular case in point was the government support for the De Lorean car company in the hope of providing employment in Northern Ireland. Again the decision to put £53 million of taxpayers' money into the scheme was political rather than economic and was pushed through Cabinet by the Northern Ireland Secretary Roy Mason in the teeth of Treasury opposition. The decision was a fiasco, with the bills eventually coming in for the Thatcher Government. John De Lorean's business ethics and the firm's financial probity were to be seriously questioned, raising doubt as to the validity of the rescue in the first place. Mr Mason had acted out of the best of intentions – providing jobs in a province with a higher rate of unemployment than any other part of the United Kingdom – but, as was the case with British Leyland and Chrysler, customers and not governments provide real jobs in manufacturing industry.

Another Northern Ireland Minister, Stanley Orme, who favoured a radical industrial strategy, recalled that 'we had factories in Northern Ireland that came to us for money. They wanted to be a cooperative or to get £x million grant but they made products no one would buy.'[41] John De Lorean was in essentially the same position except that his greater financial experience, and the prospects for employment he held out, were sufficient to persuade the British Government. The customers, however, were not forthcoming and consequently nor were the long-term prospects for secure employment.

A similarly depressing story of industrial strategy intervention concerned the nationalised steel industry. The problems were all too familiar – overmanning, low productivity, unimaginative management and lack of competitiveness in world markets.[42] Throughout the course of the 1974–9 Labour Government the economic position of BSC deteriorated and the need for rationalisation became ever more urgent. The government's prime concern was job losses and thus subsidised BSC to remain overmanned and hence uncompetitive. BSC's spiral of decline was eventually, like De Lorean's, inherited by the Thatcher Government, which was required to take drastic measures to return a semblance of financial reality to the industry.

The British aircraft industry was another recipient of huge sums of public money. In September 1978, £750 million was allocated to balance the industry's books. Rolls Royce received £240 million to develop the RB211/535 engine.[43] Thus, seven years after the Heath Government had bailed it out, Rolls Royce was still in need of injections of taxpayer's money. British Airways was allocated £400 million to buy nineteen Boeing 757 narrow-bodied jets and British Aerospace was permitted £100 million to collaborate with the French in building a European 'Airbus'. Such investment in the aircraft industry bore little prospect of a financial return. In 1974 work by N. K. Gardner, a senior economic adviser at the Department of Industry, showed that post-war governments had spent £1·5 billion (in 1974 prices) on the development of civil aircraft and aeroengines with less than £150 million recovered.

Government subsidies to British Shipbuilding provided another source of political controversy, particularly the £21 million subsidy to gain an order to build twenty-four ships for Poland at a cost of £115 million. Optimistically, Mr Varley in December 1977 said that the deal had warded off disaster for the British shipbuilding industry. *The Times* put it that:

As charge and countercharge thundered about the Commons, Mr. Nott, Conservative spokesman on trade, accused the Prime Minister of being willing for the sake of the love of one Labour marginal seat to ski down Everest in the nude with a carnation in his mouth. Angry Labour charges that the Conservatives were trying to wreck the agreement were met with opposition gibes that the Government was being taken to the Polish cleaners.

Mr. Michael Grylls, Tory MP for Surrey North-west, said it was supreme folly to subsidize the merchant fleet of the communist world so that it could compete against our own fleet.[44]

Even still, industrial disputes plagued the beginning of work on the deal and in December 1978 the government gave a further £17 million reprieve to the Marathon yard on Clydebank where Jimmy Reid in 1971 had led the 'work-in' which helped reverse the non-interventionist policy of the Heath Government.[45]

The key political issue in the shipyards subsidy was to prevent a rise in unemployment. The artificial preservation of jobs in fossilised industries was the central feature, in practice, of the government's industrial strategy. This much was made clear in a memorandum written by the Permanent Head of the Treasury, Sir Douglas Wass, in February 1979 which argued that seven of the government's job subsidy projects were not only unlikely to break even in any acceptable period of time but were expected to accumulate losses at a faster rate than that at which the economy would expand.

Sir Douglas's memorandum accurately described the flawed logic of seven particular projects. The Rolls Royce RB 211–535 engine development was regarded as 'an inherently risky project and on optimistic assumptions not expected to break even until 1993',[46] while the British Aerospace 146 was estimated to cost £300 million to launch with a subsequent loss of from £90 million to £210 million. The participation in the A310 Airbus jet was calculated to involve a negative cash flow of £300 million by 1983 and the proposal to provide cheap electricity to Anglesey Aluminium was expected to cost losses of £130 million to £150 million. Other losses were envisaged in the memorandum for the Sidewinder missile chosen by the Ministry of Defence (£17 million) and the British Aircraft Corporation's Milon missile (£40 million).

The most wasteful example of the seven was the Polish ships' subsidisation. The £21 million subsidy or 70 per cent of the selling price was calculated to amount to more than £6800 million for each man-year of employment. Sir Geoffrey Howe the Shadow Chancellor spoke of the 'notorious Polish shipbuilding deal'[47] and other commentators, not necessarily Conservatives, were also critical. Commenting in the *Guardian*, where Sir Douglas's memorandum was leaked, Frances Cairncross correctly analysed the reality of the Polish ship subsidy as unjustifiable:

> But what about saving jobs? Might not the Polish shipbuilding order, which will eventually allow the Poles to undercut British shipping, be justified on the grounds that it is a cheap alternative to paying out unemployment benefit in regions where jobs are scarce?
>
> The answer is no. All the projects listed in the Wass memorandum show a loss even after allowing for the saving of unemployment benefit.
>
> To pay skilled shipbuilders to clean out canals or lay out parks may seem an appalling waste of skills. But it would be cheaper than paying them to build ships which we have to pay other countries to buy. And sadly, it may have more future in it.[48]

A final example of the subsidy growth sanctioned by the industrial strategy occurred in November 1978 when the Kirkby Manufacturing and Engineering (KME) workers' cooperative, championed by Tony Benn when he was Industry Secretary, was taken over by a private firm with the help of £4·3 million of public funds. Originally Mr Benn had provided £3·9 million to KME and a further £860 000 was granted in April 1977. However KME's financial position continued to deteriorate and a £700 000 loss in the first half of 1978 became a £1 million loss by the time the private firm Worcester Engineering took KME over with a further £4·3 million of public money. The problem was therefore to be inherited by the Thatcher Government.

Although the Labour left can criticise the 1974–9 industrial strategy as not going far enough and are correct to point out that the Cabinet effectively neutralised the scale of intervention drawn up by the left in opposition, the ineffectiveness of the industrial strategy is arguably an ineffectiveness not of too little state intervention but of too much.

The first myth that underlay the industrial strategy was that if only the level of investment could be increased, by such institutions as the NEB, the future growth potential of British industry could be assured. The argument was flawed from the beginning. The share of output devoted to fixed investment, according to the NIESR, was only 6 per cent to 10 per cent from the Victorian era to the 1929 slump. During the Depression investment still did not fall below 10 per cent and by the 1950s it had risen to 14·5 per cent and further still to 18·3 per cent at the beginning of the 1960s. Indeed investment was at 21·8 per cent in 1975 as the immediate effects of the oil crisis were still affecting the economy. Thus investment, at levels reflecting a growing proportion of an expanding total output, was not at the depressed levels that supporters of the industrial strategy claimed.

But more importantly the huge increase in public investment in industry between 1974 and 1979, which has been chronicled in this chapter, failed to produce any adequate rate of return on the capital sums invested. Investment by itself is of no merit – indeed the opposite is true – if that investment is unlikely to satisfy a customer and therefore to generate further funds. This was the story of British Leyland, BSC, Chrysler, British Shipbuilding, the Kirkby Coop and many other chronic loss-making nationalised industries such as the railways. The problem was not too little investment but too much without sufficient economic justification. It is, arguably, difficult to justify such industrial investment even on socialist grounds as the money invested could have been better spent on the welfare state, the environment, education and so forth, which socialists have often argued, rightly, contribute to an improved quality of life.

The second myth that underlay the industrial strategy was that it was 'saving' jobs which would otherwise have evaporated into longer dole queues. There is no evidence, not least with such major rescue cases as British Leyland and British Steel, to believe that the net number of jobs in the economy was increased by such subsidisation. Ultimately, as both BL and BSC discovered, if the customers are not forthcoming and profitability proves illusory there is no way of safeguarding jobs except by further subsidy which itself reinforces the spiral of decline. A new and successful product range only would have 'saved' British Leyland jobs in the mid 1970s, not further injections of public money. Had the government wished simply to create jobs, irrespective of financial criteria, it would have been better advised to increase spending in health, education and environmental services generally, where social and recreational benefits to the public at large would have resulted.

These individual cases, however, raise the wider point that throughout the industrial development of Britain, and other countries for that matter, the creation of new jobs has been a process associated with the decline of old jobs. The industrial revolution itself helped to 'destroy' jobs in agriculture. The workers who flocked to work in car production in its boom years left other jobs to do so. As the number of blacksmiths, saddle manufacturers and stage coach construction firms declined, so the number of workers in the car industries and on the railways increased. All such economic and social changes and advancements involved a continuous process of job losses in old industries. But the *net effect* was an increase in employment, even with an increase in population growth, as new industries came to take their place. One economic commentator put this point particularly succinctly at the time of the British Leyland 'a million jobs lost' scare:

> Mr. Wilson made it very clear time and again that critics of the rescue operation will have 'a million jobs' thrown in their faces; and they will deserve it if they allow themselves to be so intimidated. It really is not good enough for a prime minister who once taught economics to play up to the illiterate assumption that if some particular jobs disappear, no others will take their place. Anyone with knowledge of the future looking ahead in 1959 would have been able to predict job losses far exceeding anything involved in BL. Between 1959 and 1973 the fall in the numbers employed in agriculture – or 'jobs destroyed' in the populist jargon – was 325,000. Over 400,000 jobs disappeared in mining; nearly 230,000 in textiles and over 200,000 in the railways. But although these jobs were not 'preserved', total employment expanded by 1·2 million over the period.

The fallacy is that there is an entity called 'the UK' which decides which industries should expand or decline, and by how much. The motor industry was not created by a government decision. Nor were most others. The Government does not have to decide which product 'we' opt in or out of. There are any number of halfway houses, such as manufacturing trucks and specialised cars, or components, or final assembly, or leaving small car production to Ford; but if the motor industry declines, other industries will take its place, provided that government policy allows a market return on capital.

Harold Macmillan, although far wiser than his successors, displayed the essence of the politician's (or industrial states-man's) approach when, discussing 'demand management' with some economic journalists, he asked: 'Demand for what?' It is a mistake even to try to answer from the centre how consumers at home and abroad are going to spend or invest their income. They will decide for themselves – it is not governments that create jobs but customers, here and abroad.[49]

The third myth which underlay the industrial strategy was that the economy as a whole was dependent overwhelmingly on manufactured industry and that in manufactured industry, not the service sector, lay Britain's future employment prospects and hopes for prosperity. As Alan Budd has argued, in this respect 'the value of the Industrial Strategy is its very vagueness: people feel that the decline in British industry must be bad; a policy to rescue it must be desirable'.[50] Such feelings are, indeed, natural but, alas, they are misconceived. Again, the assumptions associated with this argument are fallacious, particularly when the question of exports is raised. In reality Britain has always had a visible trade deficit which has been covered by invisible earnings. Britain has never been a net manufacturing exporter, indeed quite the reverse. As W. A. P. Manser has rightly argued from his research into Britain's trade based on statistical evidence dating back to 1826:

from the present day back to the beginning of our national life, back successively through the maturity, growth and infancy of our industrial economy and through the rural ages that preceded it, Britain appears to have been a net importing country . . . The notion, then, that Britain would be exporting a surplus is misplaced. Equally misplaced is the notion that she ever, in fact, did export a surplus.

This leads to the first question. How, through all these centuries, did Britain run a trade deficit and survive; and not only survive but grow from economic insignificance into mature propserity? Clearly, though she had an unbroken deficit, she was not economically weak.

The answer is simple. Her 'visible' deficit was covered by her 'invisible' surplus. In other words, her shortfall in the exchange of physical commodities was made up by an excess of income on the sales of non-physical necessaries: banking, insurance, shipping and the like. Throughout her history Britain's 'invisible' earnings have generously exceeded her deficiency in 'visible' incomes.[51]

Moreover, the general trend away from manufacturing employment towards service industries was clearly marked between 1974 and 1979 despite the rhetoric and injections of public money into the manufacturing sector. Not only was there the prospect of North Sea oil income but also the huge expansion of tourism. Bernard Nossiter has pointed out that given Britons' alleged preference of 'leisure over goods' the growth of the tourist industry makes good economic sense. Nossiter argues that:

> Apart from oil, as we have seen, the fastest growing component in Britain's balance of payments is tourism. There were 8·8 million tourists in 1975, 10·1 million in 1976 and an estimated 11·4 million in 1977. They spent £2·2 billion in 1976, enough to rank as Britain's sixth export industry; for 1977, their outlays probably reached £3 billion, a gain of more than a third. That pays for a lot of imported food and raw materials . . . The choice of leisure over goods may yield rewards in that most competitive of markets, the struggle for tourist exchange. As other industrial nations rise to ever-higher levels of income, there is every reason to believe that at some point they too will devote more and more of their income to leisure. Tourism is a modern grown industry. Britain, for a variety of reasons, is well-equipped to profit from it.[52]

Because of its class-rooted background of trade unionism and industrial struggle the Labour Party was not prepared to accept the necessary, and economically advantageous, deindustrialisation that was proceeding during the 1970s. The industrial strategy itself was a retreat to a mythical age of manufacturing industry's supremacy at the expense of future patterns of economic development. Nossiter, an outsider, an American economist, recognised this in Britain in the late 1970s even if the Labour Government did not. He, rightly, analysed the changes required in the economy, and consequently in society, as transforming Britain:

> It is transforming the heritage of the industrial revolution, shedding the plants, the mills and some of the values that made them work. It is slowly becoming a post-industrial society where a decreasing number of men and women are concerned with the production of goods, and an increasing number with things of the mind and spirit – services in the economists' accounting. This transition is eased by the fortuitous discovery of North Sea oil, an old-fashioned process of mineral extraction made possible by new and advanced technology . . . But more and more, Britain will earn its way by trading its skill with words, music, banking, education and leisure for the products of more traditional societies. This can't and won't happen overnight. But the day that the last mine, mill and assembly line close should be an occasion for national rejoicing, not despair.[53]

Labour's industrial strategy 1974–9, and incidentally, a more extreme version of it favoured by Labour's left, have little to commend them except good intentions. Ultimately the total failure of the industrial strategy ironically contrasted with the total enthusiasm with which it was launched.

CHAPTER IV

Wilson's Last Months

TUC SUPPORT FOR THE £6 POLICY

As is often the case with the initial stage of a compulsory incomes policy, the £6 pay policy received strong support from the TUC, particularly from its architect Jack Jones who was the stoutest defender of the policy both in public and private. At meetings between the TUC and the Labour Party Jones 'asserted his Cromwellian New Model Army authority'.[1]

The TUC's overwhelming support was confirmed at Congress in September 1975 with the miners – arguably the *primus inter pares* of the powerful unions – backing the £6 policy. General opinion was that even if the unions didn't like the policy there was no alternative to it. As a result the policy held well and the increase in earnings was restricted to 14 per cent between July 1975 and July 1976. The rate of price increases was 13 per cent. Such statistics must not be seen in isolation and still less in a causal relationship. Public expenditure, checked in April 1975, was further brought under control in February 1976 and a semblance of financial discipline returned to the money supply. Thus, as one economic analyst put it in relation to the £6 pay policy, 'Emergency clamp-downs of this kind nearly always seem to lead to a temporary favourable deviation of inflation from the path suggested by monetary and exchange rate factors.'[2]

However, having given their support, the TUC certainly exaggerated the economic, as opposed to political, benefits that the £6 policy could deliver. Free collective bargaining had been suspended but bargaining with the government continued with the unions, in a throwback to the Social Contract days, trying to trade off wage restraint in favour of government action to reflate. That such an outcome would have simply meant renewed inflation was obscured to trade-union leaders by their self-denying belief in the £6 policy. This paradoxical approach is best described by Barbara Castle at a joint Labour Party/TUC Liaison meeting in November 1975:

> Len Murray came in firmly. He hoped the TUC would have a chance to discuss the contents of the package. The situation was obviously deteriorating. Measures were going to be needed to stimulate consumption. 'The main bulwark against inflation is the pay policy,' he said. 'We want it to go on sticking.' David Basnett was equally stern. 'We accept the argument that now is not the time for general reflation, but we shall be coming back to you about another package.'[3]

Given the massive support for the £6 policy at Congress in September it was not surprising that the 1975 Labour Party Conference also supported the government because the trade union block votes dominated policy decisions. There was some hostile criticism from the left of the £6 policy, more so than at Congress, given the Constituency Labour Parties' considerable move to the left. This criticism from the left boiled over at a fringe meeting in a huge row between Jack Jones and Ian Mikardo, the veteran left-wing member of the NEC. The *Guardian* described the event as:

> a fantastic public confrontation between Mr. Jack Jones, the leader of the Transport and General Workers' Union, and Mr. Ian Mikardo. It happened at the annual Tribune Rally which is traditionally a revivalistic occasion for the Socialist faithful. But this time it was reduced to uproar by Mr. Jones as he responded with uncontrolled bitterness to a violent attack on himself and other trade union leaders by Mr. Mikardo.[4]

Barbara Castle recalled that:

> Mik proceeded to read the speech he had handed out, piling selective statistic on selective statistic to give a hostile distortion of the work of the Government. Suddenly out of the crowded aisle where he had been standing leapt Jack Jones, up onto the platform, jabbing an accusing finger at Mik like an Old Testament prophet pronouncing his doom. As Mik had the microphone and Jack had not, all we could hear were a few snatches of what Jack said. 'I detest these attacks on the trade

union movement' was all I caught. But he stood there for a full
minute, jab following jab with inarticulate shout after inarticulate shout. It was electrifying. The audience split into pro- and
anti-Mik arguments and there was pandemonium, which Dick
Clements in the chair eventually managed to quell, appealing
to Jack as an 'old friend' and saying that Michael would be
answering Mik. Jack sat down heavily on the end seat on the
platform to which Dick Clements invited him and didn't utter a
word after that. Mik finished rather lamely to tumultuous
applause from parts of the audience. A few people tried to give
him a standing ovation.[5]

Mikardo, and the far left generally, were unable to take
compulsory pay restraint, which involved a cut in living standards, at the same time as what they regarded as a dilution of
Labour Party policy on the industrial strategy, and the fundamental transfer of wealth in favour of working people. The left
regarded any economic crisis as the opportunity for radical
socialist policies, such as taking over the 'commanding heights' of
the economy, not an excuse for postponing them. Inflation, or a
sterling crisis, were not to be tackled in the conventional way that
Labour Governments had previously tackled them, but by
socialist transformation. To the far left the endorsement of the £6
pay policy at the TUC Conference and at the Labour Party
Conference represented a defeat.

For the government the £6 policy, while a political victory, did
not constitute an economic panacea. The position of the pound
had to be closely monitored, unemployment was rising, and
public expenditure after the excesses of the Heath Government
and the overenthusiasm of the Social Contract, required further
scrutiny. The pressure on the economy of financing the PSBR was
a major constraint on every aspect of economic policy and Denis
Healey, in the autumn of 1975, prepared more substantial public
expenditure cuts. One Treasury minister recalled that 'we came
up against constraints on borrowing. You can't just have the
borrowing requirement you want.'[6]

THE QUESTION OF PUBLIC EXPENDITURE

Excessive public expenditure, resulting in huge financial deficits
which were unjustified in view of Britain's economic situation,

had been part of Mr Wilson's 'dual inheritance'. The Social Contract had not tackled this problem and had arguably made it worse. So it is to the credit of Mr Healey and the Labour Government in general that a major attempt was made in 1975/6 to control the public expenditure deficit – the source of so many other economic difficulties.

In August 1975, with the summer sterling crisis still fresh in the memory, and with the £6 pay limit imposed, the Cabinet and senior ministers met at Chequers to discuss spending priorities which obviously in reality meant cuts in public expenditure. For any Labour Government such a policy causes great heart-searching because of the misconception that the level of expenditure already existing is preferable to the level that ought to exist. Cuts in expenditure are thus invested with much rhetoric about betrayal of socialist principles as well as offering 'spending' ministers the opportunity to safeguard their budgets at all costs. The process of achieving the required cuts was – and still is for any government – a long one, involving a war of attrition between the Treasury and spending departments.

The background to the spending cuts exercise in late 1975 was dominated by concern about the pound and the balance of payments deficit. In November Denis Healey told the House of Commons that the government was applying for a drawing of initially 1000 million Special Drawing Rights (£575 million) and then a further 700 million SDRs (£400 million). As Joel Barnett commented: 'Although he was not pressed to spell out the detailed consequences of what we would need to do to meet the requirements of the IMF, informed opinion had a pretty good idea, even if it did not wholly appreciate the difficulties involved.'[7]

The scale of the cuts presented an obvious problem in that the Cabinet's judgement would be more closely influenced by strictly political repercussions, such as the strength of trade union feeling. After the initial April 1975 cuts the principle of spending cuts was not in doubt, at Cabinet level at least, since it had occasioned no resignations. To many on the left it was the principle of public expenditure cuts, not their degree of severity, that was crucial. One MP put it that 'once we said we could bring down inflation by cutting public expenditure and the welfare state, it was a betrayal of socialism'.[8]

Denis Healey, who appreciated more than any other minister the serious position facing the economy, estimated that a £3¾ billion public expenditure reduction was required for 1978–9. He was, however, prepared to settle for £3 billion for 1977–8. It is worth recording, however, that expenditure plans for 1976–9 were to remain inviolate, a decision that was later overtaken by events.

The crucial Cabinet meeting occurred on 13 November, with the Chancellor seeking approval for cuts worth £3¾ billion. Barbara Castle, on the left of the party and a major spending minister at Health and Social Security, and Joel Barnett on the right of the party and Economic Secretary, have both provided highly enlightening accounts of the Cabinet discussion. Mrs Castle recalled that:

> the first trial of strength with the Chancellor in his bid for the global sum of £3¾ billion. Denis opened with his now familiar analysis. During 1977–79 output would be 'rising very quickly indeed'. (I have never understood the basis for this claim.) If we didn't get 10 per cent investment a year during that period we should be finished, 'and that is less than in the Labour Party document'. We must achieve a balance in our payments by 1978 otherwise the burden of debt interest would wipe out the gains from North Sea oil and gas. It would be a 'recipe for disaster' to accept Tony C's proposal for cuts of only £2 billion, with another £500 million of cuts 'kept on the shelf'. At present the public sector was borrowing 20 pence for every pound it spent, and the burden of debt was becoming crippling. We couldn't continue with a borrowing requirement of anything approaching the present £12 billion. Even if public expenditure over the last three years had risen by more than 18 per cent in real terms, while GDP has probably risen by only 1½ per cent. We still weren't properly controlling public expenditure. The increase in 1975–6 would probably be up by 4 per cent instead of the planned 1½ per cent. It was a formidable case and Tony spent a lot of his speech acknowledging it. His main point was that the Treasury's forecasts of upturn in the economy would probably be falsified, so there would be no pressure on resources by 1978 and the Chancellor would be digging a hole with nothing to fill it. He was prepared to accept the formula cuts of £1 billion as 'politically tolerable', with the commitment to review the position in six months' time. I backed him strongly, but Harold Lever jumped in to back the Chancellor. 'Barbara and Tony would put our full employment strategy in

jeopardy.' The PM pointed out that Cabinet had already agreed to reduce public expenditure below this year's level . . . Wedgie had made his usual speech. Meanwhile Eric and I had been totting up our usual calculation of where the votes had fallen. We made it ten clearly in favour of Tony's figure of $2\frac{1}{2}$ billion; nine for the Chancellor's figure, including Harold himself, and two wobblers: Bob and Jim. We thought the Chancellor had lost, but Harold summed up that there was a 'very slight' majority in favour of the £$3\frac{3}{4}$ billion. Eric kept whispering to me that he thought Denis would have resigned if he had been beaten. What interested me was how close a thing it had been. 'My guess is that in the end the Chancellor will settle for £3 billion' said Tony C contentedly to me afterwards.[9]

Tony Crosland's guess was entirely correct. Joel Barnett in his memoirs recalled that:

we had to obtain Cabinet approval for the cuts of £$3\frac{3}{4}$ billion for which Denis was aiming, or rather the £3 billion for which he was prepared to settle . . . At the Cabinet meeting there was much heart-searching about the size of the cuts proposed. Those who supported us, like Roy Jenkins, who spoke with great authority, were able to point to the statistics Denis Healey and I had provided. In the last three years, public expenditure had grown by nearly 20 per cent, while output had risen by less than 2 per cent. On top of that, the ratio of public expenditure to gross domestic product (GDP) had risen from 50 per cent to 60 per cent, having been only 42 per cent fifteen years earlier . . . At the end of the long Cabinet discussions with few, if any, Ministers seriously influenced by colleagues' speeches, we achieved a small majority for cuts of £$3\frac{1}{4}$ billion. But given that I then had to have bilateral meetings with spending Ministers, I knew I would be fortunate to achieve £3 billion . . . I was not entirely surprised when my meetings, and a final Cabinet meeting, still found us short by £140 million of even the minimum target of £3 billion. There was then a long wrangle, with no Minister prepared to concede another penny. Normally Harold Wilson would have pressed for the comparatively small balance to be shared across a number of programmes, and I had submitted a paper showing precisely how this could be done.

To my surprise, he came up with a wholly new proposition. He suggested that the balance be found by a straight percentage cut in the size of the civil service. My officials had obviously not been warned that this might come up, so either it was genuinely out of the blue, to avoid what he feared might be the last straw for some Ministers if he had pressed for more cuts, or he had discussed it as a possibility with just a few of his top officials. Whichever it was, the idea was accepted as one worth looking at further, and the long and difficult meeting ended with a deep collective sigh of relief. We later got the civil service cuts, and I had sewn up my first big public expenditure package without a single ministerial resignation.[10]

Thus by bluff and improvisation rather than by rational planning, the £3 billion figure was reached. Far more than the £6 pay limit, the cut represented a large step in the right economic direction, given its political sensitivity, and proved a dry run for further, equally necessary, restraints on excessive public expenditure taken a year later at the height of the IMF crisis. But if Cabinet approval for the £3 billion cuts had been difficult the indication was that the parliamentary Labour Party would be even more divided. The Public Expenditure White Paper, which detailed the cuts, was published in February 1976 and was for the Tribune Group a 'White Paper of Shame'. The government faced a humiliating Commons defeat unless the rebels could be forced to back down. The Conservatives opposed the White Paper as not going far enough – it is, after all, the purpose of the Opposition to oppose and under Margaret Thatcher's leadership rather than Edward Heath's attacks on excessive government expenditure did not seem two-faced.

Joan Lestor had already resigned from her post as Under-Secretary of State for Education because of the £620 million cut in education spending and the left of the party did not conceal its intentions when the time came for parliamentary approval. Thirty-seven Tribune Group MPs abstained in the vote on the government motion: the government was consequently defeated 284 to 256. Harold Wilson, absent at his sixtieth birthday party, dodged the immediate political storm which broke on Ted Short, the Leader of the House. The government could withstand the pandemonium that followed its defeat as part of the Commons ritual, but it faced a dilemma over whether or not to risk a vote of confidence. Harold Wilson, within a week of resignation – a fact unknown to the vast majority of his Cabinet colleagues – opted for a vote of confidence in the hope that the recalcitrant left-wingers would not feel able to abstain if doing so would precipitate a general election. Barbara Castle described the Cabinet meeting when the decision was made:

> In the event, the atmosphere in Cabinet was remarkably calm. Harold looked refreshed and disposed of the 'confidence' matter quite briskly for him. One would never have thought he had been 'humiliated'. Having thought things over during the night, he had concluded that the best thing was for us to take the vote right away today on the Motion for the Adjournment, which he would then make a question of confidence. Some of us were a bit taken aback by this: it looked rather weak and might be misinterpreted. Surely we needed a substantive Motion reaffirming the Government's policy? We were then informed that it was too late for that: the Motion should have been tabled last night. (This reinforced my astonishment at Harold's behaviour last night. He had received full warning that we were going to be beaten and ought to have had his strategy thought out, if necessary calling a quick Cabinet after the vote.)
> A long discussion ensued as to which was the lesser evil: to act today without a substantive Motion, or to postpone a vote till Friday or Monday, with all the risks to sterling. I had been fulminating last night that we ought to resign: I could see us drifting into the position in the 1960s when we just couldn't get our policies through the House, but Roy pointed out that an election wouldn't solve anything. Even if we won, the unresolved clash would still remain. All I did was to ask Bob if the abstainees had realized we would be defeated, to which he replied, 'No doubt at all. They are counting on a vote of confidence to bail them out.'[11]

The Chief Whip's assessment proved correct and the vote of confidence was carried by 297 to 280 and with it approval for the government's public expenditure programme, a fact which both Harold Wilson and Denis Healey[12] made clear in their speeches during the debate. The vote on the White Paper and on the subsequent vote of confidence had put the left in a dilemma as well as the Cabinet. The left was unable to vote to bring down a

Labour Government, though its public expenditure policies had become vastly different to those of the Social Contract, for fear that a general election would usher in a Conservative Government led by Mrs Thatcher and committed to monetarist policies. In this regard the left reacted in the same way as had Jack Jones to this electoral threat – they did enough to keep the Labour Government in office. While the Tribune Group delivered in the division lobbies, Jack Jones and the unions delivered the £6 pay policy. Both these factors, though in different ways, enabled Denis Healey to exert some control over public expenditure and to concentrate attention on reducing inflation and financing the balance of payments deficit. But before attention could turn to the April 1976 budget the political limelight focused on Prime Minister Harold Wilson, who announced his resignation on 16 March.

HAROLD WILSON: AN ASSESSMENT

Harold Wilson was never far from controversy during thirteen years as party leader, and eight as Prime Minister and during five general elections of which Labour won four. His resignation was no exception and for some observers of British politics it was Wilson's greatest controversy of all. It deserves some detailed attention in this account. Joel Barnett recalled that:

> The Prime Minister came out of the Cabinet Room after a few minutes and I went in for my items, with Ted Short, the deputy leader, presiding. It was an astonishing scene as I sat down next to Denis Healey. They all seemed dazed. I understand that of the potential new leaders Jim Callaghan and Denis were only told of the Prime Minister's plan to resign just a few minutes before going into Cabinet. I cannot vouch for the truth as far as Jim or anyone else was concerned but, having seen Denis earlier that morning, I am sure he did not know.[13]

James Callaghan like Denis Healey was barely prepared for the news. He had discounted it as unlikely when Wilson told him in December 1975 that he was 'considering' resignation. Thus early in 1976 he remarked to one surprised British ambassador abroad: 'the Prime Minister has been saying he will retire shortly. He told me again last week. But you know, I look at the calendar and I see the Queen's Jubilee coming (in 1977) and the Commonwealth Prime Ministers' Conference and the first European summit in London. And I say to myself, surely the little beggar won't pass those up.'[14] Another cabinet minister similarly recalled that, 'I'd heard a number of rumours that Wilson was resigning so I tended to discount them. He was in moods when he'd put it about that he would resign but people disbelieved it.'[15] Barbara Castle, likewise, who had discussed with Wilson the likely successors as party leader and Wilson's future plans on 4 March 1976, described the shock in Cabinet on 16 March when the resignation was announced:

> I arrived at Cabinet, all unsuspecting that Harold's time-bomb was about to go off. As we settled down in our seats, Harold said calmly that he had just come from the Palace and had a statement to make to us. He then read a lengthy statement announcing his 'irrevocable' decision to give up office . . . Harold then embroidered his statement with a few casual and almost inaudible explanations. He had made up his mind to do this when he won the election two years ago, he told us. There was never a 'right time' to carry out such an intention, but he thought he had chosen the best possible. He had considered resigning before the last party conference, or at Christmas, but decided the pay policy was in too delicate a balance. However, it was right to go before we became embroiled in the next pay policy round. He had thought of his sixtieth birthday as an excellent moment, but unfortunately there turned out to be two by-elections on that day. He had thought of waiting till the summer, but decided that would be awkward for his successor, who ought to have a chance to play himself in before the House rose for the recess and before the next party conference. So there it was.
>
> The silence which followed this was, I thought, the most moving tribute we could have paid to him. There was no rush of ready falsities. Ted Short blurted out something almost incoherent about what an appalling shock and blow this was. Another silence, then Jim hesitatingly took up the theme. He didn't, he said, want to 'pre-empt' what anybody else might want to say. There would be other occasions to pay proper tributes. But he couldn't let this pass without expressing his thanks to Harold for all the generosities he had always showed

to him. He remembered, for instance, how, when Harold had won the leadership thirteen years ago, he had at once turned to him and said: 'Of course you'll carry on, Jim, as shadow Foreign Secretary.' Jim concluded haltingly, 'Thank you, Harold, for all you have done for us.' More silence. I felt near to tears. I don't quite know why. Tears of farewell to the friendly familiar? Eric passed me another note: 'It's a very emotional moment.' To which I replied: 'What's your reaction?' Eric: 'I think he's wrong.' Me: 'I think it will prove how difficult it is to replace him.' Harold then asked us to excuse him, as he had various people to talk to, including the chairman of the PLP with whom he had to discuss the quick holding of an election for his successor. He told Ted Short to take the chair and disappeared just as, once again, the waiters filed in with those welcome cups of coffee.[16]

Although Wilson, in the course of many controversies, attracted many critics, not least among his own party, he also attracted much respect and admiration, the latter albeit often grudgingly consented. Wilson's greatest ability was to keep his party together. It is arguably no coincidence that the Labour Party has split, with the defection of many on the right to the Social Democratic Party, after Wilson relinquished the leadership. One trade union leader recalled that 'Dell, Williams, Short, Healey and Barnett, I found had little understanding of the trade union movement. Wilson wanted to do the right thing in the Social Contract with the principle of a platform of commitment to a social programme based on cooperation.'[17] Similarly one cabinet minister noted that 'Wilson was always in control. I think he was a very good Prime Minister. He listened to us and tried to get a reasonable sense of responsibility.'[18] Wilson's skill in keeping his party together over the issue of the Common Market was a prime example of his leadership abilities and Wilson, rightly, notes in memoirs how Roy Jenkins said 'how much he misunderstood what I was doing – a reference to my handling of the Common Market issue which had ended with the party, with whatever individual misgivings accepting the decision to remain in Europe'.[19]

Of course Wilson's critics have never been short of ammunition. The press and the Conservatives always found fault, as arguably Wilson himself should have expected, more than he publicly seemed to do. Many in the Labour Party, too, were not sorry to see his departure. Tribune Group MPs resented the demise of the Social Contract and the radical industrial strategy while one MP commented that 'Wilson didn't have any strategy. There just were no new ideas in 1974 unlike in 1964.'[20]

Many of Wilson's critics in the Labour Party, while admiring his skill at keeping the party together, have felt let down by the achievements of the governments over which he presided. This line of argument is, of course, dependent on the expectations of socialism that should be realistically held about Labour governments.

To a Tribune Group MP Wilson's governments are, therefore, bound to be disappointing. Many on the left remember that Wilson was the left's candidate against George Brown in 1963 and whilst they would not agree with *The Times* that George Brown drunk is better than Wilson sober, feel a great disappointment that Wilson's administrations were too conventional and insufficiently radical. Again such an analysis depends on the viewpoint of the critic.

One factor that is amenable to a more objective judgement is that without Harold Wilson there would have been no Labour administration anyway in 1974. It is arguable that Wilson's electoral skill was particularly demonstrated in the February 1974 campaign when by widening the issues to cover the EEC, inflation, unemployment, housing and so on, he weakened Edward Heath's appeal of 'who runs the country – government or unions?' By fighting on a traditional, rather than Mr Heath's single-issue, campaign Wilson undermined the Conservatives' approach and contributed to the lack of authority which the last weeks of the Heath Government displayed. Similarly in October 1974 Wilson's electoral skills far outshone the Conservatives', whom Wilson tarnished with the same confrontationist brush as in the previous February.

An assessment of policy advocated by Wilson between 1974 and 1976 presents a difficult problem in that Wilson was never really free from his 'dual inheritance'. In the circumstances, however, a relatively strong case for the defence can be put up, at least by those not on the left of the Labour Party. Wilson may be criticised for allowing the left too much influence on policy-making in opposition but once in government the more extreme left-wing programmes were shelved. Wilson belonged to Labour's 'old left' not the fist-clenched 'new left' which became visible particularly at party conferences. Barbara Castle recalled that Wilson told her shortly before his resignation that: ' "There are three groups in the Left," he continued. "There is what is now called the 'soft' Left, to which you and I and Michael always belonged. There is a middle group and then there are the really vicious group."[21]

Wilson knew the truth about the direction his party was taking and, in office, did his utmost to prevent it. The decision to demote Tony Benn reflected Wilson's fear that the nature of the left in the Labour Party was changing.

There is evidence too, that Wilson knew the truth about the economy and the irrelevance of the left's strategy.

This is not to argue that Wilson made no mistakes, such as an initial overreliance on trade union leaders, and an initial inaction on excessive public expenditure. Wilson knew, however, that inflation was a threat to the economy both in terms of Britain's perilous external payments position and in terms of employment. It was Wilson, not Keith Joseph or Margaret Thatcher who, quite accurately, told the NUM conference that

> The action the Government has decided to take is not in pursuit of some economic textbook or theory. It is not a question today, in the crisis that Britain faces, of choosing between inflation and unemployment. Inflation is causing unemployment. We cannot have a little of one and less of the other. The more inflation we have the more unemployment we have. And if we were to tolerate the rates of inflation reached in recent months, then no industry would be secure, no job safe.
>
> The battle against inflation is a battle for exports, for a greater measure of economic independence in an interdependent world. But, no less, the battle against inflation is a battle for full employment. Lose the battle against inflation and the battle for full employment is lost before you begin. Lose the battle against inflation, and there is no hope of stopping unemployment rising much higher.[22]

It was Wilson's Labour Government, not the Conservative Heath Government that preceded it, that realised that inflationary expansion of the economy could endanger, not preserve, jobs. The Public Expenditure White Paper, presented in February 1976, sought to remedy this economic failing. Wilson's crucial support for it in Cabinet, which proved decisive, does not suggest the action of a natural inflationist. Although he may not always publicly have said so, as and when he felt it politically damaging, the evidence suggested that Wilson knew the truth not only about his own party but also about the economy. Wilson did not relish his 'dual inheritance' nor, arguably, did he relish the £3 billion of public expenditure cuts presented in February 1976 – but he knew that the latter course was economically unavoidable.

CHAPTER V

The IMF Crisis

CALLAGHAN TAKES OVER

It is not the purpose of this account to describe the campaign for election of Harold Wilson's successor as Labour Party leader and, consequently, Prime Minister.[1] Suffice it to say that James Callaghan, who became Prime Minister on 5 April 1976, was the leader least objectionable to the parliamentary Labour Party as a whole in that the left preferred him as leader to Healey, Jenkins or Crosland and the right preferred him to Foot or Benn.

Although Callaghan had been Chancellor of the Exchequer, Home Secretary and Foreign Secretary and was well known in the Labour Party for his opposition to *In Place of Strife* in the late 1960s, his fame was limited outside the establishment and the labour movement. No biography of him appeared before he became Prime Minister and indeed only one biography, critical but not particularly convincing, has appeared since.[2] The satirical magazine *Private Eye*[3] launched an attack on him shortly before he became Prime Minister but came up with nothing more sinister than Callaghan's business friendship with Julian Hodge which, though possibly misguided, was hardly politically incriminating.

If Callaghan the villain sounded unconvincing so also did Callaghan the avuncular, 64-year-old non-smoker and chapel-goer of 'Sunny Jim' mythology. Callaghan was neither a villain nor an easy-going, relaxed chapelgoer. Rather he was an experienced politician with a considerable love of power who was not usually overawed by establishment habits despite a working-class, non-university background shared by few of his cabinet colleagues. His ministerial experiences had involved tough decision, particularly his time as Chancellor from 1964 to 1967 which culminated in the political defeat of devaluation. One Treasury minister recalled that Callaghan was 'bruised by his time as

Chancellor in the 1960s',[4] and a left-winger commented that 'Callaghan's experiences at the Treasury left their mark'.[5] Harold Wilson recalled that 'Jim learned from his experience as Chancellor as does someone who has had a severe operation'.[6] With hindsight, however, it may be argued that many of Callaghan's difficulties in that period were caused by the near-catastrophic handling of the economy by his Conservative predecessor Reginald Maudling. In short Callaghan had always made up with political acumen what he had missed in educational and intellectual background. Moreover evidence suggests that this political acumen was central to his political career and not least to his leadership triumph in 1976. Peter Jay, who as Callaghan's son-in-law knew him well, detected a profound change in the style of government once Callaghan took over. Jay recalled that, 'In the twenty years of the two Harolds we had frivolous, facetious government. From the moment Callaghan took over the frivolity came to an end. He saw elections as a means to an end rather than an end in themselves.'[7]

Callaghan was not to know that within a year of becoming Prime Minister he would have to face the severest economic and political crisis for a Labour Prime Minister since 1931 – the great IMF crisis. This was not obvious however in April 1976 though the origins of the crisis are evident with hindsight. Stage I of the incomes policy, Jack Jones's £6 policy, was holding, public spending had been put under a measure of control in the February White Paper, and financing the balance of payments deficit had not proved too difficult for Chancellor Denis Healey. One senior Treasury official put it that 'we had not deflated in 1974–5 along with the rest of the world. The 1975 budget was mildly deflationary and arguably by early 1976 the economy was in better balance and not out of kilter.'[8] The question of just what was, or became, out of kilter dominated the rest of the year.

The origin of the problem can be traced back to the last two weeks of Wilson's premiership. By then the pound was moving between $2·02 and $2·03, having been below a crisis line of $2·20 during the sterling crisis of June 1975. The fear, quite naturally, was that foreign holders of sterling, such as the Nigerians with their newly-found oil wealth, would withdraw their funds precipitating a sterling crisis which would seriously endanger Britain's ability to finance the balance of payments deficit. The scenario was a falling pound out of control and exhausted reserves. One Treasury official recalled that 'the basic problem at the start of 1976 was that we didn't have enough reserves. I remember that it fell to me to tell the Chancellor.'[9]

To even the most casual observers of British politics such balance of payments and sterling crises were not new. The 1964–70 Labour Government had wrestled with the problem almost perpetually and both Callaghan and Wilson knew the attendant danger signals which precipitated the severest moments of such crises.

In early 1976 the Treasury, under Sir Douglas Wass's promptings as Permanent Secretary, sought to engineer a controlled devaluation of the pound, first to encourage exports and secondly to enable the balance of payments deficit to be eased. The Treasury argument was that such a devaluation had worked before in 1967, bringing a balance of payments surplus by 1970, and would be appropriate to the circumstances of early 1976. One Treasury minister who was less than convinced by the argument put it that 'we were not yet an oil backed currency and we had to finance the balance of payments deficit. The Treasury had this thing about devaluation on the 1960s Jenkins precedent.'[10] According to one senior cabinet minister: 'The Treasury bought too entirely the view that devaluation was the correct way to improve competitiveness. They were influenced by the Cambridge school – that is pre import controls – of Kaldor which believed in devaluation. I only favoured parity changes as a last resort.'[11] One dissenting Treasury official recalled that 'some Treasury officials tried to persuade themselves that the devaluation strategy was the answer to everything. A fetish isn't too strong a word for one or two individuals. Douglas Wass was hypnotised that you could get out of it all by devaluation.'[12] Another senior official confessed that 'the current Treasury doctrine was to keep the rate down. Douglas Wass was in favour of a lower exchange rate.'[13]

Harold Wilson recalled in his memoirs that Callaghan was aware of, and disapproved of, the Treasury's intentions:

> James Callaghan, about to go abroad for an extended tour, had voiced his anxieties to me. The Treasury weren't bent on forcing the £ down further, were they? Would I perhaps call a meeting on his return of the key ministers who dealt with these matters, to make quite sure there was no fatal slide? I told him

that I, too, was carefully watching the decision. Certainly no decision had been taken, and the Treasury had given no hint of any move below the two dollar market. We would be meeting on this and other questions, but not until he returned.[14]

Evidence suggests, however, that the Treasury did engineer a fall in the pound which, sliding further downwards than had been anticipated, really marked the opening moves of the 1976 crisis which ended with the IMF. On 4 March, in the hope of disguising the policy of controlled devaluation in case it became uncontrolled, the Bank of England began selling pounds after the price of sterling had started to rise because, it was later speculated, of Nigerian buying. This was not in itself remarkable but as the Bank began to sell, other sales made quite separately had their own effect of forcing the rate down. Dealers were unaware that this was coincidental and assumed that the Bank was 'committing the cardinal sin of central banking: selling the £ on a falling market'.[15] Thus although the authorities had sold sterling to prevent it rising too far above the $2·00 level the impression was the opposite. Harold Wilson noted that 'it was only later that I learnt that the markets had for long heard rumours that the Treasury had been harbouring a fetish based on the belief that the real value of the £ should be $1·88'.[16] One cabinet minister, close to events, similarly recalled that: 'There were too many generals in the Treasury and the economists in the Treasury were generalists not specialists in international money. The market men all knew the Treasury was in favour of devaluation.'[17] According to one senior Treasury official 'sterling was strong in the morning of the fourth, but in the afternoon the mistake was not to detect the change in sentiment in time to stop the change in interest rate'.[18]

It may be argued that the secret devaluation strategy was of dubious benefit even if it had worked, leading to higher inflation, with imported goods costing more, as well as threatening the sterling balances.[19] But, as it had failed, the crisis developed a dimension of its own. This was reinforced on 5 March when Minimum Lending Rate was cut by a quarter of a point which the exchange markets, naturally apprehensive, interpreted as a sign that a decline in the pound was official policy. The Governor of the Bank, Gordon Richardson, had considered cancelling the planned MLR reduction but the Treasury advisers warned that this would 'cause more panic than letting it through'.[20] Given that the Treasury actually wished to achieve a devaluation this advice was predictable. Although Richardson and Sir Derek Mitchell, the Head of the Treasury overseas side, were sceptical as to the devaluation strategy – quite rightly as it turned out – the devaluers seemed to have achieved their aims when the pound fell below $2 for the first time and within a week was $1·90 or a 5 per cent devaluation. How enthusiastic Denis Healey was about this strategy is open to question. Although one official thought 'Healey was a lower exchange rate man'[21] another senior official felt that 'my impression is that Healey managed to stay on the fence. He was careful never to say it was to do with him.'[22]

However the slide did not halt there. The decline continued through to the $1·70s and the Bank did not have sufficient reserves to hold the pound at the point the Treasury would have preferred. Keegan and Pennant-Rae have noted that:

It has to be emphasised that the exchange-rate strategy was fully endorsed by the Chancellor, Denis Healey, but that the incident had its biggest impact on the new prime minister, James Callaghan, who had to live with the result: a run on the sterling balances which brought back unhappy memories of his 1964–7 chancellorship. Indeed, the consequences of a decision he had not been party to were to dominate the first year of Callaghan's premiership.

At first the decline in sterling was rationalised as the result of 'leads and lags' – the dramatic effect on a country's reserves when, for confidence reasons, payments from a currency are speeded up, and payments into it delayed, in the course of normal commercial transactions. Denis Healey was later to blame leads and lags for about a third of the outflow; what he did not say was that two-thirds was caused by a wholesale withdrawal from the sterling balances.

The mere fact that devaluation had become known as the official policy was bad enough for confidence, so that the depreciation soon went way beyond the 5 per cent or so fall the Government was seeking. What the Government had managed to do was open a Pandora's box.[23]

With the reactions of foreign exchange markets, opinion in the United States Treasury began to crystallise. Treasury Secretary

William Simon and Ed Yeo, President Ford's nominee to oversee America's international economic relationships, were alarmed in both economic and political terms at the pound's uncontrollable slide. Yeo was particularly apocalyptic, fearing that 'if a country like Britain blew up, defaulted on its loans, introduced foreign exchange controls and froze convertibility, we could have a real world depression . . . The trouble in Britain was that people had a higher standard of living than the country was earning. The Tories had lost control of monetary policy and after 1974 Labour lost control of budgetary policy . . . Our role was to persuade the British that the game was over.'[24]

Denis Healey's budget in April was an opportunity to restore confidence and put the economy back into kilter, but the opportunity was missed. Although Denis Healey described it as the most crucial of the present Parliament, it failed to consolidate the greater sense of economic reality which had emanated from the February Public Expenditure White Paper. The budget's most noticeable measure was that income tax cuts from 35 per cent to 33 per cent in basic rate were made conditional on the success of the pay talks with the TUC on Stage II of wage restraint. Given the background of the sinking pound there was no economic reason for such action and in political terms it simply transferred responsibility for inflation away from the government to the unions which was hardly fair to the unions who had not been party to the 4 March devaluation. Urgent action to reduce the PSBR was given an heroic pretext by the fall of the pound which was allowed to pass. The decision, however, was not avoided – only delayed. Joel Barnett recalled that in his budget speech:

> Denis spoke of the need to limit public expenditure demands to make room for exports and industrial investment and for improvement in net take-home pay. There were not cuts, indeed there were minor increases in expenditure on employment schemes and social security benefits. The only essential point made on public expenditure was the need for stability and to avoid 'short-term disruptive cuts'. The main criticism of the Budget from the Opposition was on constitutional grounds, fastening on the fact that the second stage of tax reliefs was made dependent on the success of the agreement with the TUC on pay.[25]

Following the April 1976 budget the pound continued to fall. Not even the Stage II incomes policy agreement, concluded in May, appeased the exchanges. The incomes policy agreement was in any case linked by the Chancellor himself to a budget that did not help to reduce inflation. Brittan and Lilley put the incomes policy agreements into their correct perspective by arguing that:

> The apparent short-term success with wage control strengthens this belief, and leads, in anything but the shortest of short runs, to more monetary expansion rather than less. To coin a useful slogan: the more control there is of pay, the less there is of cash.
>
> A classic example occurred in the Budget Speech of 6 April 1976 when the Chancellor of the Exchequer, Mr. Denis Healey, offered some tax relaxations without corresponding cuts in government spending and did so when the economy was clearly moving out of recession. The relaxations were granted in return for a TUC pledge on wage restraint and were justified by the classic words: 'I believe it is well worth accepting some increase in the Public Sector Borrowing Requirement to achieve a lower rate of inflation.' That is like saying 'It is well worth exposing the patient to the flu virus as long as he promises not to catch a cold.'[26]

The details of the Stage II agreement had been worked out to the background of the falling pound and politically this made it easier for the government, as it had the previous July, to set a seemingly tough policy. Negotiations between the government and the key union leaders were not essentially about the necessity for another year of strict wage control – that was conceded – but about the type of wage restraint. In talks with Denis Healey, Jack Jones, Hugh Scanlon and David Basnett made the running in the key negotiations. Jones and Basnett favoured another flat-rate increase, the former because he believed it to be socially fairer and the latter because it would particularly help his members. Scanlon, with the known support of many other unions, favoured a percentage increase in order not to further upset relativities already distorted by the £6 policy.

The final deal produced the formula of £2·50 to £4·00 per week depending on the level of earnings, which roughly translated to a $4\frac{1}{2}$ per cent increase, and was therefore nearer to Scanlon's

preference. Such a percentage increase represented a high degree
of trade union compliance since only eighteen months before 30
per cent increases had been commonplace. Stage ɪɪ, in fact, was as
well observed as Stage ɪ, with money earnings declining for the
second successive year. However much such an incomes policy
may be regarded as a political success its economic benefits were
dubious. As has been convincingly argued, the 'success was on
pay alone and had no corresponding impact on inflation itself'.[27]
For as long as the economy was 'out of kilter', with public
expenditure too high, the PSBR a constant burden and the
pound's value in international markets uncontrollably declining,
inflation was bound to continue at a damaging level irrespective of
a wage squeeze. In short the Stage ɪɪ agreement could not take the
place of effective action against inflation by the Chancellor. The
April budget represented more than just a missed opportunity; it
represented the Chancellor's failure to see clear danger signs
which later led to necessarily more drastic action. Thus following
the April budget and the Stage ɪɪ agreement the pound continued
to fall.

In May sterling reached a new low of $1·70. For the Chancellor
options seemed to close as advice poured in. Many on the left of
the party were already beginning to think in terms that were later
to emerge in a coherent form as the 'alternative strategy'. One
Tribune Group MP recalled that 'it didn't matter that the pound
was falling. Healey's explanation was *ex post facto*.'[28] Jeremy Bray,
one of Labour's ablest backbench economic experts, thought that
'the pound was falling too much to ignore',[29] a view that was
widely shared as long as the process of decline showed no end. On
the right of the party Reg Prentice, then still a cabinet member,
noted that 'you can only live with a lower pound up to a point.
There was a danger to the economy and society.'[30]

A key opinion that carried weight was Harold Lever's. Lever's
approach to the problem, for which his Cabinet brief ideally
suited him, tended to scorn what was regarded as the deflation
orthodoxy. Earlier loans from the IMF had not lasted long, as
withdrawals continued from the sterling balances in April, May
and June, so Lever thought that a larger loan would prove to be
the vital stabilising factor. Neither Derek Mitchell nor Gordon
Richardson initially thought a loan viable unless accompanied by
public spending cuts and they feared that 'the request would raise
suspicion that the government was determined to evade the

discipline of the IMF – which would actually sharpen the threat to sterling'.[31] Lever's view was that not only was the threat of public spending cuts economically harmful but that their imposition from outside was politically unacceptable. Borrowing on the right scale would evade such unacceptable consequences. As one Treasury minister put it, 'Harold Lever thought the only thing was to borrow – he was a great borrower'.[32] One senior Treasury official recalled bluntly that 'Lever's view wasn't really credible. The most we could get from overseas governments was only short-term credit.'[33]

In June the borrowing option was tried. A $5·3 billion stand-by credit was arranged by central banks as an alternative, or so the British Government originally thought, to going to the IMF. However the $5·3 billion loan was the US Treasury's 'chance to ensnare the British government'.[34] The loan was therefore 'deliberately limited to six months, because the countries concerned, and particularly the United States, were adamant that Britain put its own house in order and that if it did not do so it should be forced to go to the IMF and accept IMF conditions'.[35] The Chancellor and the Prime Minister were surprised to learn that the loan was repayable in full by December 1976, as this severely restricted their options. One cabinet minister noted that the $5·3 billion loan 'turned out to be a self castration'.[36] Fay and Young rightly stress that far from being an alternative to tough IMF terms the June loan was actually a way the US Treasury could bring IMF control nearer:

> But everyone reckoned without the US Treasury. What Healey presented to the House as a helpful coil of rope for sterling halfway down a precipice turned out to be a noose. As Ed Yeo candidly says, the Americans and especially Arthur Burns put up the money 'for the bait' – i.e. to hook the UK economy into IMF control when it had to be repaid. By inference, Healey also conceded this in his private letter to Bill Simon and, unemphasised, in his statement to Parliament.
>
> What is certainly true is that Callaghan, that June, saw the implications of the terms. He had fought against them, and failed; and later complained to Ford about Yeo's intransigence. Foreseeing the conflict, the American State Department too had become involved, acting out its traditional role as the soothing defender of allies against the hard men of the US

Treasury. 'They didn't like waves,' says Yeo. 'But there were going to be waves. The only question was whether they would be tidal waves.'[37]

Similarly Joel Barnett is right to argue that the loan was not altruistic in that the Americans wished to avoid an international financial crisis caused by sterling's problems.[38] Given the six-month repayment insistence the Chancellor needed to take swift action to restore confidence as confidence in sterling was weak and the rate of drawing on the stand-by consequently considerable. Joel Barnett noted that 'temporarily it did the trick . . . but no serious observer of our economy really thought a $5·3 billion credit was all the action needed'.[39] Denis Healey, therefore, prepared an emergency July package involving the politically sensitive question of public expenditure cuts.

THE JULY PACKAGE

Denis Healey faced a familiar dilemma: 'how to reconcile the conflicting demands of the currency market, which obviously wanted more cuts in public spending, with the increasingly brittle tolerance of the Labour party for any more assaults on its commitment to full employment'.[40] On 6 July he told the Cabinet he was seeking a public expenditure cut of £1 billion for 1977–8 which he justified by reference to the Treasury's belief that with the domestic economy and world trade recovering, cuts would be necessary to prevent over-heating in 1978–9. The argument, which was based on the Treasury model, envisaged a 5 per cent growth rate leading to bottlenecks in manufacturing industry and a large increase in imports. The £1 billion cuts were therefore presented in a politically less sensitive way than if their sole justification had been foreign confidence in sterling.

It must not be inferred that the Treasury presented a monolithic view. Different Treasury ministers took different lines and the officials were divided over the principle and the degree of deflationary action. Derek Mitchell thought a £3 billion public spending cut necessary and Sir Leo Pliatzky, the second Permanent Secretary, was carrying through a comprehensive review of public sector practices which 'cut a lot of ground from beneath spending ministers'.[41] However, according to one senior Treasury official, 'Leo Pliatzky took the view that all the fat had been removed from Public Expenditure'.[42] The Permanent Secretary Sir Douglas Wass took the view, which predominated in the Treasury, that public expenditure was under adequate control and that deflationary measures were not required. With hindsight this view could not have been more inaccurate.

As it was, Cabinet agreed on the £1 billion figure Denis Healey had requested but the details were left to the discussions between the Treasury and spending ministers. On 13 July the Cabinet duly endorsed the £1 billion cuts despite the political divisions in Cabinet which had led to Tony Benn putting forward an 'alternative strategy'. However the 'alternative strategy' of import controls and greater industrial investment and planning was still in its infancy, and as much opposition to the cuts came from the Croslandites, to whom increasing public expenditure was a matter of faith. Both the Croslandite right and the left were critical of Healey's package when he addressed the PLP on 20 July.

One cabinet minister, who was unconvinced by the Chancellor's arguments, put it that 'I didn't share the view that public expenditure was too high. I took the view that government spending was sustaining the economy anyhow and was counter-recessionary in a Keynesian sense.'[43]

The £1 billion public expenditure cuts were not the full extent of the July package unveiled in the Commons on 22 July. Denis Healey also raised another £1 billion by the subterfuge of a 2 per cent increase in employers' national insurance contributions. This proposal was tacked on as a *caveat* to the public expenditure cuts in Cabinet and ideologically, as a tax on employers rather than workers, it evaded more general Labour Party opposition. The Cabinet, when it finally realised that Healey had railroaded the increase without proper consultation, was furious. Thenceforth Healey's colleagues kept a closer watch on Treasury proposals, and insisted on greater Cabinet debate. The NIS surcharge itself was well-intentioned enough in aiming to increase foreign confidence. But it emerged in the following years as a tax on employment with obvious deleterious effects on the unemployment level as well as failing in its immediate aims. Sir Ronald McIntosh, the head of the National Economic Development Office, thought the surcharge 'Catastrophic. The important thing was the nature of the cuts. They should have come out of the non-productive soft underbelly of public spending.'[44] The July package therefore emerged as an inadequate £1 billion cut in public expenditure and an economically self-inflicted wound to industry in the form of the NIS surcharge. To the background of the pound's continued decline the July package was an unmitigated failure. One minister bemoaned that 'I would have had a strong July budget to avoid the IMF, with a clear intention to support the pound and the means to do so.'[45] One senior Treasury official commented that 'few of us on the inside thought the July package would do the trick'.[46] Not surprisingly the Americans, anxious to see signs that effective action had been taken after the $5·3 billion loan, were disappointed.

The failure to act on the monetary side was another distinguishing feature of the July package. A number of economic commentators thought that if interest rates had been raised a further sterling crisis could have been avoided. Samuel Brittan rightly argued that:

It is probable that the July package would have been sufficient without further measures if it had been announced at the time of the April Budget and been accompanied by a firm monetary budget. Even when it was announced, it would quite likely have been enough if the Treasury had not muffed the monetary side of its measures. The July statement was originally supposed to contain a commitment to a 12 per cent limit on monetary growth in 1976–7; but this was vetoed at a late stage at a high official level, and the 12 per cent figure became something between an aspiration and a forecast. The potentially favourable effects on confidence and on inflationary expectations were thus thrown away ... Indeed, the effect of delaying the announcement of a firm monetary objective was to worsen expectations about inflation and sterling and thereby make necessary emergency increases in MLR and further fiscal restraints which could otherwise have been avoided. The monetary explosion of the summer and early autumn of 1976 did more than anything else to confirm the suspicions that the three previous years of stability had been an accident due to the ease of financing the Budget deficit.[47]

The monetary explosion that was apparent by August, with M3 showing its fastest rise since 1973, was immediate proof of the

inadequacy of the July package and propelled the crisis, which
had begun in March, to sterling's further disadvantage.

THE IMF MEDICINE

The decline in sterling continued in September and after another
$400 million of foreign currency had been spent to hold the rate at
$1·77 in the first week of September, Healey gave instructions to
the Bank to stop supporting the pound. The fear that the whole
loan would be used up by the time it had to be repaid in December
was paramount in official considerations even with $4 billion left.
Action to raise interest rates was now unavoidable and on 10
September the MLR was raised to 13 per cent, which provided a
brief respite as a result of the attractiveness of gilt-edged stocks.
The hope that any subsequent IMF loan would not have too
many strings attached again surfaced in the same way that earlier
optimism regarded the $5·3 billion loan avoiding difficult deci-
sions. According to Fay and Young, Denis Healey shared the
sense of optimism and expected no major change in policies to
result from the forthcoming IMF conference in Manila.

The optimists were again proved wrong. With the unsupported
pound still falling the Labour Conference met at Blackpool. The
left was already seething over earlier public expenditure cuts and
the abandonment of the radical industrial strategy. For many on
the left the crisis meant the opportunity for socialist solutions not
their postponement. Thus the NEC voted to support a motion to
conference calling for bank nationalisation, which, while the
notion of Cabinet government still exists in Britain had no chance
of being implemented, did serve further to weaken Healey and
undermine confidence in sterling. The pound fell 3 cents on the
Monday of the party conference and on the Tuesday it was down
$4\frac{1}{2}$ cents at $1·64.

Denis Healey himself heightened the drama by cancelling his
visit to Manila at Heathrow airport and dashing to Blackpool to
address the conference. In dramatic terms he spoke of having
come from the 'battle front' and pledged to negotiate with the
IMF 'on the basis of our existing policies'. In political terms
Healey's performance in Blackpool was courageous but in terms
of appreciating economic realities it was Prime Minister Jim
Callaghan who, later in the same week, made a crucial interven-

tion. With the decision to apply to the IMF already made on Wednesday, 29 September, Callaghan analysed the failure of Keynesian economic policies which had so undermined sterling's position. He told the conference that: 'We used to think you could spend your way out of a recession and increase employment by cutting taxes and boosting spending. I tell you in all candour that this option no longer exists, and that in so far as it ever did exist, it only worked by injecting a bigger dose of inflation into the system.'

As an indictment of post-war economic policies Callaghan had summed up the case for the prosecution impeccably. Callaghan's speech could be rightly interpreted as reflecting a decisive change in the intellectual climate. It is not an exaggeration to ascribe to it the much over-used description as a watershed in economic policy direction. Peter Jay recalled of the speech that 'there was more to full employment than demand management and nothing to be ashamed of in admitting that Keynes wasn't a truth for all time. The 1976 speech was very important. It was the beginning of what I called the New Realism in Britain.'[48] Callaghan's speech devastated the philosophy of post-war Keynesianism in a way that had previously been unthinkable for any Prime Minister, Labour or Conservative. But more than that, Callaghan was blaming the profligate early eighteen months of the Labour Government when public expenditure and inflation raced out of control. Callaghan, to some in the Labour Party, may have appeared to be speaking for effect, or aiming his comments at foreign speculation and the US Treasury. The evidence, however, does not indicate that Callaghan disbelieved what he said. As a former Chancellor he had reined back Reginald Maudling's ill-judged expansion when Labour took office in 1964. The diaries of neither Richard Crossman nor Barbara Castle portray Callaghan as an expansionist, let alone a deliberate inflationist. Furthermore since becoming Prime Minister, Callaghan had backed – though with the reluctance shared by all in the Labour Party – Denis Healey's previous public expenditure restrictions. Callaghan's socialism was the kind under which working people moved from poverty to affluence with the backdrop of the welfare state for those who needed it. Callaghan realised that inflation, as Harold Wilson had earlier pointed out, can create unemployment as well as harming the poorest in society, and far from being the mainstay of socialism can actually generate greater inequality.

Callaghan's repudiation of Keynesian economics was not a repudiation of its intentions but of its results. Callaghan was preparing his party for the IMF medicine.

The pound meanwhile was continuing its downward path, reaching an all-time low of just over $1·50 on 6 October having fallen 12 cents since 8 September. Healey decided that further action on the interest rate front was necessary. Fay and Young describe how the decision to raise the MLR to 15 per cent came about:

> On October 6 the Chancellor and the Governor asked to see the Prime Minister: Healey informed Callaghan of the diagnosis of the Treasury and the Bank, but the Prime Minister saw it differently. He was concerned by the political implications, by the inevitable rise in mortgages, and the deflationary effect on industry. By the end of the meeting he appeared to have battered them into submission.
>
> Healey retired, but he did not lick his wounds. Within hours he was back in No. 10 to tell the Prime Minister that unless the rate did go up as he proposed he would not be responsible for the currency. The disastrous consequences of Healey's confession of impotence at the height of the crisis concentrated Callaghan's mind admirably. He grudgingly consented to the 15 per cent interest rate. That was the day the pound nearly died.
>
> But the new rate impressed the market, and purchasers at home and abroad rushed to buy gilts; with a return of 15 per cent annually for every pound invested, they needed little persuasion. But to men such as Crosland, Lever and Benn, the 15 per cent interest rate did not save the pound; it was a blow to hopes for growth and jobs.[49]

The decision received less than full Cabinet backing. One dissenting minister recalled that: 'It's hard to tell if there would have been less worry if interest rates had been higher – they were very damaging to industrial development. The Treasury was against intervening on interest rates.'[50]

After discussions in Washington with IMF officials to gauge their requirements before they arrived, the IMF team, under former Bank of England official Alan Whittome, arrived in London on 1 November. Although it was clear to many observers that the IMF would require further public expenditure cuts, the question became the degree of severity of the cuts themselves. But as has been noted, 'by this time even the hard-line Keynesians in the Treasury were resigned to some further public spending cuts'.[51] One Treasury official commented that 'the IMF were here for months. It was like having your in-laws to stay. Being here for a whole quarter meant that the economy changed and the figures [changed].'[52] To the Labour Party and the Cabinet the question of cuts was a source of great political *angst*. Callaghan realised this, and as a party leader of wide political experience and possessing considerable political acumen, he sought to minimise the IMF conditions.

To this end he sought international support for a solution to the sterling balance problem. Callaghan, who had originally grown to dislike the sterling balances during his tenure as Chancellor, 1964–7, thought that if other countries would take the responsibility of moving money into London when sums were being withdrawn from the sterling balances, a safety net would be created and the pound would not be threatened. At first the German Chancellor Helmut Schmidt was sympathetic but by the time Ed Yeo visited him in late October, the German view was that the IMF must not be undermined in recommending, if need be, strong medicine for the British economy. One cabinet minister, who was shocked by the Germans' tough approach, recalled that: 'I thought it was right to borrow through the IMF partly because it was a way of making the major trading partners face up to their responsibility to keep world trade going. I was appallingly disappointed with West Germany's attitude. I heard Schmidt in Oslo at the Socialist International and it might have been an orthodox economic lecture.'[53] Another cabinet minister explained Schmidt's reluctance by arguing that 'the Germans have a horror of inflation, from pre-war experience and the Hitler period and they wouldn't back us'.[54]

Yeo's view was that the sterling balance issue was a diversion and that once appropriate action had been taken in accordance with the IMF 'the sterling balances will look after themselves'.[55] (Yeo turned out to be absolutely correct as was demonstrated during 1979 when the balances were rising fast, thus making a strong contribution to financing the balance of payments deficit.) Callaghan's next gambit in resolving the sterling balance problem was to send Harold Lever to Washington to win the approval of the Americans, particularly President Ford. Lever, in turn, saw key officials from all the important American departments of state, including Kissinger, and tried to portray a disaster scenario if the British economy collapsed and injured the whole Western financial system. Having seen Ford, Lever thought he had reason to believe a sterling balance deal would be forthcoming which would avoid harsh IMF terms. But the intricacies of Washington's interdepartmental politics ruled this out and in the end only a limited safety net for sterling was agreed in early January 1977, by which time the IMF medicine had had to be taken. One senior Treasury official thought that 'Lever exaggerated his own importance. He's the nicest of people but he can be naive and simplistic. One example was his one-man mission to the Americans. It never had a hope in hell. I know the pressure on Kissinger to send him away with a flea in his ear.'[56]

Central to the IMF medicine was 'the price we would have to pay to obtain the IMF funds'.[57] The negotiations between the IMF team and the Treasury were conducted in an atmosphere of bluff, improvisation and, from the Treasury's side, delay. Essentially the Fund took the minority Treasury view, advocated by Derek Mitchell from the beginning of the crisis, that large public expenditure cuts were necessary to reduce the PSBR and restore confidence. This view saw the PSBR as representing an economy out of kilter from previous inflationary excesses. The IMF team suggested a £4 million reduction in the PSBR over two years and a stricter control of the money supply and of domestic credit expansion. Not surprisingly the IMF medicine was not well received by many in the Cabinet. One minister who was close to events commented that 'the PSBR was an absurd concept. It only achieved market importance because the Treasury attempted to give it importance.'[58]

Controversy also surrounded the Fund's intentions for the exchange rate. IMF officials took the line that a low rate for the pound was preferable – ironically, the very argument that on 4 March had induced the Bank to sell on a falling market. One Treasury minister confirmed this by recalling that 'when the IMF came – and this is not generally known – they wanted a $1·60 pound with falling inflation. I always said $1·65 was the best figure.'[59] Indeed before the IMF arrived Malcolm Crawford suggested in the *Sunday Times* that the IMF were aiming at a level of $1·50. Strenuous denials were officially offered by the IMF as the pound slumped to $1·55. Essentially the episode was bluff and counter-bluff and few doubted that a lower rate for sterling was one of the Fund's aims, as, indeed it later transpired.

The slow pace of negotiations between Healey, Callaghan and the IMF was ended by the IMF's managing director Johannes Witteveen who gave Downing Street only twelve hours' notice of his arrival on 1 December. As Yeo put it, 'we decided to flush the PM out'.[60] Healey had already been convinced that there would have to be extensive public expenditure cuts and now Callaghan, while regretting the fact, had to agree. Witteveen said the Fund would be content with £2·5 billion of public spending cuts over two years plus the sale of £500 million of BP shares as suggested by the British Treasury. This was £1 billion less than the original figure of £4 billion and Callaghan, who had not received satisfaction over the sterling balances issue, was realist enough to accept.

The debate now shifted to the Cabinet. Essentially the Cabinet was divided into three groups – those who supported the Chancellor, the Croslandites whose political philosophy abhorred public spending cuts and the left who advanced the 'alternative strategy' of import controls, direction of investment and a *de facto* siege economy. Tony Benn put the 'alternative strategy' case in Cabinet on various occasions during the 1974–9 government but at the 2 December Cabinet Benn needed not just a brilliant analytical exposition but a convincing realistic remedy. The 'alternative strategy', to many on the left, had now reached the stage where it had emerged from the realms of theory to the practical world. To the right of the Labour Party the 'alternative strategy' was neither an alternative nor a strategy. One Tribunite MP recalled that: 'In 1975 the Tribune Group put forward an alternative strategy which was printed in *Tribune* at the end of 1976. We were like a government in exile. When Brian Sedgemore saw Healey to put the alternative strategy, Healey just fell about laughing.'[61]

In Cabinet Benn argued the case for the 'alternative strategy' using the familiar 1931 analogy to add political weight to the argument. But the thoroughness of a full Cabinet examination exposed Benn's arguments and according to Fay and Young 'without a Treasury behind him, Benn was pulverised. Even non-economic ministers primed with briefs from No. 10 joined in to expose the weakness of his argument . . .'[62] To some members

of the Cabinet the decision was now clear cut. Fred Peart thought
that 'we had no alternative with the IMF. I backed the Cabinet's
line.'[63] One cabinet minister who supported the 'alternative
strategy' recalled that: 'Callaghan chaired the Cabinet brilliantly.
Whatever side of the Cabinet you were on you couldn't feel you
hadn't had your say. I was convinced the alternative strategy
could have worked given a will to do it. I did believe at the time,
that it would have meant a rough run for six months.'[64] Similarly
another minister argued that 'eighteen months of import controls
would have seen it through so we could have avoided the IMF.
But we were dominated by the City. Our financial system is the
most open in the capitalist world. The City tail wags the dog.'[65]

But in Cabinet, at least, the left had lost the battle for Benn's
version of the 'alternative strategy' and now switched to a
watered-down version of it in the form of Peter Shore's plan for
selective import controls. This idea had the further advantage of
not ideologically antagonising the Croslandites.

Crosland and his supporters, Roy Hattersley, Shirley Williams
and Harold Lever, essentially wished to avoid what they regarded
as swingeing and unacceptable public expenditure cuts. Reg
Prentice, then a member of the Cabinet, recalled that 'We went
through weeks of meetings and at the beginning when Denis put
the case for cuts only Edmund Dell and myself supported him.
Gradually the intellectual force of his arguments and the sheer
weight of hard facts was decisive. But at first the Cabinet right
wing – people like Crosland – were against the cuts.'[66] Joel
Barnett noted that at the 2 December Cabinet meeting 'Crosland
said he still believed it wrong to deflate . . .'[67] One of the
Croslandites recalled that:

> The IMF was a dead end course. Though I'm the enemy of
> profligacy I'm the enemy of the meat-axe. Certainly public
> expenditure should have been cautiously and consistently
> reduced but there was no need for the meat-axe. Tony Crosland
> was a consistent opponent of the meat-axe. Once he was
> rebuked by the Prime Minister for opposing it. Callaghan said
> that when he was Foreign Secretary he backed the Chancel-
> lor.[68]

Crosland and his supporters therefore came to regard the
possibility of import deposits as an alternative to spending cuts

without really being in favour of protectionism *per se*. This paradox proved fatal when individual Croslandites considered it in detail. Shirley Williams feared that any form of protectionism would harm the Third World, which it undoubtedly would have done, and Harold Lever thought that import deposits would be deflationary, a view confirmed by Denis Healey.

Callaghan and Healey had effectively won the Cabinet battle on the principle of cuts of £1 billion in 1977–8, £1·5 billion in 1978–9 plus the sale of BP shares to cut a further £500 million off the PSBR. Both the left and the Croslandites had to face up to supporting Callaghan or resigning, with the latter possibly precipitating a general election. The left however, still retained their faith in the 'alternative strategy' as a realistic proposal for a future Labour Government – a faith they have since strengthened. But for Tony Crosland and his supporters acceptance of the IMF terms was an ideological defeat. Fay and Young recorded that after Cabinet had backed the Prime Minister and Chancellor the left found the surrender of Crosland galling:

> 'Everyone ran for cover after that', says one of the left. 'We realised we'd either have to accept or get out, and if we went we'd have lost the election.' . . . 'As we argued, a myth grew up about the opposition organised by Crosland,' says the same left-winger 'but he collapsed like a pack of cards. It was a pathetic thing, quite frankly.'
>
> Another leftist is more detached and sympathetic: 'That was the day Croslandism died. He said to me: "This is nonsense, but we must do it." He knew it meant the abandonment of his position as a revisionist theorist. He knew he was going up a cul-de-sac. It was a tormenting time for him. I watched him, torturing himself.'[69]

Similarly Stanley Orme, a Cabinet opponent of the IMF medicine, recalled that 'The centre collapsed. Tony Crosland went to see Jim before the final meeting. I could see the signs on the horizon. Crosland lacked bottle. He, Shirley and the centre collapsed and capitulated.'[70] Jeremy Bray thought that 'the IMF deal was the last nail in the coffin of Croslandism',[71] which was a verdict consistent with the emergence of the left's 'alternative strategy'. One left-winger accurately summed up the dilemma – arguably for both the left and the Croslandites – by arguing that

'The IMF crisis wasn't necessary. The battles in the Cabinet were about the degree of cuts not the principle – that's the question they didn't address themselves to. Lever was essential to the acceptance of the IMF terms. He understood the economic reasons but was not aware of the political consequences.'[72]

Following Cabinet's decision to impose the cuts in principle on 2 December, further Cabinet meetings agreed the details of where the axe should fall, a task that was equally as difficult for a Labour Cabinet. Joel Barnett noted in his memoirs that the 14 December Cabinet was very difficult:

> At 1 pm Jim appeared to lose his patience. I say 'appeared' because he was always cool on these occasions, and in total command, so I assumed it was carefully planned. He said, as we could not agree, he and Denis would go away, make up a package and present it to the House and the Parliamentary Party. If it was thrown out by the Party, that would be that; if it was approved, then those Cabinet Ministers who wanted to resign should do so then, but not before. There was an appalled silence before Michael Foot, Peter Shore and a number of others said there was no need for that and that we were not far from agreement.[73]

Ultimately agreement was reluctantly reached with the unwillingness to cut the welfare state necessitating greater cuts from overseas aid, housing, roads, defence and the nationalised industries. On 15 December Denis Healey presented the 'Letter of Intent' to IMF to the House of Commons and outlined the £3 billion spending cuts to the unenthusiastic Labour Benches and the derision of the Conservatives. For Labour MPs, particularly those on the left, the IMF package presented a dilemma which reoccurred during 1974–9 – support the government in the lobbies or face a general election which would sweep Mrs Thatcher to power. So for many Tribune MPs it was a question of reluctant acquiescence in a policy they believed to be inimical to their version of British socialism. The same may be said of the trade unions who were loyally sticking to the Stage II restrictions of about $4\frac{1}{2}$ per cent. Jack Jones stated that he 'opposed the IMF cuts; the general feeling in the TUC was that the cuts were too great'.[74] It is also arguable that the left were further trapped as Denis Healey found it useful to retain the Fund as a bogeyman to threaten the left and in the autumn of 1977 IMF surveillance of the economy was retained. One cabinet minister thought that Healey 'saw the IMF as an invaluable aid for controlling a turbulent and profligate Cabinet and Labour Party'.[75]

The central question of the whole IMF crisis, for the left, for the Croslandites, for the Treasury, and for the British people was, and in many ways remains, the question of whether the acceleration of the crisis could have been prevented from reaching its December climax. Evidence, both with hindsight and at the time, suggests that the development of the IMF crisis was a story of blunder and lost opportunities.

The Treasury's conduct at the beginning of the crisis in March was seriously at fault. It is arguable that the strategy of seeking deliberately to devalue the pound was unsuited to the conditions of greater exchange rate volatility that existed in the 1970s and which had not been the case in the 1960s' world of fixed exchange rates. Moreover the theory of devaluation was flawed in 1976 by the threat it would pose to the inflation rate which was arguably the largest single danger to the British economy. Apart from a few senior Treasury officials such as Sir Derek Mitchell and Sir Leo Pliatzky the Treasury consistently ignored the inflationary threat posed by an exaggerated PSBR and the consequences thereof to external confidence in the pound. The failure to take appropriate action in 1974–5, as other Western nations reacted to the oil crisis by reducing growth rate expectations, may be blamed for storing up the crisis of 1976 so that the inevitable public spending cuts would seem more drastic. The IMF crisis dramatically illustrated the failure of Keynesian policies to maximise economic welfare in the context of a shift in economic wealth and power from the industrialised countries to the member states of OPEC.

Denis Healey's role in the development of the crisis deserved sympathy given the poor advice that was often forthcoming from the Treasury Keynesians. Healey knew that the British economy needed to reduce its inflation rate in 1975/6 and he also knew that sterling was vulnerable if foreign confidence in the economy was undermined. Intellectually Healey dominated his Cabinet colleagues and was able by the power of his arguments to defeat his critics, as was the case over Tony Benn's 'alternative strategy'. One cabinet minister recalled that 'Healey was a good Chancellor and he had a sense of humour, unlike Benn',[76] and a junior Treasury minster thought 'Denis was in some ways a very good

Chancellor. He had a tendency to jump around.'[77] One critic of Healey's policies argued that 'You can't take Healey's ability from him but the stance wasn't right from the start as the strategy we agreed was never put into operation.'[78] Regarding Healey's relationship with the Treasury officials one cabinet minister recalled that 'Denis was intellectually more than a match for his officials. He believed that there was some validity in monetarist arguments but that didn't mean he was totally in favour of the Friedman line.'[79]

While it may be argued that Healey never had any intention of adopting the strategy of the Labour left, it would be unfair and inaccurate to argue that Healey embraced the IMF without a fight. Indeed evidence suggests that tougher measures earlier, for example in the April and July budgets, might have restored confidence in sterling and prevented the crisis developing the momentum of chilling inevitability which it developed. Tougher measures to restrict the excessive level of public expenditure, or to raise interest rates, earlier in the crisis would have fundamentally altered the course of events and averted recourse to the IMF. But in political terms such action was difficult for a Labour Chancellor whose Cabinet colleagues, as well as the PLP, had failed to recognise the seriousness of the crisis and the imbalance in the economy. Political as well as economic constraints limited Healey's action during 1976 and made the temptations of borrowing difficult to resist. It is to Healey's credit that when such borrowing clearly only postponed, rather than cancelled, the necessary solution of public expenditure cuts, Healey was prepared to face political condemnation by his party rather than duck the issue.

For Labour voters, and the electorate generally, public spending cuts were presented as a betrayal by the left of the whole philosophy of the Labour Party. One Tribune Group MP put it bluntly that 'Healey was anti-working class.'[80] However the alternative to public expenditure control was increasing inflation, a falling pound and a collapse of business confidence which would have led to higher unemployment. Such an outcome, with inflation possibly at 50 per cent or more, would have been extremely damaging to Labour voters and the British people. Nor would import controls have benefited the working-class consumer who would have suffered higher prices and loss of purchasing choice. Ultimately, both Healey and Callaghan knew that the IMF medicine, while tasting foul, would benefit the patient in economic terms. But in political terms, and as practising politicians, the same assumption could not be drawn while the Labour Party was at odds with the Labour Government. Healey and Callaghan knew that the IMF deal was only supported in the division lobbies because the prospect of a general election victory for the Conservatives was too horrific for most Labour MPs to contemplate.

CHAPTER VI

Callaghan's New Dawn?

LABOUR'S PARLIAMENTARY ARITHMETIC

Electoral volatility at by-elections is a strong feature of recent British politics. Harold Macmillan in the days of 'you've never had it so good' saw Torrington and Orpington fall to the Liberals and Mr Heath's government faced a series of by-election debacles at the hands of the Liberals. Between 1964 and 1970 Labour's by-election performances, with one or two exceptions, were abject. However until 1974 governments could take by-election losses in their stride because their overall majority was sufficiently comfortable to allow them to do so. Even Labour's loss of Leyton in 1965, while humiliating for Patrick Gordon Walker, did not precipitate a threatened general election.

Labour's failure in October 1974 to secure a larger working majority made the government's parliamentary survival a matter of dispute should by-election results go against them, which indeed they did. Under both Wilson and Callaghan Labour lost by-elections to the Conservatives in seats which, at a general election, would be expected to return a Labour member with a large majority. Moreover electoral volatility was developing a logic of its own in that the safer the seat the greater was the by-election threat to it. In June 1975 the Conservatives gained Woolwich West from Labour and in November 1976 the Conservatives won both Walsall North and Workington from Labour. At Walsall North the swing was 22·6 per cent and at Workington 13·2 per cent to the Conservatives. By January 1977 the government's overall majority in the Commons had fallen to one, given the support of the two members of the break-away Scottish Labour Party and the two non-Unionist, Northern Ireland MPs. (In March 1977 the Conservatives gained Birmingham Stechford and, in April, Ashfield from Labour to further weaken Mr Callaghan's hold on power.)

The government had the problem of not only a combined vote

103

of the Conservatives and minor parties, which would leave Labour vulnerable to a general election on a vote of no-confidence, but also the worry about a left-wing revolt on key policy issues. Many Tribune Group MPs were deeply disillusioned with the performance of the government following the IMF spending cuts and what they regarded as the betrayal of many radical policies agreed in the Social Contract period. The government's parliamentary arithmetic was, at best, finely balanced, which was a serious position as the Conservatives increased their lead in the opinion polls. On 17 March, less than a fortnight away from the budget, the government's expenditure White Paper, which dealt with the terms agreed with the IMF, was defeated following a backbench revolt, by 293 votes to nil. The government, knowing that many Tribunites would abstain, had also instructed Labour MPs to abstain in order to allow the House to adjourn. However the Scottish Nationalists forced a division and Margaret Thatcher duly put down the ritual vote of no-confidence following the government's defeat. The government's immediate problem of Tribune Group rebels had now become a wider problem of cobbling together a majority to prevent a general election.

THE LIB–LAB PACT

Like the government, the Liberals had a good electoral reason to fear a general election. Their opinion poll popularity had plummeted since the heady days of 1973–4 and in by-elections the humiliation of a series of lost deposits had been exacerbated at Walsall North in November 1976 when the Liberal candidate, despite good credentials, had been beaten into fifth place by independent and National Front candidates. At Stechford in March 1977 the Liberals again failed to gain as many votes as the National Front candidate, proving the extent of electoral volatility in by-elections yet again. Such a depressing outlook for the Liberals inevitably made them as unenthusiastic for an election as Labour and more than any other factor, made the possibility of a parliamentary pact with the government seem attractive.

The Liberal leader David Steel was a man ideally suited to the task of 'doing a deal' with the government. Unlike many Liberals Steel did not regard the survival of the Liberal Party as the sole aim of its existence, and he was naturally attracted to any scheme which would allow the Liberals access to, if not direct control over, the governmental process. Like most Liberals Steel had little original or profound to say on policy matters, but he had a shrewd understanding of the political realities of Commons infighting and he knew that a share in power was more important to the Liberals than the details of policy.

Indeed, Steel's most recent political experiences in 1976 had been his skilful, and rather ruthless, campaign against John Pardoe for the Liberal Party leadership and his attempt to prevent the Liberal Party being smeared with the details of the Thorpe affair – Bessell, Scott, homosexual allegations and so on. In this latter operation Steel was to conduct himself and his party with utter probity in contrast to Thorpe who became more and more involved in the scandal. Although it is open to speculation, the Thorpe affair did not inspire electoral belief in the Liberals and gave Steel another reason for seeking an accommodation with the government. With the threat of the vote of no-confidence concentrating minds talks began between the government and Liberals.[1]

It is not the purpose of this account to trace the details of the talks that led up to the pact but emphasis needs to be given to the fact that the pact was essentially about Liberal support in the vote of no-confidence on 23 March rather than about significant policy changes. The ritual of speaking for the effect and jostling for bargaining positions that led up to Steel's meeting with Callaghan to agree the pact dramatised the process, but did not advance the rationale of the pact. Thus as part of the ritual the Liberals put themselves forward as the moderate party of the national interest, as opposed to the Labour and Conservative 'extremes'. David Steel, recalling the pre-pact manoeuvring, had issued a statement that:

'Either the Government now proceeds on the basis of agreed measures in the national interest for the next two years, in which case we would be willing to consider supporting such a programme, or else we have a general election.

'The one thing we cannot do is stagger on like last night with a lame duck Labour programme. The political decision as to which course to take therefore rests squarely with the Prime Minister and the Labour Party.'

On Saturday, in a further statement designed to put the

screws on via the Sunday papers, I said that if the Labour Party does not 'acknowledge the political reality that it cannot continue to push on with full blooded Socialist government because there is no mandate for it, then the 13 Liberal votes will be bound to be cast against the Government in the confidence debate in favour of a general election, at which we would put our case for an end to the domination of Parliament by any one extreme – Socialist or Thatcherite.'[2]

In the event when Steel began the meetings with Callaghan to work out the pact there was only one item of real contention, the Liberal proposal for a Bill for direct elections to the European Parliament with a free vote on the type of election system to be used. This issue aroused strong feelings in the Labour Party with many anti-marketeers ideologically opposed to anything to do with the EEC. Steel, however, as a political realist knew this and a compromise solution was not too difficult to reach. Steel recalled that:

> The sole source of disagreement was the European paragraph. It seemed a pity that our failure to agree this one issue should vitiate the prospects of everything else. We talked round and round the subject, with me doodling drafts, which were then sent next door for instant typing. Eventually we came up with a revised paragraph which, I said, I was prepared to commend to my colleagues.
>
> It promised introduction of a Bill, a choice of election systems in the preceding White Paper and account to be taken of the Liberal Party's strong views on the matter. The Prime Minister had patiently explained that he could not promise what he could not get Labour MPs to deliver, and I accepted his private assurances that when the time came he would back PR himself.[3]

The other features of the pact were a consultative committee to be set up between the parties, a meeting between John Pardoe and the Chancellor to discuss economy policy, an end to nationalisation and legislation for devolution on the lines approved by the Liberals. The pact's terms were anything but draconian given the government's predicament, and though there was considerable Cabinet disagreement over the terms there were no resignations.

Michael Foot, an enthusiastic backer of the pact, helped to convince the left in the Cabinet[4] and Tribunite backbenchers in marginal seats needed little encouragement to see the pact's merits. One left-wing backbencher, who thought differently, recalled that: 'I was against the Lib/Lab pact but I didn't have a backer. People said "you're all right with a 22 000 majority", but I replied that if we left it the electoral position could get worse not better.'[5] Another critic of the pact, Stanley Orme, recalled that 'I opposed the pact. It sustained us but only for a major defeat. What happens is that governments become terribly pragmatic.'[6]

In the event in the crucial vote on 23 March 1977, the government won by 24 with 322 voting with them and 298 against. Had the Liberals voted with the Conservatives the government would have lost by two and a general election would have ensued. The pact's first hurdle had therefore been overcome to the mutual advantage of both Labour and Liberal parties. The second hurdle, the March 1977 budget, proved more difficult as it concerned a central feature of the economic policy-making process.

Although only three months after the IMF medicine, the budget was mildly reflationary with income tax reductions totalling £2·25 billion, of which £960 million was contingent on satisfactory arrangments for Stage III of the incomes policy due in July. Personal allowances were raised and the level of entry to higher tax brackets raised by £1000 to £6000. There were also the traditional increases in taxes on drink, tobacco, vehicle excise duty and a 5½p increase in petrol tax. As a whole the budget could not have been more in line with what the Liberals had urged; but the 5½p increase in petrol duty, while making excellent economic and conservationist sense, was politically unacceptable to the Liberals. With no advance warning of the budget, in keeping with the custom of budget secrecy, the Liberals had not had the opportunity to bargain away the petrol tax increase with the government. The prospect of an unpopular petrol tax rise in rural Liberal constituencies only a week after the pact had saved a Labour Government was too much for Steel and Liberal MPs. Steel himself, alert to the political rather than the economic consequences, recalled of the budget that:

To our horror it included a 5½p increase in fuel tax as well as increases in vehicle excise duties. Liberal constituencies are

predominantly rural and would be those most affected by the
increases. We could scarcely vote to make life difficult in our
own seats in the name of our new political agreement.

The problem was discussed next day at the first meeting of
the Lib–Lab Committee, by John Pardoe and Joel Barnett,
Chief Secretary to the Treasury, and once again when I saw
the Prime Minister early in April.

He reiterated what Barnett had told Pardoe: that while
sympathetic, no Government could lose its Budget resolutions
and stay in office. We therefore faced the embarrassment of
abstaining in the Budget debate on the transport tax resolutions while remaining determined to do something about it in
committee stage of the Finance Bill.

In the discussions that followed it became painfully obvious
that Ministers who ought to have been consulted (e.g. Roy
Hattersley at Transport) simply bowed to Treasury diktat and
had no real information on such a matter affecting their
departments before the Cabinet briefing. Indeed on the whole
question of rural transport, our David Penhaligon (Truro)
seemed to be conducting regular tutorials with Bill Rodgers,
whose Stockton-on-Tees constituency provides no background
on the subject.[7]

Joel Barnett's view of the dispute was that the Liberals had not
appreciated the reality – that opposing the 5½p increase would
lead to the very general election the pact was designed to prevent.
In this matter Barnett is right to talk of the 'naivety of the
Liberals'[8] and only after the Prime Minister had made the
situation clear did David Steel take the appropriate evasive
measures. He simply announced, without prior agreement with
his parliamentary colleagues, that the Liberals would abstain,
rather than vote against the vote on the petrol tax, which gave the
government victory in the lobby by 290 votes to 281. This tactic
removed the threat of a general election but did not remove the
dispute itself.

Discussions between Pardoe and Barnett, which were relayed
back to the Liberals and the Cabinet respectively, took nearly six
weeks to reach a compromise solution. On 5 May the Cabinet
agreed to a reduction of 5½p on petrol, but not derv, and only from
5 August in return for Liberal support on all other aspects of the
budget. In the end the government did not seek to raise the lost

revenue in another way when economically it had every reason for doing so. This situation was further compounded when two left-wing Labour MPs, Jeff Rooker and Audrey Wise, voted with the Conservatives on the Finance Bill Committee for higher tax relief.

John Pardoe, who was also on the Committee, voted with the government in accordance with the agreement on the $5\frac{1}{2}$p petrol tax compromise, but the combined votes of the Conservatives, Rooker and Wise were sufficient to defeat the government and cost the Exchequer £450 million in a year. Both the petrol tax row with the Liberals and the Rooker–Wise defeat helped to create the impression that the government was not in full control of its economic strategy which added extra importance to the negotiations on Stage III of incomes policy control.

The mood in the TUC as well as the mood on the shopfloor had hardened considerably after two years of pay restraint. The ritual of negotiations with Denis Healey over a mutually satisfactory norm had not been able to replace the ritual of negotiations under conditions of free collective bargaining – to which trade unions, quite rightly, attach status and importance. Jack Jones, still a staunch supporter of continuing the pay policy, faced a revolt from his own T & GWU rank and file who voted, at their summer conference on the Isle of Man, to throw out the twelve-month rule despite Jones's recommendation of it.[19] The twelve-month rule itself simply sought a commitment from each union not to seek an increase less than twelve months after receiving one. To the government the advantage of the twelve-month rule was that it prolonged and regulated incomes policy in the hope of avoiding a pay 'explosion' similar to that of 1974–5. The TUC ultimately reaffirmed the twelve-month rule, but it could not come to any formal agreement on a pay norm.

Undaunted by the lack of formal collaboration Healey hoped that the TUC General Council would acquiesce in the government's policy of a 10 per cent norm which was therefore a relaxation on Stages I and II. Healey made it clear that as well as imposing the 10 per cent in the public sector, the government would impose sanctions against private companies which transgressed the 10 per cent limit, a policy, it may be argued, which is totally alien to the rule of law.

One Treasury minister recalled that as the incomes policy developed, more and more regulations and anomalies arose so that 'there were areas where incomes policy was ridiculous. Denis Healey chaired a special committee deciding what percentage plumbers in central London should get for more bogus productivity. A committee sat on percentages for lift operators.'[10] Such facets of incomes control were publicly hidden by the emphasis on the 10 per cent norm, which, for political reasons, had to be regarded as tolerable, if not agreeable to the unions. As well as the 10 per cent policy the government's White Paper *The Attack on Inflation after 31st July 1977*[11] contained a statement published by the TUC in June advising negotiators not to delay settlements under Stage II, or reopen Stage II negotiations when Stage III began. Barnes and Reid noted that the government 'had fixed a norm with an assurance that the General Council would not dissent and in the hope that it would influence the coming wage round'.[12]

Healey's confidence in TUC acquiescence may be gauged by the July mini-budget which increased child benefits, reduced income tax from 35 per cent to 34 per cent – though not to 33 per cent as suggested in the April budget – increased aid for industry and raised personal allowances as a result of the Rooker–Wise amendment. The July package thus added a further reflationary stimulus which, while of dubious economic benefit, was politically tempting given the possibility of a sudden general election resulting from a breakdown of the Lib–Lab pact. Many union leaders were not fooled by the July package and the pressures for return to free collective bargaining continued to grow, though not as yet to the point of explosion. Hence the 10 per cent policy was not achieved as wages rose 16 per cent to July 1978 while prices rose 8 per cent. It is arguable that such a rise in earnings was politically acceptable within the context of the language of incomes policy. Jack Jones commented that the '10 per cent was not agreed but tacitly accepted by the unions. By and large there wasn't *too much* [emphasis added] evasion and trouble.'[13]

ECONOMIC RECOVERY?

By the autumn of 1977, barely nine months after the IMF trauma, the Labour Government had not only survived but now appeared to be witnessing a remarkable economic revival. The problem of sterling being too weak had so evaporated during 1977 that by October the Treasury announced the pound was free to float upwards, which it did, until it was eventually just short of the $2 parity, in stark contrast to the crisis levels of 1976. This astonishingly successful turnaround helped to improve living standards and reduce inflation. Predictably the CBI were unhappy. According to one Treasury official, 'the CBI really wanted to keep the exchange rate to $1·60 to $1·70. It's true they had kittens when the pound floated upwards.'[14] Similarly, one cabinet minister recalled with some irony that 'the CBI told us they couldn't live with the pound above $1·70 as it would be too difficult to export'.[15] Such a view, long held by many in the Treasury, failed to realise that the British people export to live rather than live to export. Without tackling underlying problems of poor management, overmanning, strikes and low productivity, devaluation *per se* is of temporary value only to exporters as well as exacerbating inflationary pressures. Far from being a handicap the rising value of the pound was a sign of real economic recovery.

A similarly encouraging picture was emerging in the external account. The balance of payments, which had been in deficit in the second quarter of 1977, showed a £483 million surplus in the third quarter and a £351 million surplus in the fourth quarter. Boosted by the much anticipated North Sea oil revenues, the Chancellor's headache of financing the external balance had been transformed into a prospect for genuine economic recovery. Foreign currency reserves rose from $7196 million to $20 557 million during 1977 and the intention of keeping the pound artificially low to assist manufacturing exports was jettisoned.

Inflation during 1977 continued to fall, not because of incomes policy, but because of the measures taken, at the IMF's behest, to control public expenditure and the money supply. Cash limits were introduced and money supply targets treated with respect. The PSBR, which had exceeded £10 billion in 1975–6 was further assisted by a measure of public sector underspending in relation to the targets set by the government. This added £1·6 billion restraint and greatly contributed to the improved economic situation. One minister recalled that 'the PSBR assumed more importance as the mood in the City was for publishing money supply targets'.[16] Indeed, a Treasury minister, Robert Sheldon, who opposed the new strategy, nearly resigned in protest: 'Monetary targets were to please the City. I sent a memo to Denis not to accept targets. I went to resign but my political friends talked me out of it. They said nobody would know what it was all about. I regret enormously not resigning. It was the greatest mistake of my political career.'[17]

To many in the labour movement the period after the IMF medicine confirmed their opinion that the City was too powerful *vis-à-vis* a Labour Government. Hugh Scanlon thought 'there was a strike of capital . . . all the might of the unions was nothing compared to the might of the City and the financiers'.[18] Jack Jones recalled that 'Labour ministers tended to be overinfluenced by top management and the City. Wilson and Callaghan were unduly impressed by big business and finance.'[19]

Despite such misgivings the improvement in the inflation rate was impressive during 1977. From the 30 per cent levels of 1975, inflation was down to under 10 per cent by 1978 so that, as King has speculated, 'it is doubtful whether any other democratic government in history has ever succeeded in reducing a country's rate of inflation by such a large amount in so short a time'.[20]

With the parliamentary life-line granted by the Lib–Lab pact and the improved economic position it was not surprising that the Labour Party, while not about to settle its differences, could feel more optimistic about its electoral chances. In August Labour held Birmingham Ladywood in a by-election with only an 8·8 per cent swing to the Conservatives compared to the 20·8 per cent swing which had lost Labour Ashfield in April 1977. In the press the turnaround in the government's economic fortunes did not go unnoticed. Hugo Young, in an article aptly entitled 'Is this the Labour miracle?', caught the political mood:

> In the past few days I have talked to three Cabinet Ministers. Such conversations are not usually amazing and one rarely learns any sensational State secrets worth putting on the front page. What can always be divined however, is at least the collective state of mind. And sometimes this discovery itself constitutes a small sensation.
>
> This I believe, is such an occasion. For in one respect the Callaghan Government is much misunderstood. Divided in the Cabinet, impotent in Parliament, buried under a catastrophic record of inflation and unemployment, it might be expected to be in despair. At best it should be waiting in stoic resignation for the end. Outside Westminster there are few people who hold it in confident regard and fewer still who would make it an even bet to win the next election.

Yet this is far from being the mood of the Cabinet. I think my Ministers are a good cross-section and what they all exhibit is optimism. They feel thoroughly pleased with themselves and speak about the future with a positively glowing confidence. Winning or not losing the election is now a thought which in all sobriety they allow to cross their lips.

What then has done the trick? The first factor is mere survival. The political year begins with the party conferences and twelve months after the last lot the Government lives on. Given the forces at work against it inside and out, abroad and at home, in Parliament and the country – this is pretty surprising. Seen from the Cabinet, it can be almost completely divorced from the delicate question of what the Government has actually done or not done with its time.

Furthermore, there is now some impression that Britain's economic destiny is back under her own control. This may be illusory but it does wonders for the self-esteem. Next week's Labour party conference will be very different from last year's, when Denis Healey did not dare to leave the country, and the seat of government lurched between the VIP lounge at London Airport and a rostrum of ranting trade unionists at Blackpool. Moreover SOD – Sod-Off-Day, as Mr. Healey designates the moment Britain sheds the IMF yoke – may be approaching.

Again, after months of decline, the economic graphs are climbing. The trade surplus was a record, inflation is going down, money has become very cheap, the 12-month rule has been signed up. There also seems certain to be an autumn reflation at a time of the Chancellor's calculated choosing.[21]

One economic statistic that was not politically encouraging in autumn 1977 was unemployment, which stood at 1·6 million in September. However while such a figure – though representing only a 6 per cent unemployment rate – would once have haunted a Labour Government, this was clearly not the case in the late 1970s. Indeed the Callaghan Government showed few signs of the panic, irrespective of the ill-advised industrial strategy, which had gripped Mr Heath's administration.[22] Labour had realised that a 6 per cent unemployment rate was not a recipe for electoral disaster in an age of welfare benefits, earnings related supplements, a growing black economy and a small core of long-term unemployed[23] as opposed to job changers.

'Mass unemployment', in terms of unused capacity on a 1930s scale, was conspicuous by its absence. One backbench MP recalled that 'the public reaction against unemployment was less extreme. I organised a march in my constituency against unemployment and only 1000 employed people turned up and virtually none of the unemployed.'[24] Another MP commented that 'unemployment is only an issue when it affects Coventry and Surrey – there's always been unemployment in places like Hartlepool'.[25]

Joel Barnett, similarly, noted in his memoirs that

> If anybody had told us in 1974 that we in a Labour Government would preside over levels of unemployment of that size, we would have derided them. But not only did we do so, we did so for years and, despite criticism from the trade union movement and our activists inside and outside the House of Commons, we did so with comparatively little trouble. Remarkably enough I do not recall a single letter in the whole of that time complaining specifically about this terribly high level of unemployment. I know from talking to other Ministers and backbenchers that the same quietist mood applied in their constituencies. Although the subject of unemployment came up from time to time in my constituency party meetings, frequently we went many months without referring to the subject. It could be that they had so many other issues they wanted to raise but, even allowing for that, the low level of feeling on such an emotive subject remained a constant source of surprise.

> How was a Labour Government able to live with such levels of unemployment? The answers we gave ourselves were never wholly satisfactory. But no doubt there was some validity in all of them. The level of benefits was undoubtedly a factor, especially in the first six months of unemployment, when they were related to earnings. These not only cushioned the blow, but also enabled a worker to take his time in accepting another job. There were many more married women on the unemployment register than would previously have been the case, and undoubtedly there must have been a large number of workers 'moonlighting'. Many other explanations were offered, of greater or lesser plausibility, but none was entirely satisfactory, particularly to Ministers in a Labour Government. For even

without outside pressures of the kind we might have expected, we felt badly about unemployment at such high levels.[26]

In summary, while the Labour Government was politically unhappy with the level of unemployment, it did not find the 6 per cent level politically damaging and after October 1977 when the trend was, temporarily, downwards, the political connotations were even less pronounced.

The government's economic 'new dawn' also received the blessing of the IMF and the Fund's managing director told a Washington press conference given jointly by himself and Mr Healey that Britain's financial policies had been an 'astonishing success, providing the basis for much more satisfactory development of the real economy in the near future'.[27] Mr Healey thus began to prepare a substantial October mini-budget aimed at reflation, or rather at its political advantages. Those monetarist voices urging restraint, or arguing that the improved economic position was the result of reducing demand rather than expanding it, were not to the Chancellor's liking. The strictly political consideration of tax cuts was now concentrating Mr Healey's mind. The advice of CBI director-general John Methven that 'again and again Britain has moved forward too early. We have got to be sure the rate of inflation is under control before we start reflating',[28] was economically accurate but politically unappealing.

The reflationists, who had been routed both intellectually and politically a year earlier, now made the running in the build-up to Mr Healey's October package. The Chancellor himself betrayed his intentions by warning against '*excessive* [emphasis added] stimulation of demand' a clear indication to those familiar with Treasury jargon that a stimulation of demand was on its way. The trade unions hoped for, and urged, a considerable expansion. NUPE called for a £2 billion reflationary package to reduce unemployment and other public sector unions expressed a similar view. Calls for reflation dominated the advice to the Chancellor from the Labour Party Conference with David Basnett, general secretary of the G & MWU, predicting 'political catastrophe' if unemployment was not reduced. The TUC duly followed the same line urging a £2 billion reflation to reduce unemployment by 250 000 over a year.

Mr Healey's twelfth budget, unveiled on 26 October 1977, went half way towards the TUC's target, injecting £1 billion into the economy. Tax allowances, backdated to April, were increased, and of several public spending increases, £400 million was allocated for the construction industry because of the 'exceptional difficulties' it faced. Mr Healey's optimism contrasted with the pessimism of the IMF medicine of ten months before. The contrast was deliberately fostered by Mr Healey who put it that:

The Government has made it clear that it aims at a steady and sustained expansion and is determined to avoid the risk of overheating the economy with the damaging consequences for growth, inflation and the balance of payments which we saw four years ago.

For this reason the decisions I shall now announce are part of a programme for economic expansion spreading over 18 months. Our main objective must be a continuing fall in the level of unemployment . . . In our present circumstances it would clearly be wrong for us to take up any further drawings on our standby with the IMF. We will therefore not take up at the end of November the 310 million dollars which then become available. The managing director of the IMF has been informed of this decision.[29]

Although a number of trade union leaders went through the ritual of criticising the mini-budget for not reflating enough, the package reinforced the political optimism that had preceded it and significantly Jack Jones hinted that the winter pay climate would be more conducive to restraint because of the Chancellor's measures. The euphoria of the government's 'new dawn' reached its apogee when at the end of October the pound leapt 6½ cents to $1·86. As the IMF crisis of 1976 suddenly seemed light years away, the prospect of 1978 being Labour's election victory year was far from unrealistic.

CHAPTER VII

The Missed Opportunity

RESUMED EXPANSION

The period from October 1977 to the expansionist April budget of 1978 was one of near euphoria for the government. Politically the prospects were more optimistic than anyone had expected so soon after the IMF nadir and economically there was evidence of falling inflation and a favourable external balance.

In December 1977, the Prices Secretary, Roy Hattersley, was confidently predicting single-figure inflation by mid-1978 with the prospect of permanent single-figure inflation dependent on continued wage restraint. Although Mr Hattersley, like other enthusiastic believers in incomes policy, missed the point that the fall in inflation had resulted from the government's deflationary policies in 1976, he was correct in observing that in the winter of 1977/8 there was no evidence of a 'wage explosion', a euphemism for the collapse of incomes policy.

The December 1977 unemployment figures showed a drop of just over 18 000 since November and while the total figure of 1 428 822 was politically worrisome to many in the Labour Party this represented a mere 6·2 per cent of the working population. Even in Northern Ireland the percentage rate was only 10·5 per cent. Mass unemployment on a 1930s scale was conspicuous by its absence.

The balance of payments showed a £218 million surplus for November in contrast to the forecast of a year earlier in the Letter of Intent of a £500 million deficit for the second half of 1977. For the first time in six years both the visible and invisible balances were in surplus for four consecutive months. On 15 December 1977 Denis Healey's Letter of Intent to the IMF confirmed that Britain was virtually free of active constraints imposed by the IMF and while controlling the money supply was mentioned no specific ceiling was targeted. Moreover in January 1978 the

Chancellor announced that Britain was to make an early repayment of $1 billion of its $4·9 billion of borrowing from the IMF shortly after a $500 million overseas loan to the Electricity Council, which was not due for repayment until 1982, had been repaid. Given the improvement in the balance of payments, the increase in reserves, and the revenue from North Sea oil, such repayments made good sense in order to avoid unnecessary interest payments. The OECD, normally an unreliably gloomy forecaster, shared the government's sense of optimism. Its forecast in the 1977 year-end Economic Review predicted a rapid growth in living standards, inflation in single figures and a large balance of payments surplus. In January 1978 the government itself announced that living standards had risen 1 per cent in the three months to the end of September 1977.

The economic picture therefore looked optimistic and allowed the government to think in political terms of a traditional pre-election boom. This temptation was made greater by the uncertainty of the government's parliamentary arithmetic, dependent as it was on the Lib–Lab pact. However the position at the start of 1978 deserves fuller appraisal. The economic improvement was due to the policies initiated at the behest of the IMF which centred round reductions in public expenditure and proper monetary control. The rightness of the IMF's case was demonstrable a year after the great crisis not only in the external balance but in the domestic economy. Living standards were shown to have been protected, not reduced, by exercising public expenditure restraint. Inflation, which Harold Wilson had rightly stated in 1975 to be the enemy of employment, had been reduced to manageable proportions. The vindication of the IMF medicine lay in the patient's recovery not in any purely theoretical monetarist dogma. Without the IMF medicine, 1978 would have been ushered in by a weak pound, possibly hyperinflation, lack of international competitiveness and high, rather than nominal, unemployment.

In economic terms the last thing that was required was a dose of inflation, however disgruntled individual taxpayers may have felt and however persuasive the political arguments for reflationary tax cuts. The feeling that 1978 was the likely election year added the crucial dimension to policy formulation. The temptation to buy votes by reflating had been too strong for Reginald Maudling to resist in 1964 and for the Conservatives to resist in 1972 when unemployment reached one million. That both governments subsequently suffered electoral defeat perhaps shows even the political folly of such a strategy. However in 1978 a similar situation faced the Labour Government which had a long way to make up in the polls on the Conservative lead. Resumed expansion generated a political rationale of its own irrespective of its potentially long-term adverse economic effects.

One key factor in the strategy of resumed expansion was incomes policy. The 10 per cent policy, despite the threats of industrial action from a number of unions, including the miners, was crumbling gently rather than exploding. Sanctions against private sector firms were an ineffective and inefficient way of policing the 10 per cent but the TUC was prepared to acquiesce up to a point in backing the government. Thus although the policy was not actually working it looked as if, in the language of incomes policy, it was 'sticking'. The crucial factor in this appearance of success was the defeat of the firemen's strike which lasted for eight weeks from mid-November 1977. The only official national strike against Stage III was unsuccessful, though at times bitter, which lent support for the government's position.

The course of the strike and its outcome is one of the most intriguing in recent British politics not least because a Labour Government used troops to undermine the firemen's position as monopoly suppliers of labour. The dispute deserves particular attention.

The firemen's claim was for 30 per cent, a figure that was reminiscent of the level of settlements in 1975, and which could not be countenanced by the government without totally abandoning Stage III. Furthermore in economic terms the government was right to stand firm as at their current pay levels there was no shortage of firemen given the high job satisfaction and job status attached to firefighting. The difficulty lay in the use of troops, manning the veteran Green Goddesses, as strike breakers – an aspect of the dispute that aroused great passions in the Labour Party. As one trade union leader put it, 'the use of troops in the firemen's strike was regrettable'.[1] Mr Callaghan, more than once, received a stormy reception from striking firemen, when he visited various parts of the country. In Cardiff the Prime Minister was booed and jeered when he told strikers that the £72 a week they were being offered was a lot more than many Cardiff people earned.

At the end of November 1977 the firemen's leaders rejected a government formula that released the firemen and local authority employers from future pay restrictions in return for accepting 10 per cent but the failure to receive TUC backing effectively consigned the firemen to continuing their battle against the government alone. First the TUC Finance and General Purposes Committee rejected the plea of the firemen's leader Terry Parry for a campaign against the 10 per cent limit and secondly the TUC General Council voted 20–17 to support wage restraint in defiance of the firemen's call for TUC opposition to Stage III. The TUC, in a statement, argued that 'the General Council do not believe that a public campaign would be of assistance to the FBU in this very difficult situation'.[2]

Thus without the backing of the TUC and with troops containing the decreased number of fires quite proficiently the firemen were effectively defeated in their attempt to break the 10 per cent policy. In early January the FBU's executive urged a delegate conference to accept the employers' offer of 10 per cent immediately and staged increases to the level of skilled industrial workers' pay over two years. Len Murray thought the offer a deal many other groups of workers could justifiably envy, 'a real achievement out of the dispute'.[3] It was a tactful way of advising the firemen to concede, which they duly did.

The real winner in the firemen's dispute was the image of the 10 per cent policy. It had been seen to have won in contrast arguably to those settlements above 10 per cent in the private sector that did not receive publicity. If the strategy of resumed expansion needed the political backing of Stage III observance then the firemen's defeat provided it. The January Public Expenditure White Paper and the April 1978 budget typified the government's expansionist gamble.

The Public Expenditure White Paper was presented as a plan for 'resumed and continuing expansion',[4] £1614 million was added to 1979–80 and £1830 million to 1980–1. Although the White Paper went through the motions of stressing the importance of adequate public expenditure control, in effect it added up to a considerable reflationary impetus. One aspect of the White Paper that caused consternation in the Labour Party was the degree of underspending during the previous two years. Given the massive problems of financing the PSBR this should have been cause for congratulation but in the Labour Party the reaction was the opposite. In the previous two years spending had turned out to be 4 per cent or £2½ billion below the level anticipated.

The impact of cash limits had contributed significantly to the underspend and consequently for many on the left of the Labour Party they became a symbol of the government's lack of a radical socialist policy. The underspending by the National Enterprise Board, revealed in the White Paper, was particularly criticised by the left who saw it as evidence for the demise of the industrial strategy. In reality the element of underspend had contributed to the economic recovery but its existence also contributed to the political pressures on the government to compensate for underspending by introducing a more expansionary April budget.

Joel Barnett, recalling the mood of optimism in early 1978, noted that:

> At Cabinet, in early February, Denis Healey gave his analysis of the economic situation, stressing the great uncertainty about the amount of stimulus we needed or could afford. He cautiously told colleagues: 'I don't want to generate too much optimism.' There was probably too much optimism already, and even the ultra-cautious Edmund Dell could not dampen it. For Edmund, the great danger was doing too much and our being faced with a crippling balance of payments deficit. Tony Benn, at the other extreme, felt there had already been an element of overkill in cutting back public expenditure and reducing PSBR.[5]

The Benn alternative, envisaging a £4 billion boost to the economy, was put before the Home Policy Committee of the NEC in February. It advocated the maximum use of statutory powers to compel the 100 top manufacturing companies to make planning agreements with the government, 'import penetration ceilings', higher public spending on education, housing and the health service, and tax cuts by increasing personal allowances.

The question of tax cuts also enjoyed wider political support. To the Conservatives cuts in income tax were a matter of faith. In political terms such a policy was attractive to the Conservatives and in economic terms it ran parallel to the desire to reduce public spending and inflation. The Liberals, who by now faced the least optimistic electoral prospect of all the parties, were attracted to tax cuts to boost the popularity of the Lib–Lab pact. Meetings between Denis Healey and Liberal spokesman John Pardoe revealed differences in both policy and personality which could not be reconciled. The threat that the Liberals might vote against aspects of the budget, as they had done over the petrol increase a year earlier, was a permanent restraint on budget strategy. Michie and Hoggart noted that:

> Throughout the talks with Pardoe, the Chancellor had insisted that if his Budget strategy was ruined, there would be a general election. The warning had begun a long period of bluff and double bluff, as the Liberals announced that they did not fear an election, and that they would do better in spring with a platform of tax cuts to fight on than they might in October when the issue would be largely forgotten. Again, this was not believed by most Labour ministers whose constant belief has been that the Liberals in the last resort will not face an election, a belief buoyed up frequently by the party's failure to do anything to prove them wrong. For their part the Liberals did not believe that Callaghan would contemplate an election as long as the opinion polls were not pointing his way and while the two devolution bills were still working their way through the Commons.[6]

The budget that was actually presented on 11 April 1978, while not of the magnitude of the Benn proposals, did give a sizeable boost to demand. As one senior Treasury official put it, 'the 1978 budget was expansionary. Denis felt he was putting the economy on a path which would mean expansion making some inroads on unemployment and not boosting demand inflation.'[7] Another Treasury official recalled that 'the theory was that Denis was letting things go – on the fiscal side things were a good deal laxer – in preparation for an October election. By the end Geoffrey Howe and Co. inherited a head of inflationary pressure.'[8] Politically, not economically, the budget was astute, in that while reflating the economy by £2·56 billion, the emphasis was on increasing tax thresholds leaving basic income tax unchanged at 34 per cent. A lower tax band at 25 per cent was introduced on the first £750, which along with the threshold increase removed 360 000 people from the tax net entirely and 4 million people from the standard rate. The PSBR was set at £8·5 billion – within the limit agreed with the IMF – pensions were increased, child benefit raised to £3.

Minimum lending rate increased from 6½ per cent to 7½ per cent, school meal prices frozen and as a sop to the Liberals a small profit-sharing scheme introduced. Mr Healey also phrased his remarks to take account of the forthcoming pay negotiations for a fourth stage of incomes policy. In contrast to many of his previous budgets, Mr Healey's optimism was scarcely constrained:

Now that the inflation rate is stabilising at a level well below the increase in earnings, living standards and personal consumption should both rise substantially.

Private investment in manufacturing industry, rose about 14 per cent in volume last year and is expected to show a similar increase this year.

Public expenditure on goods and services is planned to rise significantly. It is more difficult to forecast how our trade performance will develop since assumptions about our competitiveness are crucial here . . . Earnings in fact will be the key to the inflation rate next year. Although earnings have increased in the current round far less than most observers expected a few months ago, they are still growing faster in Britain than in most of the countries which compete with us, and our productivity is growing more slowly.

So we shall be unable to prevent our rate of inflation from rising significantly next year unless we can achieve much lower levels of increase in wage costs than we have achieved this year . . . I therefore propose early discussions with the representatives of both sides of industry to see first whether they agree with the Government that we must keep inflation moving down next year and second, what policies are appropriate both in the field of prices and of earnings to ensure that we achieve this objective . . . The objective of the measures in my Budget today is to provide additional support for our industrial strategy partly in the form of direct help for business particularly for small firms and partly by strengthening the incentive to effort at all levels in industry through cuts in income tax.

I also believe that by using tax cuts to increase the real value of the pay packet during the coming year I can encourage further moderation in pay settlements and a continuing fall in the rate of inflation.[9]

The Liberals did not seek to defeat the budget resolutions but, eager to reap the popularity of seeking further tax cuts, they were prepared to call Labour's election bluff by voting with the Conservatives on 8 May to cut 1p off the basic rate of income tax at a full year cost of £370 million. The Conservatives, as well as the Liberals, shared a political interest in tax cuts which was intensified after Mr Healey's budget. Margaret Thatcher having described the budget's tax cuts as 'election deep' was eager to inflict damage on the Finance Bill especially if, with Liberal support, the Opposition could reassert itself as the tax-cutting party.

Because of the imposed 1p income tax reduction the Chancellor sought to recoup the lost revenue in June with a $2\frac{1}{2}$ per cent surcharge on employers' National Insurance contributions. Although the Liberals abstained to give the government a 287–282 vote victory in a no-confidence motion, they successfully limited the actual increase to $1\frac{1}{2}$ per cent. Michie and Hoggart accurately noted that: 'Callaghan and Healey had absorbed that if they wanted to survive they had to swallow their pride and accept the realities of the parliamentary arithmetic. The Liberals perhaps too late had learned to compromise their policy ideals and use persistent bloody-mindedness to win popular concessions.'[10]

Thus despite the budget defeats and the compromises with the Liberals the policy of resumed expansion, born out of the mood of optimism at the end of 1977, was well under way by the time the government had to face the question of Stage IV of incomes policy. With the June Gallup Poll showing Labour and Conservatives neck-and-neck, Stage IV was crucial to the government.

THE BATTLE FOR 5 PER CENT

The emergence of the 5 per cent norm for Stage IV of wage restraint was, and to an extent remains, one of the most intriguing episodes in recent British political economy. The origins of the policy are shadowy enough not to fit in to the conventional model of policy determination based on Whitehall, Westminster or the unions themselves.

It may be surmised that a 5 per cent policy would be a logical successor to a 10 per cent policy that had gradually crumbled despite the defeat of the firemen in the winter of 1977–8. However, while such a supposition later came to be a useful justification for the government the origin of the 5 per cent policy is to be found in chance events and comments at the end of 1977 when the 10 per cent policy still had seven months to run.

In December 1977 it was certainly the case that the government had decided on a fourth round of pay restraint rather than the return to free collective bargaining that the unions preferred. Denis Healey, in an interview with *Socialist Commentary*, repeated the approach to Stage IV he had outlined earlier to the Manifesto Group of Labour MPs. He argued rightly that high labour costs without correspondingly high output would lead to greater unemployment. However, he preferred the incomes policy remedy rather than that of allowing workers to price themselves into jobs. Such a policy, or what Mr Healey contemptuously called a free-for-all, was dismissed. The Chancellor argued that:

> More and more people are coming to realise that no Government can avoid having an incomes policy as far as its own employees are concerned. It must have an attitude about what is the appropriate level of wage increases in the various parts of the public sector where it is either employer or paymaster. But, of course, to have a pay policy for the public sector and a free-for-all in the private sector can be very unfair to the public sector.[11]

As well as the Chancellor, Mr Callaghan made clear his preference for continued incomes policy restraint by obliquely noting that he had 'ceased to worship' free collective bargaining ten years ago. Mr Callaghan, though, went much further than the Chancellor in a New Year broadcast when, for the first time, the figure of 5 per cent was publicly aired. Almost as if he was thinking aloud Mr Callaghan had said, on BBC radio's 'World This Weekend', at Sunday lunchtime, 1 January 1978 that: 'Thirty per cent wage increases, roughly 30 per cent price increases; 5 per cent wage increases, roughly 5 per cent price increases; 10 per cent wage increases, roughly 10 per cent price increases . . . 1979 is the year I am now looking to . . . I want to see 5 per cent price increases.'[12]

The political appeal of such reasoning could not conceal its economic illiteracy. One junior Treasury minister recalled the broadcast as being the first time he had heard 5 per cent mentioned:

The first time I heard 5 per cent I was having Sunday lunch and Callaghan came on the radio – he had just come back from seeing Schmidt whom he got on well with – and said that in Germany they had just had a 5 per cent settlement and inflation was only 4 per cent. He said that if we could have 5 per cent settlements we could get 5 per cent inflation.[13]

The 5 per cent norm therefore took the Treasury, as well as the unions by surprise. One senior Treasury official recalled that 'I say, with hesitation, that Schmidt did influence Callaghan – Schmidt and Callaghan in the kitchen at Hamburg had an effect.'[14] Another Treasury official bluntly put it that '5 per cent was definitely not a Treasury idea. Callaghan originated the 5 per cent.'[15] A Treasury minister explained the origins of the 5 per cent policy in terms of Callaghan's genuine desire to restore prosperity rather than a temporary economic improvement. To Robert Sheldon, 'Wilson would have been happy with the *appearance* of success but Jim actually wanted the real thing and to get success you needed 5 per cent. 5 per cent would have produced the goods and Jim wanted nothing less than the genuine article.'[16]

The evidence suggests that the 5 per cent pay limit, which was formally announced in July 1978, originated in Mr Callaghan's thinking at the end of 1977 well before the 1978 budget, the talks between Denis Healey and the TUC over Stage IV, and the ending of the Lib–Lab pact in June 1978. The 5 per cent policy prejudged, rather than originated from, the events of 1978.

Those events, however, were not without consequence; on the contrary they contributed to the failure of the government to obtain even a level of reluctant acquiescence similar to that pertaining in Stage III. Constant appeals from ministers during the early months of 1978 did not suggest that a Stage IV agreement would be forthcoming. Joel Barnett urged a Stage IV settlement 'well below 10%' to beat inflation and William Rodgers the Transport Minister was even more blunt, arguing that:

In the national interest and not least in the interest of maintaining and improving public services it must be understood that if public sector wages take a bigger share of the national cake then – if we are not simply to finance inflation by printing money, as our predecessors did – the consequences are clear.

And surely, as night follows day, so excessive public sector wage settlements must be followed by cuts in public services. The alternative of financing higher public sector wages from higher taxation is not an option open to us.[17]

Such ministerial warnings did not produce any enthusiastic union response. In May David Basnett, the TUC chairman, firmly opted for a 'responsible and flexible' return to free collective bargaining. Clive Jenkins's ASTMS voted overwhelmingly against further wage restraint and Alan Yates, the president of NUPE, prophetically declared that 'we do not want a further stage of incomes policy in any size, shape or form'.[18] Although the NUR, GMWU and NALGO favoured an acceptable Stage IV, the miners and the T & GWU were committed to a return to free collective bargaining.[19]

The T & GWU's opposition to further pay restraint held a deeper significance for the government in that in March 1978 Jack Jones had retired to be replaced by Moss Evans. In May Terry Duffy, the right's candidate, was elected to succeed Hugh Scanlon as the AUEW president[20] which meant that the inner circle of union leaders, which had previously delivered wage restraint, was broken up. The retirement of Jones removed from the union leadership the government's greatest ally. Unlike his successor Moss Evans, and a number of other union leaders, Jones was committed to the survival of a Labour Government in preference to a return to free collective bargaining, especially if a wage explosion and industrial action ensued. Significantly Moss Evans had declared in January 1978 that he was opposed to pay policy 'either imposed by the government or by voluntary agreement'.

Furthermore Jones's retirement left a political vacuum not only in his own union but in the TUC as a whole given the lack of stature of General Secretary Len Murray. Without Jones the political will, and a sense of political urgency, to seek a Stage IV policy was diminished. One minister, who was typical of many, recalled that 'the retirement of Jones and Scanlon was a factor – there was then less comradeship. There would have been no 5 per cent with Jones and Scanlon.'[21] Jones himself, with hindsight thought that '5 per cent wasn't very sensible – the government was overcommitted to the Liberals. I warned in 1977 of too rapid a return to free collective bargaining so not to risk disaster in the form of a Thatcher Government.'[22]

In the months immediately preceding the announcement of the 5 per cent norm the government's resolve to declare a tough Stage IV was increased by the knowledge that the annual rate of earnings was rising at 14·4 per cent, rather than 10 per cent. However although such statistics were only confirmed in July 1978, well after the 5 per cent limit had been targeted by the government, they did allow Mr Callaghan to warn the unions that another pay round similar to Stage III would cause inflation and unemployment. The CBI, who also sought a more flexible Stage IV, received little encouragement for their hope of less restraint on differentials. In short, 'adherence to incomes policy was rapidly crumbling'.[23]

On 21 July the government duly set out its policy in a White Paper, *Winning the Battle against Inflation*,[24] arguing that to reduce the level of inflation below 8 per cent a 5 per cent norm was necessary. The 5 per cent policy, according to Joel Barnett, received a 'silent acclamation' in Cabinet largely because ministers were certain an election would occur before the pay round got underway.[25] One minister recalled that 'I was the only one in Cabinet who opposed 5 per cent. I said it wouldn't work but the rest were ready to go along with it.'[26]

The White Paper, running to a mere eight pages, was an electoral gamble but also an economic gamble in the face of the policy of resumed expansion which had dominated 1978. It stated that:

> The Government has decided to adopt a pay policy to apply from August 1 in which the guideline will be set at five per cent.
> This may seem an ambitious objective. But in many of our competitor countries settlements have been at or below this level. With determination there is no reason why we cannot return to the same standards ourselves . . . It would be neither fair nor practicable for the Government to set a guideline for the public sector and leave the private sector subject only to the constraint of market forces. Britain has a highly structured and interlocking pay system, each section of which has repercussions on others. These considerations make it necessary for the Government to give the guidance for the whole economy.[27]

The 5 per cent policy was not greeted with acclaim. The TUC as expected was critical. The General Council voted, with only

Tom Jackson dissenting, to reject the 5 per cent policy and instead demanded a 35-hour week, a better deal for the low paid and the resolution of anomalies arising from the erosion of differentials. Ministers, however, were also focusing their attention on rank and file reaction which they hoped would be less critical than that of TUC leaders. As one minister explained, 'despite the opposition of the TUC the 10 per cent was quite successful. This led to our downfall in that we thought despite the opposition of union leaders the members would accept [5%].'[28] Sir Harold Wilson recalled that '5 per cent didn't sound realistic. You can run a wages policy for a year or so – particularly if there's a crisis with jobs at stake – but in the second year it goes at the edges and in the third breaks down.'[29]

One minister noted that 'Denis thought he had pulled off a deal with the TUC committee for 5 per cent. He had but it didn't work out like that.'[30] Neil Kinnock, who favoured a flat rate Stage IV, recalled that 'In July 1978 I told Callaghan we must go for another £6 policy only now it must be £8 which was the same in net terms. But I asked, "Jim, why 5 per cent?" and he replied "because it's half of 10 per cent". 5 per cent was too little even for negotiations.'[31] Joe Ashton put it simply: the government 'had used up its goodwill. It had traded on the unions for four years.'[32]

The 5 per cent policy was, of course, designed to run up to the end of July 1979 by which time a general election could either have been forced on the government or opted for if Labour's popularity were to increase by the same magnitude as it did in, say, 1970. The test of the 5 per cent policy would be known during the winter pay round and, given that the policy was clearly a gamble, the temptation for the Labour Party and the unions to think in terms of an October 1978 election was virtually impossible to resist.

THE ELECTION DILEMMA

If the emergence of the 5 per cent policy can be seen as one of the most bizarre episodes in recent economic policy-making, the decision not to go to the polls in October 1978 can be seen as equally bizarre in electoral terms. In the event Jim Callaghan decided not to risk a general election that was both widely anticipated by most observers and widely advocated by many in the labour and trade union movements. However it is arguable that the decision whether or not to call an October election was more of a dilemma for Labour than has been popularly thought.[33] Both Harold Wilson in 1970 and Edward Heath in 1974 had opted for early general elections, when they still had comfortable parliamentary majorities, only to lose. Callaghan, however, had no majority and had therefore not only the task of holding Labour marginals but also that of winning seats from the Conservatives. Although the economic indicators were more favourable than at any time since Labour's victory in October 1974, for the Prime Minister the key question was whether the economic indicators would be insufficient in October 1978, but sufficient in spring 1979 to return Labour to office. Callaghan faced the further dilemma of whether Stage iv would hold or disintegrate and how far Labour's relationship with the unions was crucial to electoral credibility.

There was certainly much available evidence in the summer of 1978 to those who predicted, or advocated, the October election option. In July David Blake, the economics editor of *The Times*, argued that the government had created the conditions of a pre-election boom and that with inflation at only 8 per cent and earnings rising about 15 per cent the advantage lay in an October poll before the economic statistics moved less favourably for Labour. Blake argued that delay would seriously hinder Labour's chances as inflation would move upwards into double figures by 1979.[34]

In August Mr Healey, in an analysis of the economy similar to Blake's, envisaged a 3 per cent growth rate for 1978, and continuing single-figure inflation with the economy in 'better balance' than at any time since 1945. Similar optimism was evident at the TUC Conference in September and many observers believed that a 5 October election campaign would be launched after a relatively harmonious conference. David Basnett, the TUC chairman, made an electioneering speech on 4 September calling on trade unionists to 'work and vote for Labour'; the pay policy dispute with the government was studiously downplayed, with Mr Basnett stressing the political importance of the 1978 campaign and the importance of the next election.

On 5 September Mr Callaghan, in his famous 'singing' speech, stated that he would make an announcement about the general election 'very shortly' which was universally taken to mean that 5 October was indeed to be the preferred date. Ian Aitken, the political editor of the *Guardian*, confidently asserted that 'the General Election date is likely to be announced today [7 September]', a view that was widespread in Fleet Street. Aitken's reasoning, far from journalistic speculation, was a rational appraisal of Mr Callaghan's electoral options:

> Although he theoretically has a full year in hand the demise of the Lib–Lab pact has robbed him of anything remotely resembling a majority in the Commons.
>
> He has little hope of rigging up a substitute alliance with other minority groups and many things could go wrong between now and next spring or summer.
>
> He faces two dangers in delay. The first is that he would be humiliatingly defeated in the Commons this winter, precipitating an unplanned general election in December or January. The other is that his government's remarkable recovery in public esteem could begin to crumble during the winter.
>
> He therefore goes to the country with crossed fingers and considerable faith in his own ability to beat Mrs. Thatcher in the personal confrontation which is bound to be the centre piece of the election campaign. Even Conservatives are prepared to give him a fair chance of pulling it off.[35]

Mr Callaghan did not share such an appraisal. At the Cabinet meeting on 7 September he informed his colleagues that there would be no election until 1979. Joel Barnett later noted that Callaghan's decision:

> was a total surprise to all but a handful of his closest colleagues. There was a startled silence, as mixed feelings sorted themselves out. On the one hand, there was relief at not having to fight an election which few could be confident of winning. On the other hand, most of us felt in our bones that hanging on was a mistake. We little knew how big a mistake. The Prime Minister had no objection to our discussing his decision but he said: 'I told the Queen of my decision last night.' In those circumstances, and as he had the right to make the decision anyway, there was not much to discuss.[36]

Similarly one MP recalled that 'Stan Orme told me the Cabinet was poleaxed when Callaghan told them there wouldn't be an election.'[37]

Orme himself confirmed this adding that 'I wanted an election and two-thirds or three-quarters of the Cabinet did but Denis, Michael and Jim didn't want an election at all. There was nothing we could do once it had been decided.'[38] One Treasury minister commented that: 'Not going in 1978 was utterly wrong. We were working on the basis at the Treasury that we were hanging on for the October election. In 1979 we knew that inflation would be higher, not by very much, but the trend would be up.'[39]

Despite the misgivings of his colleagues Jim Callaghan had exercised the prerogative they did not share – the ability under normal circumstances to decide general election timing – and in a televised broadcast he explained his reasons. He stated that he was 'not proposing to seek your votes because there is some blue sky overhead today . . .'

> We shall face our difficulties as we come to them. I can already see some looming on the horizon. I cannot, and I don't promise that we shall succeed. I can say that we shall deserve to.
>
> I shall not be calling for a general election at this time. Instead I ask every one of you to carry on with the task of consolidating the present improvement in our country's position. Let us see it through together.[40]

The reasons why Callaghan opted to delay the election are still open to some speculation. One cabinet minister recalled that 'Jim was innately cautious – conservative with a small "c" – and he genuinely thought an autumn election would not lead to an overall majority.'[41] A factor that weighed considerably was the advice of Michael Foot who strongly advised spring 1979. Foot argued that Labour stood a good chance of avoiding defeat in the Commons during the winter and that the Queen's Speech would face little risk of defeat. However, it is likely that, as Dick Leonard has argued, Foot 'was pushing Callaghan in a direction in which he very much wanted to go'.[42] A similar analysis may be made regarding Denis Healey's advice to the Prime Minister that inflation would not be that much different in spring 1979. Both Foot and Healey, as senior members of the Cabinet, helped to convince Callaghan that delay would not be disastrous.[43]

Furthermore opinion poll information did not give Callaghan, by nature a pessimist,[44] much confidence in Labour's ability to win any Conservative marginals. A MORI poll showing Labour doing worse in key marginals than in any other parts of the country confirmed Callaghan's pessimism. The same poll, in September 1978, showed a two-point Conservative lead which would have been sufficient to defeat Labour irrespective of a swing to the Conservatives during the campaign. Foot and Callaghan were not prepared to risk an election in which the Conservatives started with a lead even if the economic indicators were pointing Labour's way. Denis Healey's confidence in the economic situation, assuming the success of Stage IV, similarly suggested to Callaghan that an October election was a greater gamble than holding on for the spring, or at the latest, autumn of 1979.

A further factor in the delay may also have been the personal one that Jim Callaghan, Prime Minister for only 2½ years, did not wish to jeopardise his position. Callaghan's route to the top in British politics had been a long march, an endurance test. The prospect of defeat may well have concentrated his mind more than any other factor. It is not necessarily a criticism of Mr Callaghan to say that he was scared of losing. Nor is it a valid criticism to assert that his decision to postpone was irrational or politically naive. Although it may be argued with hindsight that Callaghan made the wrong decision, at the time, to Callaghan at least, that decision was a dilemma. Nevertheless the fact remains that Labour could have won in October 1978 and, if they had lost, would not have lost as comprehensively as they did in May 1979. To those in the Labour Party who preferred October, especially those MPs who lost their seats in 1979, Callaghan's postponement has seemed less justifiable. One backbench MP recalled that 'Callaghan was absolutely wrong on what makes people vote Labour. He asked me about the election and I said autumn 1978, but others advised him the other way.'[45] A junior minister's comment that 'we were all prepared for October 1978', was typical of the PLP as a whole.[46] Reg Prentice, by October 1978 a Conservative MP (though not a Conservative candidate) recalled that 'From what I heard Callaghan thought he could make a successful appeal for pay restraint with an eventual ideal date of October 1979. But he has made more strategic errors than anyone contrary to his public image of an avuncular personality.'[47]

Ultimately the decision to delay the general election proved fatal for Labour. Some of those who urged postponement now acknowledge their mistake. Hugh Scanlon, who argued for the spring, confessed that 'I was wrong, and most of the leadership was right on the election. I argued for a late election so that the government would reap the benefit of three periods of wage restraint in the spring.'[48] The rationality of such a view in October 1978 was not open to question as long as Stage IV proved effective. However the unions had already made clear their implacable opposition to the 5 per cent policy, having supported, or reluctantly aquiesced in, the previous three stages. It was more rational to believe that incomes policy would break down – as previous incomes policies had done – in the face of both union opposition and the economic effects of reflation, which, during 1978, had been quite considerable. Having sacrificed the appropriate economic policies of continuing financial restraint during 1978 for short-term electoral benefit the postponement of the election represented a double missed opportunity. On the one hand it was the missed opportunity for continued real economic progress – as opposed to a reflationary binge – and on the other hand it was the missed opportunity for Labour to reap a potential electoral benefit. In both senses 1978 represented a missed opportunity.

CHAPTER VIII

The Winter of Discontent

THE INITIAL CHALLENGE

The wave of strikes in both the public and private sector against the 5 per cent Stage IV policy proved economically damaging and politically disastrous for the government. The widely held view that a Labour Government meant less industrial disruption than a Conservative Government turned out to have been a myth. The extent of the strikes, both in the length of their duration and in their individual bitterness, was the most acute since 1926.

The initial challenge to the government over the 5 per cent policy came in the private sector. The government hoped that sanctions against private sector firms would encourage them to stand firm and as early as September 1978 Denis Healey publicly declared that the government would not help companies who deliberately broke the guidelines. The first challenge to both the 5 per cent policy and the sanctions retaliation came when Ford car workers came out on strike in rejection of a 5 per cent offer. On 26 September the AUEW declared the dispute official and after a nine-week strike the company settled for 15 per cent. Unlike British Leyland and Chrysler, Ford were profitable and relatively efficient, with such an excellent product range that at the start of the strike there was an eight-to ten-week waiting list for all Ford models. There was no economic or moral reason why Ford workers should have been subject to the same 5 per cent norm as British Leyland or Chrysler workers. If ever there was a strong case for free collective bargaining it was over the Ford dispute. However, as Ford chairman Sir Terence Beckett rightly commented, the strike was 'made into a political rather than an industrial issue'.[1] Nor, given the sanctions policy, was the political dimension removed when Ford conceded the 15 per cent settlement. The decision to apply sanctions was, in any case, largely symbolic. Joel Barnett noted that:

Like the nuclear weapon, they could be counter-productive if used. Their use in this case was complicated by the fact that Fords had few direct contacts with the Government, other than supplying a small number of cars, ambulances and vans. There was, it is true, an agreement to provide large cash grants to build an engine plant in South Wales, but to cancel that would lose many jobs in an area of heavy unemployment. In any event, we could not cancel if we had wanted to, as the money was already legally committed. Still, we felt we must be seen to be taking some action, if sanctions, and possibly the whole pay policy, were not to collapse. To the intense anger of the Ford UK chief, Sir Terence Beckett, we imposed a fairly ineffective sanction of not buying Ford cars.[2]

The sanctions policy did, indeed, prove counter-productive and in December Parliament voted against it, adding further humiliation on the authority of the government. On 13 December, four left-wing Labour MPs abstained and the opposition parties united to defeat the sanctions policy by six votes. It had been possible for the government to ignore the Labour Conference's rejection by a 2:1 majority of the 5 per cent policy but parliamentary defeat could not be sidestepped. The government duly won the vote of confidence on 14 December but Jim Callaghan conceded at the start of the debate that the sanctions policy had been jettisoned. Moreover Mr Callaghan's subsequent appeal to the CBI to hold back excessive pay settlements served only to undermine the government's authority still further. Thus, as Peter Shore put it, the sanctions defeat 'stripped us of moral power on public sector pay'.[3] The way was open for the 5 per cent pay policy to be effectively challenged by a multitude of unions on a multitude of different issues – low pay, comparability, differentials, productivity deals or catching up with the lost ground of Stages I to III.

THE DAM BURSTS

The petrol tanker drivers were the next group of workers to defy the government although other groups, particularly in the public sector, had given notice that they would strike rather than accept 5 per cent. The drivers were T & GWU members and their militancy can be partly ascribed to the lead given by Moss Evans, particularly at the October Labour Conference, in opposing pay restraint. Although an official strike was avoided the settlement was in excess of the guidelines and helped to precipitate industrial action by the lorry drivers, also T & GWU members. Strike action was at first unofficial, but no less effective in disrupting supplies and inconveniencing the public before Moss Evans made the dispute official, commenting that 'there is too much obsession with percentages. It is the rate for the job that matters.'[4] Another factor that mattered in the dispute was secondary picketing, with lorry drivers' pickets denying access to depots when neither lorries nor depots were involved in the dispute. Public reaction was swift in its condemnation. Moss Evans lacked the authority to deal with the abuses of secondary picketing, despite prodigious efforts to do so, so that, as Barnes and Reid note 'the effects of the initiative by the union varied according to the militancy of those involved in different areas . . .'[5] Whether the declaration of a State of Emergency would have helped is doubtful. The Heath Government had declared five States of Emergency in $3\frac{1}{2}$ years with little beneficial effect on the disputes in question.[6]

By mid-January the extent of the crisis was self-evident. Both Callaghan and Healey appealed in vain for moderation and exuded a measure of public optimism that belied the scenes of disruption televised daily to the electorate. Some road haulage employers were prepared to concede the drivers' claim of 22 per cent, food shortages developed, factory workers were laid off, and in the north-west an unofficial strike by water workers left thousands of homes without water supplies. The government's embarrassment was intensified by Mr Callaghan's injudicious remarks on returning to Britain from the Guadeloupe summit on 10 January. He played down the grave industrial situation and when questioned about the chaos replied 'Please don't run down your own country by talking about mounting chaos. If you look at it from the outside you can see that you are taking a rather parochial view. I do not feel there is mounting chaos.'[7] Politically the damage was done. It did not help that the tone of Mr Callaghan's remarks became immortalised by the phrase 'what crisis?' allegedly uttered to newsmen at the airport. Joel Barnett, assessing the political damage, recalled that:

We were to live with that phrase for some time to come. Months later, during the election campaign, I found at first hand that it was still remembered with anger. Jim's popularity instantly slumped to an all-time low. An opinion poll gave the Tories a 19 per cent lead, with Margaret Thatcher, for the first time rated ahead of him as a leader. It did not do much for the Prime Minister's morale, nor for the morale of the Government as a whole.[8]

It did not matter that Mr Callaghan's gaffe had been prompted not by the degenerating road haulage crisis but by the removal of the threat of the tanker drivers' crisis. 'What crisis?' became to Mr Callaghan what 'at a stroke' had been to Mr Heath and 'pound in your pocket' had been to Mr Wilson. Wilson later shrewdly recalled that 'I never allowed a Prime Minister's conference in winter in a sunny climate. I knew what the press would make of it and Callaghan didn't look to be in charge.'[9] In electoral terms Labour suffered badly. As Peter Jenkins rightly put it describing the Commons clash between Mr Callaghan and Mrs Thatcher on 16 January:

> Mrs. Thatcher knew well that no eloquence of hers could speak as loudly as the televised behaviour of some of the trade unionists gangs, that nothing she could say would woo votes as effectively as the appearance on the box of Mr. Moss Evans or Mr. Alex Kitson. Oppositions don't win elections, Governments lose them and the Callaghan Government was busy losing the next election with the powerful assistance of the trade union movement.[10]

The winter of discontent was, despite action by the water workers, lorry drivers and train drivers, still not at its most disruptive point. That situation only occurred with the public sector low pay strikes which began at the end of January. The unions involved were the GMWU, COHSE and NUPE, the latter adopting the most militant line in what they regarded as the scandal of low pay. The fact that other groups had already breached the 5 per cent guideline did not affect the dispute nor soften the government's line. Peter Shore, the Environment Minister, in an apt metaphor noted that while the government had lost the battle it had not lost the war against inflation as the pay round was still at an early stage.

As a result of the strike action by NUPE and other unions,

public services were seriously disrupted in hospitals, schools, refuse collection, universities and local government as cleaners, cooks, ancillary staff, attendants and porters all followed union instructions to strike on 22 January. A NUPE spokeswoman described the response from members as 'phenomenal' and 'successful beyond what we ever expected'. Meetings between the government and TUC leaders were unable to prevent the strikes escalating, and Mr Callaghan openly defended the right of people to cross picket lines if they disagreed with the arguments put to them. The picketing of hospitals by NUPE members, where the victims of such action were the patients not the employers, caused grave public resentment and Mr Callaghan, in sharp contrast to his Guadeloupe gaffe, attacked 'free collective vandalism'. In Cabinet, according to Joel Barnett, Mr Callaghan said it was a plain fact that Mrs Thatcher 'had struck a chord with a public heartily sick of the trade unions'.[11] One particular strike that contributed to the public mood was that of gravediggers in the north-west. Bodies awaiting burial were simply stored in temporary warehouse mortuaries.

Unlike the earlier disputes with Ford and the road hauliers, where the traditional unions versus management battle lines could be drawn, the NUPE disputes were of a different dimension. Inconvenience to particular individuals such as hospital patients, or to the public at large, became not a side-effect of strike action but its rationale. The employers seemed irrelevant to a dispute in which the union was fighting the government by maximising public distress. In such circumstances public reaction was understandable and public condemnation fell not only on the unions but on the Labour Party and the government. NUPE emerged as the Conservatives' best election ally since Zinoviev.

The reasons why NUPE, led by Alan Fisher, acted as it did deserves further attention. Fisher himself carried little weight on the TUC General Council and his approach to a Labour Government, as opposed to a Conservative one, was the opposite of the Jack Jones approach of keeping in power at almost any cost. Fisher was so personally determined to lead a campaign against low pay, which he regarded as evil, that he was prepared to ignore the means by which that campaign developed. Later in 1979, after the Conservatives had won the election, Fisher attacked those who had called NUPE a nasty four-letter word[12] but he should not have been surprised. Fisher may have been in touch with his members but he was out of touch with the vast majority of essentially apolitical people who resented inconvenience or unnecessary suffering.

Members of the Cabinet and MPs, through their postbags, realised that above all, it was the NUPE strikes that were damaging Labour most. The Cabinet exchange on 1 February quoted by Joel Barnett is particularly revealing:

> the Prime Minister summed up what many of us wanted to say, when he put a question to Tony Benn: 'What do you say about the thuggish act of a walk-out without notice, from a Children's Hospital?' Tony replied that: 'When decent people become irrational, something else must be wrong if they are driven to such desperate acts.' Jim Callaghan's response was that he 'had never in fifty years been so depressed as a trade-unionist,' Denis Healey, more pointedly said: 'We should not allow middle-class guilt to blind us to what's going on.'[13]

One cabinet minister, assessing the electoral damage, thought it likely that 'We would have lost in 1978 but not as badly. The winter of discontent made it worse, and of all the strikes the hospital strikes created the greatest resentment. It put ordinary people's backs up.'[14] A Treasury minister's comment that 'the NUPE strikes horrified us all'[15] was typical of many. Another cabinet minister thought that 'the NUPE disputes were crucial – the dead unburied and the hospital strike affected the main line of the nation'.[16]

Joe Ashton, who was a government whip at the time, recalled that 'NUPE was important. Fisher had taken over a tame union up to 1968 then came great recruitment but the recruits, tea ladies, cleaners and the like, weren't union officials. The officials were got from Ruskin and were militant and wanted to [prove it]. Suddenly ambulance men and hospital porters on strike found they were headline news and were on TV – like the miners.'[17] Another left-winger, Neil Kinnock, made a similar point about the NUPE leadership – 'The graduate officials in NUPE thought about the working class as if they had stepped from the pages of a history book. They fitted the working class into economic models which were political science fiction.'[18]

Hugh Scanlon, who had retired only a few months previously, conceded that the winter of discontent 'was terrible in its social effects. The public image of the unions was dented so there was a vote against Labour.'[19] Another union leader, who also perceived the political damage of the NUPE strikes, pointedly recalled that 'some union leaders thought they could browbeat the government and still allow Labour to win'.[20]

Many on the left of the party, including Tony Benn who sat in Cabinet, totally agreed with NUPE's objective and acquiesced in supporting the nature of the industrial action. However the unpopularity of the NUPE action could not be disguised by the left's defence of NUPE's original case. NUPE further widened the political rift with the government by targeting the constituencies of cabinet ministers for special disruption by local authority workers. The cabinet ministers who were in London were not personally affected but their constituents of course were. The lesson of not antagonising the public was learnt by the civil service union, the CPSA, whose general secretary Ken Thomas said that unlike NUPE his members' strike action would be aimed at the machinery of government and not the public.

A further complication with the NUPE strikes was that Alan Fisher's main role was the running of the strike rather than negotiating with the government. Albert Booth, one of the cabinet ministers sympathetic to NUPE, recalled the negotiating difficulties:

> I don't think NUPE was entirely to blame. I can't deny NUPE was a major policy concern but my criticism was not so much that the unions were bargaining too toughly but that they were running at two levels. Alan Fisher never went near the negotiating table until it got to No. 10. The number twos were dealing with negotiations – Ron Keating for NUPE – and they weren't the top officials. After two hours at No. 10 the General Secretaries wanted to reach a settlement but the number twos wanted to continue negotiating. You couldn't expect Callaghan to go through the negotiating rituals. He thought it could be settled across the table with the General Secretaries.[21]

At the height of the NUPE disputes, in order to retrieve its position, the government and TUC presented a joint concordat which dealt with some of the unsavoury aspects of trade union power which had been evident throughout the winter of discontent. The concordat dealt with all aspects of government–TUC relations including guidance to unions on picketing, negotiations and the closed shop. Barnes and Reid put it that 'desks in Whitehall and Congress House had been ransacked for good advice and declarations of intent'.[22] However the most optimistic of such declarations of intent concerned inflation, which both government and TUC aimed to reduce to 5 per cent over the next three years. That the going rate for settlements was about 9 per cent[23] not 5 per cent at the time of the concordat and that incomes policy had clearly broken down served only to undermine the concordat as an economic blueprint and as a political way out for the government it was scarcely more than a figleaf. The concordat typified the incomes policy mentality in its most extreme form. An 'independent commission'[24] was established to study the 'comparability' of pay in the public and private sector and a new initial 'norm' of 9 per cent was decreed with further comparability awards 'phased' according to an elaborate formula which bore no resemblance to the supply and demand for labour in the industries or services involved. The concordat, like previous incomes policy 'agreements', was no more than the redrawing of boundaries for the next industrial relations war. Although the concordat was overtaken by events, in the form of the electoral defeat of the Callaghan Government, it is arguable that it embodied an approach to pay policy that creates the worst of all worlds, satisfying neither those on the left who favour income redistribution nor those on the right who favour reduced inflation and greater labour market sensitivity to supply and demand pressures. Most of the Cabinet, and the union leaders who favoured the 'middle way' the concordat represented, simply blinded themselves to the past failures of concordats and incomes policy from 'Solomon binding' of 1969 through the Heath search for a voluntary policy and the Social Contract 1974–5, to the Stage IV collapse itself in the winter of 1979. Whatever its short-run political merits, the concordat represented a continuation of the crisis of the winter of discontent not an escape from it.

In view of the circumstances which brought about the concordat a number of its objectives sounded at best platitudinous and at worst cynical:

The best way of keeping price rises down is by increasing output and productivity growth and by regenerating and re-equipping our manufacturing base. Equally however, there can be no doubt that a general rise in the level of money incomes which significantly outstripped the rate of growth would be incompatible with achieving our objective of a high wage high productivity low unit cost economy.

The TUC recognises the dangers that could be caused by the escalation of pay settlements and of future pay demands which ride on the back of earlier pay increases. That would not only quickly wipe out the benefit of those who have settled earlier in the round at modest figures; it is indeed to their detriment and would take us back to the high levels of inflation from which we have painfully recovered.

It is a challenge to the trade union movement as to whether collective bargaining can indeed serve the whole community rather than a process which in effect sets one group of workers against another.

Not everyone can improve his living standards at the expense of someone else. Trade unionists should take account of the effect of their action on others – and on their own best interests.[25]

Joel Barnett, who thought the concordat 'better than nothing', has noted that doubts were raised in Cabinet at the time by both the opponents and supporters of incomes policy:

On the pay front, the new 'norm', or formula, had few admirers. Those who wanted free collective bargaining did not like Commissions and Comparability and the like. For them it smacked too much of incomes policy. Tony Benn said at one meeting that the business of looking for new 'norms' put him in mind of the King shouting 'a Norm, a Norm . . . my kingdom for a Norm!' Another colleague said perhaps the thought had some deep psychological significance relating to 'King Benn and I'. Those of us who did favour incomes policy were worried about the eventual outcome of the comparability studies, and what they would mean for this, and future, pay rounds.[26]

Despite such doubts the concordat enabled the government to settle the current industrial disputes by effectively surrendering to trade union power. The hope was that the illusion of an agreement would disguise not only the failure of incomes policy but also the nature of trade union power itself.

The concordat did not end the strike action of the winter of discontent. The NUPE dispute dragged on until the end of March and the civil servants began their strike action after the concordat had been signed. The civil servants, who had seen how profitable the militancy of other unions had been, were determined to press their 20 per cent claim to the full. Their salary scales were hardly ungenerous and there was no difficulty in recruitment at the existing rates. Furthermore they enjoyed job security and index-linked pensions usually not available in the private sector or for that matter in parts of the public sector. Diplomatic communications were disrupted and VAT repayments suspended when the two unions representing 250 000 civil servants struck on 22 February prompting Mr Callaghan to comment that 'rarely can there have been a more unnecessary and unjustified strike'. David Owen, the Foreign Secretary, told a picketing civil service clerk that 'I have great pleasure in crossing this picket line – I think it is the most irresponsible picket line I have ever seen'.[27]

Although the civil servants did their best to inconvenience their employers rather than the public – the original intention of strike action since the early days of trade unionism – there were some exceptions. The disruption at the Ministry of Agriculture's computer centre at Guildford by only twenty-two striking civil servants, delayed grants for new farm building and £1 million in compensation to Humberside farmers who lost 22 500 pigs in an outbreak of swine vesicular disease. However, the worst aspect of the civil service dispute was the settlement, which largely confirmed the civil servants' privileged position.[28] Unlike other public sector groups who would be subject to the Clegg 'comparability' commission and have their awards staged over eighteen months, the civil servants' rise was staged over a year. Joel Barnett noted that this discrepancy caused a Cabinet disagreement:

One consequence of this was an outraged Shirley Williams. As Secretary of State for Education, she argued that if the civil servants had their claim within one year, the same must apply to the teachers. The Prime Minister erupted, telling Shirley the money was not there, and we did not have to finance the full teachers' claim in one year. An unusually irate Shirley retorted that she would not remain a member of a Cabinet that settled with the civil servants in one year, and the teachers in two.

As it happens, none of use were to remain members of a Cabinet much longer. But the whole episode gave an indication of the problems involved with an incomes policy (by comparability) for the public sector alone, with free collective bargaining in the private sector. And it showed that even if one saw this as a way forward to some form of permanent incomes policy, there was a long way to go before we devised a system that would prove acceptable within, let alone between the public and private sectors.[29]

As well as the civil service strike and its outcome the NUPE dispute continued to fester long after the TUC–government concordat had been agreed. Indeed it is arguable that some of the worst examples of NUPE indifference to individual patients' suffering occurred after the concordat had outlined ways of avoiding blatant abuses of picketing. Ironically one individual patient who suffered was David Ennals the Health Secretary, who had to enter Westminster Hospital in March 1979. Although nursing staff promised to treat the minister according to his appropriate medical needs, NUPE shop steward Janice Morris declared that:

He is a legitimate target for industrial action . . . Ennals is now beginning to take his own medicine.
Don't you think he has been mean-minded? People who work in hospitals like this have to fight for a decent living wage, but the miners can walk into an office and be given 15 per cent just like that. He has attacked ambulancemen and called them names and he has victimised others.
We have to be careful what action we take against him because we don't want to hurt other patients in the ward. We could, for instance, cut off food supplies, but that would mean his neighbours would go hungry. He won't get the little extras our members provide patients. He won't get his locker cleaned or the area around his bed tidied up. He won't get tea or soup.[30]

Given such a personal approach to a Labour Cabinet Minister, it was hardly surprising that, as one junior minister commented, 'it was a major factor that we couldn't go to the country saying we could work better with the unions'.[31] The NUPE approach to David Ennals was the antithesis of the Jack Jones approach to a

Labour Cabinet. The Social Contract of 1974–5 and the union cooperation over the £6 pay policy seemed, and probably were, light years away in the winter of discontent.

NUPE also prolonged the hospital dispute by refusing the 9 per cent offer that had been accepted in March by COHSE, GMWU and T & GWU members also involved in the dispute. The other unions openly attacked NUPE's attitude fearing that NUPE had been running the dispute as a recruitment campaign by telling its members and potential recruits that the other unions, by settling for 9 per cent had prevented them gaining a better wage deal. Ultimately, with the threat of a general election imminent, NUPE accepted 9 per cent with an extra £1 in advance of the comparability study. The lessons, memories and consequences of the winter of discontent outlasted the settlements that ended the industrial action. The unions lost much goodwill with the public, the government lost its 5 per cent policy and the Labour Party lost one of its electoral trump cards, the ability to ensure more than the Conservatives, industrial harmony.

THE CONSEQUENCES

The most obvious consequences and lessons of the winter of discontent concern incomes policy. Like previous incomes policies Mr Callaghan's 5 per cent policy collapsed in ruins amid industrial strife having 'successfully' 'survived' its initial stages. To some the lesson is that 5 per cent was too harsh and a more pragmatic figure would have been acceptable enough to prevent such widespread strike action. Harold Wilson, for example, has argued that:

> Ministers bravely, but somewhat unrealistically, nailed the figure of 5 per cent pay settlement to the masthead. Whether a higher, but still austere, figure such as 8 or $8\frac{1}{2}$ per cent might have been accepted, at least as a guideline, has been the subject of much argument. But the unions, torn internally by years of imposed or induced wage restraint, with differentials dangerously narrowed, and the lowest-paid in industry after industry moving into militancy, took to the streets. Garbage piled up and rotted in the streets. Physical violence in the lorry-drivers' strike, picketing and closure of schools, and – worst of all – action preventing the burial of the dead, affronted the nation.

Three Members of Parliament (two ex-ministers and a former Party chairman), whom I asked to forecast the result of an election held at that time, separately estimated one hundred Tory majority.[32]

However even a higher norm than 5 per cent may have produced similar results given the unions' mood, the effect of previous pay rounds, the reflation of the economy during 1978, and the erosion of differentials. As was argued in Chapter II, the philosophy of wage control produced a language of its own whereby norms and percentages are invested with an authority they neither deserve nor can deliver. Whether a norm is 0 per cent or 5 per cent or 55 per cent the principle behind it – that everyone, irrespective of merit, market forces or productivity, receives the same – is an economic nonsense. Nor is there evidence that on a socialist scale of moral worth, however that may be assessed, applying the same norm to different groups is morally superior to giving a distribution according to deserts. Although it may be argued that a socialist distribution based on 'merit' or 'social worth' is inevitably only a matter of opinion such a system is preferable to the incomes policy percentage norm solution which is unfair not only to some but to all.

In economic terms what made the 5 per cent policy absurd was not only the strange circumstances, described in Chapter VII, of how the 5 per cent figure was actually reached, but also the fact that during 1978 the government, by reflating, had put an upward pressure on the very incomes the 5 per cent policy was designed to control. It is convenient and cliched to think that incomes policy in such circumstances is like trying to stop a leaking hose with sellotape while turning up the volume coming from the tap. However the analogy is accurate and, in this case, the government's measures during 1978 simply injected a dose of demand into the economy that six to nine months later emerged in higher prices including the price of labour. The Ford dispute, which effectively began the winter of discontent, demonstrated the economic incompatibility of the 5 per cent policy. The company was profitable and in the private sector; it was prepared to bargain freely with the unions to avoid a damaging strike. Demand for Ford cards had increased largely because of high design standards, but partly because the government had deliberately stimulated demand during 1978. The clear economic case was for continued production and a wage rise negotiable according to productivity, manning levels and company profitability. In economic terms the government should have kept out of the picture. The language of incomes policy decreed otherwise and the resulting strike was economically damaging to everyone concerned – the company, the unions and the customer.

A further, political, point can also be made. The use of sanctions against Ford, until Parliament decided otherwise, was an attempt by the government to punish the company as if it was in breach of the law. It is arguable that this approach is a serious breach by the government of the rule of law itself. In a democracy the key distinction is between what is and what is not lawful. The distinction is not between what is lawful and what the government thinks ought to be unlawful. The Callaghan Government was attempting to practise Oliver Cromwell's adage 'What's for their good not what pleaseth them' which has no constitutional, or moral, basis in Britain unless backed by statute. Thus, as with the Heath Government's incomes policy,[33] the 5 per cent policy helped to undermine the rule of law and in doing so extended to the political sphere the adverse effects of incomes policy already evident in the economic sphere.

From the Ford dispute, and the other disputes which followed, another consequence of incomes policy can be deduced. With each dispute the government, as well as the employer, was involved not only peripherally, which may often be unavoidable, but centrally, and in such a manner that the dispute becomes more political than economic. The consequences of such government involvement invariably exacerbated, rather than calmed, the political and hence economic position. Brittan has rightly argued that such government involvement makes the situation worse:

> The real harm both of 'hard' pay policies based on wage and price control and of 'soft' ones based on national forums now often advocated in the United Kingdom, is that they encourage the belief that each person must look to the political process for his own wellbeing. This strengthens the interest group pressures by which the citizen has to press his case under a politicized system. Thus, so far from reducing conflict, as the sponsors of nationwide policies intend, political conflict enters into every nook and cranny of personal and business life.

Governments have, for instance, staked their reputation on winning certain wage disputes, which thereby become matters of political fact. These disputes are, moreover, entered into with no satisfactory contingency plans for seeing them through, apart from relying on the weapon of public opinion – which (1) is not so important in such matters as politicians think: and (2) likes to be on the winning side. Because of the publicity spotlight turned on individual settlements, whether by Mr. Heath on the miners in 1974 or by Mr. Callaghan on Ford at the end of 1978, such settlements acquire a key status which they would not otherwise have had under an attitude of benign neglect.[34]

The condemnation of incomes policy in this context does not mean that an obvious solution exists – only a less disruptive one. The existence of free collective bargaining, with the government as far as possible from negotiations, may work in many cases. In others, especially in the public sector, the supply and demand for labour makes greatest economic sense in that an objective criteria for a wage increase can be established independently from political considerations. While the supply of, say, civil servants at existing rates is adequate, there is no argument for any wage increase though recruitment difficulties with, say, dentists or secretaries, would indicate a wage rise necessary to increase supply. Of course, government cash limits have to impose an obvious discipline in the public sector but such a discipline is enhanced by greater reliance on supply and demand. This does not mean that industrial action would not occur, and nor should it, while the right to strike is the prerogative of trade unions in a pluralist society. The strike prerogative was effectively demonstrated in the winter of discontent and while the incomes policy mentality clearly precipitated strike action and exacerbated it, the strike action itself often demonstrated not the use of prerogative but the resort to intimidation. The picketing of innocent third parties, the fact that not all picketing was peaceful as legally required, the misery caused to hospital patients and added grief to those whose deceased relatives were unburied all showed aspects of trade unionism that went beyond the simple prerogative of strike action. Whatever prerogatives NUPE exercised during the winter of discontent the prerogative of mercy was not among them.

For the Labour Party the chief consequence of the winter's strikes was electoral setback. Although this will be examined in Chapter IX suffice it to say that the party was right to feel let down by a generation of union leaders who did not share the Jones–Scanlon preference of a Labour Government above all else.

It is arguable also that a union leader such as Alan Fisher did not share the philosophy of Jack Jones in relation to strikes which affected the public. It is a fitting epitaph to the NUPE strikes to quote from Jones's 1977 Dimbleby lecture:

It is also right that I should say a word to my fellow trade unionists. The world does not owe us a living and we must not be afraid to tackle our own shortcomings. Frankly there are too many strikes – all of them have a reason, but many of them could be avoided by more discussion or conciliation.

If we are to expect reasonable treatment from employers there is surely a strong case for us to show tolerance and concern for the public. As trade unions try to force a result from employers or the Government, pressure has often been applied to the public. All too often the ordinary people have been made the victims. They have felt the brunt of industrial action. We cannot afford to be indifferent to the effects of our actions on the public – indeed such indifference would be contrary to good trade union principle. We must look for solutions which will cause the least harm to the community as a whole.[35]

Jones's advice was conspicuous by its absence in the winter of discontent. It was ironic that while no Labour Government more than that of 1974–9 had sought as much cooperation with the unions, no Labour Government experienced such industrial conflict.

The key issue of free collective bargaining was not amenable to long-term adaptation for the sake of the survival of the Labour Government. Barnes and Reid argue that this factor was central to the breakdown of shared objectives between government and unions:

By 1978 free collective bargaining had been in suspense for three years. The militants were not prepared to accept the situation for any longer; the key trade union leaders accepted this view. The terminal illness of the social contract started with the 'crisis' of 1976; its death coincided with the retirement of Jones. By 1978 the government was no longer in a position to do anything further to meet the objectives of the trade union movement.[36]

Hodgson from the viewpoint of Labour's left wing provides a similar interpretation arguing that:

both unionised and non-unionised workers lost patience with a government that could no longer obtain the voluntary agreement of the trade union hierarchy on pay policy. Furthermore, the new leadership of the Conservative Party made gains amongst the working class by stressing Conservative support for free collective bargaining. Once the union bosses could no longer claim or appear to deliver the goods by negotiation with the Labour government, then free collective bargaining seemed the attractive alternative.[37]

It may however be argued in this context that the Conservatives, rather than Labour, had learned the lessons of their own incomes policy experience in 1972–4. There was nothing sinister in the Conservatives' rejection of compulsory incomes policy and a Conservative defence of free collective bargaining is as ideologically legitimate as Labour's defence of free collective bargaining in 1974 was ideologically consistent.

The crucial issue between the Labour Government and the unions was whether incomes policy and the suspension of free collective bargaining were to be permanently, rather than temporarily, institutionalised. This incomes policy question proved ultimately too important to each side to permit a mutual agreement. One cabinet minister thought that:

Incomes policy went wrong for two reasons. The general secretaries almost to a man said our government, our Labour Government, our country was heading for the rocks because of inflation. They said 'we will sacrifice our bargaining strength for a limited period even though we know it will cause us problems'. They got away with it for a year but by then the urgency wasn't there and there wasn't the catastrophic situation. The second reason is that the government hadn't worked out with them the basis for an ongoing policy. It was a question of pulling the rabbit out of the hat before the budget. Having got the panic measures over we were up to our necks in making the policy work.[38]

In political terms such an argument is plausible; but in economic terms it ignores the government's action – rather than the unions' acceptance of Stages I and II – to reduce inflation by cutting public expenditure and controlling the money supply. Similarly the collapse of incomes policy occurred after the government had stimulated aggregate demand during 1978 which put greater pressure on the 5 per cent pay norm. The government, not the unions, was responsible for the reduction in inflation between 1975 and 1978 and similarly responsible for its increase in 1979 following the 1978 reflation. The unions' role was political rather than economic and as such the political damage to the government was extensive in the winter of discontent. The consequence of the strike action, resulting from the 5 per cent policy, was to enhance the chances of a Conservative victory which both government and unions feared. By February 1979, only eight weeks after a NOP poll gave Labour a 1 per cent lead, the Conservatives were ahead in all polls, in some cases by as much as 18 per cent and 19 per cent. Public opinion also showed considerable hostility towards trade unions with a MORI poll showing that 85 per cent of those questioned favoured a legal ban on secondary picketing and 68 per cent supported the use of troops to maintain essential services in vital industries. Anthony King, in a revealing anecdote, illustrates the effect the winter of discontent was having on the electorate:

> After the general election, a former aide to the prime minister described how one night he watched on the television news as a funeral cortege reached the cemetery gates, the camera panned to a group of pickets. They were guarding the entrance, placards aloft. The cortege turned back. The prime minister's aide knew at that moment that Labour had lost.[39]

The electoral dimension must be not be overexaggerated in an age of extreme electoral volatility and declining partisan attachment. However the decision to delay the election in October 1978 had proved very damaging for Labour. This is not a judgement made only with hindsight, as the opposition to delay in the

Labour Party at the time testifies, but rather an assessment of the risks Jim Callaghan took not only with the 5 per cent pay policy but with parliamentary arithmetic. This latter factor was to precipitate a general election thus denying the Prime Minister his normal constitutional right of timing the election to his party's advantage. The consequences of the winter of discontent in electoral terms were therefore not able to fade before the electorate's verdict was required.

CHAPTER IX

The 1979 General Election

LABOUR'S LAST WEEKS

The Labour Government fell on 28 March 1979 when it was defeated by a majority of one, 311 to 310, in a vote of no confidence. It is not the intention here to deal in detail with the parliamentary arithmetic following the Scotland and Wales referenda on 1 March which knocked away Nationalist support for the government which had been crucial since the formal ending of the Lib–Lab pact. However, as Leonard rightly points out, the failure to reach the 40 per cent hurdle in the Scotland referendum[1] may be partly explained by the government's unpopularity following the winter of discontent. The two to one majority in favour of devolution dissipated during the referendum campaign and the association in the electorate's mind between devolution, the Labour Government and industrial militancy cannot be easily explained away. Leonard argues that 'had the referendum been held in the previous December there is little doubt that a much higher positive vote (probably exceeding the 40% barrier) would have been obtained'.[2]

The vote of no confidence itself deserves some scrutiny. The SNP and the Liberals were prepared to vote against the government but Plaid Cymru's two MPs and two Ulster Unionists[3] were prepared to support Mr Callaghan. One Labour MP, Sir Alfred Broughton, was too ill to be brought to the precincts of the House to be 'nodded through' and attention thus focused on Frank Maguire, the Independent Republican member for Fermanagh and South Tyrone. Normally he could have been relied upon to vote with the government but now, disaffected with Ulster Secretary Roy Mason's alleged closeness to the Unionists, he ostentatiously abstained, standing behind the Speaker's chair and refusing the pleas of Labour MPs. Nor could Gerry Fitt the SDLP member for Belfast West support the government which provided an ironic twist to the De Lorean saga in that the government's massive investment in De Lorean cars was designed to provide employment in Catholic areas.

The general election date was fixed for 3 May and immediately the government and the union leaders seemed able to rekindle a spirit of cooperation that had been absent only weeks before. Moss Evans and David Basnett at a meeting of trade unionists for a Labour victory promised to throw trade union resources behind Labour's effort in sixty key marginals and Len Murray declared that the government 'had been good for trade unionists and working people and we want to see it sustained in office'.[4] Nor was Ken Thomas, the CPSA leader, whose members had rejected a 7 per cent pay offer and were continuing strike action, prepared to break the cordon of solidarity. He commented that 'with one hand I shall be fighting the government to try to get a bigger increase but I shall be waving it on election platforms to get it back. There is no alternative.'[5] It may be argued that such political naivety was a poor reward for Jack Jones's efforts to keep a Labour Government in office at almost any cost during the early stages of incomes policy.

The civil service strike indeed brought widespread disruption in April to remind the electorate of the winter of discontent. Tax, social security and unemployment offices were shut, the airports, ports and courts disrupted and Whitehall staff absent. As well as industrial action Ken Thomas's thoughts on the dispute were ideal Conservative propaganda. He thought that Labour ministers had shown that they expected trade unions to do everything with their power but use it, a view 'which we do not believe is shared by Labour voters'. Significantly the Conservatives did extremely well in the election among traditional Labour voters in affluent working-class areas. Ivor Crewe has noted that:

The Conservatives, on the other hand, obtained exceptionally high swings in two types of affluent working class areas. They gained against all expectations two car workers' seats – Birmingham Northfield (10·2 per cent) and Hornchurch (8·5 per cent) – and secured massive swings in Dagenham (13·4 per cent) and Barking (13·9 per cent), home of the October 1978 Ford strike. And they did unusually well in New Towns such as Harlow (12·9 per cent) Basildon (11·0 per cent) and Hertford and Stevenage (8·2 per cent) where they topped Labour's

Secretary of State for Education and Science, Mrs Shirley Williams. Conservative success in both areas was probably owed to the feelings on the part of high wage-earners that living standards were threatened by high taxes, incomes policies and possibly strikes by their own unions, although confirmation will have to await the analysis of election surveys.[6]

Labour's last weeks also saw Mr Healey's fifteenth budget, which was essentially a 'care and maintenance' budget, without overt electioneering. This situation arose as a result of collaboration between the two front benches according to which the Conservatives promised to expedite the legislation needed to enable Parliament to rise in return for minimum electioneering from the Chancellor. The irony of this situation was that in April 1978 Labour had presented a budget that engineered a pre-election boom creating the situation by October which many in the party thought suitable for a general election. Effectively the fall of the government in the vote of no confidence robbed it of the opportunity of delivering a pre-election budget only a month before polling. From such a perspective those like Michael Foot who had urged caution in October 1978 had gravely misjudged the situation.

The April 1979 budget itself provided the legislative basis for continuing tax collection and implemented a £900 million improvement in tax allowances which had already been sanctioned by the Commons in 1978. A further irony was Mr Healey's announcement that the government was making an early repayment to the IMF of $1 billion which cleared the $3·9 billion facility borrowed in 1976. Such a move was a vindication of the government's tough action in December 1976 but in the circumstances of April 1979 it was the winter of discontent, not the IMF crisis, that was fresh in voters' minds. Similarly overshadowed by the winter crisis was the balance of payments surplus and the fall in inflation.

A comparison with 1970 is not inappropriate. The Labour Government had transformed a seemingly inviolate deficit on the external account into a surplus but failed to show the electoral benefit because of other factors. In April 1979 Mr Healey announced in the budget that:

Externally we achieved a £250 million current account surplus and this in spite of the fact that the extra net help we got from North Sea oil was to a great extent off-set by a fall in invisible earnings, largely due to an increase in our contributions to the EEC budget – something we are determined to correct in future.[7]

The reference to the high cost of Britain's EEC contribution was, of course, oblique electioneering. However, the government was not in the position, feared by many Conservatives in the late 1970s, of presiding over a strong economy booming because of North Sea oil wealth. Indeed the reason why the North Sea oil contribution was less significant – EEC budget contributions – was a further irony in view of the Conservatives' enthusiasm for EEC entry. The Conservatives were set to reap electoral benefit from the stifling economic effects of EEC entry they themselves had supported. (After the election the Conservative Government's mood changed and Margaret Thatcher sought vigorously to reduce Britain's inflated budget burden.) Ultimately, like the Heath Government before it, the Labour Government did not reap electoral advantages for reaffirming Britain's commitment to the EEC.

Wisely in electoral terms, though arguably inaccurate in economic terms, Sir Geoffrey Howe, replying to Mr Healey's budget, ignored the question of the EEC and noted that Britain, despite North Sea oil, had a worse economic performance than its rivals. Mindful of the election Sir Geoffrey attacked the increase in taxation over the lifetime of the 1974–9 government and advocated 'a substantial reduction in personal taxation to restore incentives and a reduction in public spending programmes so they are in line with what the nation can afford'. During the campaign Labour spokesmen repeatedly pressed the Conservatives to be more specific on the question of where public expenditure cuts would fall and, though the point was a fair one, it never sounded really convincing following the 1978 reflation and the increase in public spending to pay for the wage increases of the winter of discontent. The extra cost of public sector pay rises totalled £1 billion and in mid-April Department of Employment figures showed earnings running at 14·9 per cent per annum. It is doubtful whether the encouraging unemployment figures – down 61 659 to 1 340 595 on 5 April – outweighed the effect of rising inflation and the memory of the winter strikes.

THE CAMPAIGN AND ECONOMIC ISSUES

It is not the purpose of this account to give a detailed description of the 1979 election campaign involving as it did non-economic issues such as law and order, immigration and council house sales. However, the importance of economic issues in the campaign is relevant to any study of the politics of economic policy in a democracy where most voters judge, and identify with, the parties in socioeconomic terms. In 1979, as in the previous three general elections at least, economic issues dominated the campaign.

The Labour manifesto, *The Labour Way is the Better Way* vigorously defended Labour's economic record and was designed to attract the votes of the mass of apolitical electors rather than inflame socialist spirit among Labour's activists.

The manifesto stated that:

> Over the past five years, the Labour Government have laid the foundations of a stronger economy.
>
> When Labour came to govern, in March 1974, Britain was facing the most dangerous crisis since the war. The Tory programme of confrontation and social injustice had brought the country almost to its knees. Unlit streets, unheated homes, shut-down factories – these were the fruits of the Tory three-day week. We were £1,000m in deficit in our national balance of payments, even before the rising oil prices. Prices were soaring month by month. Industry was enfeebled by years of under-investment. To top it all, Britain then had to contend with the four-fold rises in oil prices and the worldwide inflation and unemployment.
>
> Our inheritance was a Britain in crisis. The new Labour Government sought cooperation in place of confrontation. Instead of division, we offered social justice. In place of compulsion, we worked to win consent for the tough economic measures we knew were needed. We forged a new partnership between the Labour Government and working people.
>
> Our country has come a long way since then. The rate of inflation has been brought under control. It has become possible to improve living standards, to cut taxation and increase child benefit, pensions and benefits to the disabled to rates which more than overtake costs and inflation.

And over the past year, unemployment has at last begun to fall. Now we offer a programme to carry Britain through the 1980s.[9]

As well as Labour's plans for the future, the presentation of Labour's record in office was even more important, as the Conservatives would naturally make Labour's economic troubles central to their campaign attack. The most significant and striking aspect of the campaign concerned Labour's handling of the issue of unemployment. Five years before an unemployment rate of over 1 million would have been considered disastrous for a Labour Government but Mr Callaghan constantly emphasised that Labour represented with its jobs creation programme a 'higher-employment' party as opposed to the 'monetarist' Conservatives. In his final television broadcast Mr Callaghan stressed the threat to jobs from the Conservatives' plans and, as in other aspects of the campaign, portrayed the Conservatives as the devil the electorate did not know and could not trust. Thus as Beloff and Peele comment, Mr Callaghan 'conducted a campaign in which he projected an image of almost conservative stability in contrast to the radical challenge offered by Mrs. Thatcher'.[10]

One cabinet minister, recalling Mr Callaghan's electioneering style, thought that:

Callaghan was brilliant during the campaign. He has this incredible facility that whatever the doubts, resentments and worries in the run up to a decision – he detested aspects of decision-making – he could sell the decision once it had been made. The doubts and reservations disappeared and he had a populist side to his character and an incredible ability to present things to people.[11]

A junior minister recalled that 'Callaghan fought a superb campaign in 1979, putting forward a coherent framework'.[12] A central feature of Mr Callaghan's framework was the Conservatives' threat to employment.

However, that Labour was able to campaign as the party of less unemployment with the figure over 1·3 million reflected the public's changing attitude to unemployment as an electoral determinant. The opinion polls constantly showed unemployment as second or third to inflation as a source of public concern reflecting the fact that, at only 5·5 per cent, 94·5 per cent of the electorate of working population age had a job while inflation affected not 5·5 per cent but 100 per cent of the voters. Whilst it may be argued that not everyone is equally affected by inflation the key point is that the voters themselves identified inflation as the major policy issue. The Conservatives were thus able to concentrate on the inflation issue and snipe at Labour's unemployment record rather than attack it full on.

As previously mentioned, the Conservatives were able to benefit from the unpopularity of trade union abuses of power during the winter of discontent. *The Conservative Manifesto of 1979*, issued on 11 April promised to restore the economy and to control the unions. Postal ballots for union elections, reform of the law relating to the closed shop and the outlawing of secondary picketing were the detailed proposals but the crucial factor was that following the winter strikes, Labour could no longer claim to be the only party who could work with the unions. The Conservatives had lived down their 1970–4 reputation as the party of 'confrontation'.[13]

Inflation and trade union law reform thus featured prominently in the manifesto which stated that:

> Under Labour prices have risen faster than at any peacetime period in the three centuries in which records have been kept, and inflation is now accelerating again. The pound today is worth less than half its 1974 value. On present form it would be halved in value yet again within eight years. Inflation on this scale has come near to destroying our political and social stability.
>
> To master inflation, proper monetary discipline is essential, with publicly stated targets for the rate of growth of money supply. At the same time, a gradual reduction in the size of the Government's borrowing requirement is also vital. This Government's price controls have done nothing to prevent inflation, as is proved by the doubling of prices since they came to power. All the controls have achieved is a loss of jobs and a reduction in consumer choice.[14]

In a section headed simply 'trade union reform' the manifesto outlined the thinking behind specific changes in the law relating to picketing and the closed shop:

The crippling industrial disruption which hit Britain last winter had several causes: years with no growth in production; rigid pay control; high marginal rates of taxation; and the extension of trade union power and privileges. Between 1974 and 1976, Labour enacted a 'militants' charter' of trade union legislation. It tilted the balance of power in bargaining throughout industry away from responsible management and towards unions, and sometimes towards unofficial groups of workers acting in defiance of their official union leadership.[15]

But the Conservative campaign was far from a simple anti-union crusade. Mrs Thatcher and employment spokesman Jim Prior repeatedly appealed to trade union members to vote Conservative and hence repudiate the union leaders and an election rally of Conservative trade unionists was addressed by Mrs Thatcher with the emphasis on weakening the traditional bond between union membership and voting Labour rather than on attacking union abuses. Indeed Mrs Thatcher, stealing Labour's clothes of only five months before, pledged not to divide society but to unite it. The evidence is that the Conservative campaign succeeded in weakening the support for Labour among trade unionists. The swing to the Conservatives was 6·5 per cent among unskilled workers and 7 per cent among trade unionists compared to an overall national swing to the Conservatives of 5·2 per cent.

Cuts in taxation and a reduction of government spending also featured strongly as Conservative-pushed economic issues. On taxation the Conservatives could point with confidence to an impressive post-war record of cutting taxes while Labour by contrast had raised them. But as far as specifying public expenditure cuts to reduce both taxation and the PSBR, Labour was able to raise doubts as to the Conservatives' real intentions. Mrs Thatcher never came to terms with Labour allegations that a huge rise in VAT would be needed to pay for tax cuts, as Livingston argues:

The failure to deal with the increase in VAT was probably a tactical error on the part of party strategists. Given the emphasis on income-tax cuts, and the inability to meet them by comprehensive reductions in government spending it was obvious that VAT would have to be increased. By how much?

On what? There was no prior understanding on this, or at least no settled agreement was announced and communicated to the party. This left a big gap in the Tory defences, which Labour attacked at every turn. Healey said a Conservative government might have to double the rate of VAT. Thatcher immediately denied it, so Callaghan promptly took her to task. 'Let us assume', he said, 'that it was only increased by half. That would only leave enough to cut the standard rate of tax by 2p.' According to Callaghan, the Treasury calculated that only those earning more than £192 a week would get more back in income tax cuts than they would pay out in higher prices.[16]

The Conservatives were helped, in relation to the VAT rise allegation, by Labour's record of tax increases and the importance attached by the electorate to reducing income tax, which was largely believed to be so high that incentives were destroyed. Concentration on cutting taxes as a matter of faith – rather than stressing public spending economies – just about enabled the Conservatives to deflect Labour's question of where the money would come from.[17]

Economic issues are expected to dominate an election campaign in the same way as they usually dominate politics itself. Opinion polls regularly chart voters' reaction to the government's overall management of the economy. However in a general election campaign, as in 1979, some economic issues more than others attract the electorate's attention. As in 1970, Labour's considerable, and laudable, balance of payments success did not reap electoral benefits. As in February 1974, major industrial confrontation prior to polling did not help the government. Arguably in 1979 the winter of discontent, and the particular affect of the NUPE strike, devastated Labour's election chances.

The most crucial change in the 1979 campaign in relation to economic issues concerned the twin issues of inflation and unemployment. To be sure, inflation – or 'rising prices' as the electorate then perceived it – had played a key role in the 1970 campaign,[18] but then unemployment was only 600 000 and the Keynesian full-employment consensus dominated both parties. By 1979 the Keynesian remedy of engineering a pre-election boom was no longer regarded as sufficient for electoral victory. Labour may have lost, as Jim Callaghan feared, an October 1978 election despite semi-boom conditions. In the 1979 campaign

Labour's expansion of the economy during 1978 was not even a major issue. It has already been mentioned that the idea of Labour campaigning on its employment record with 1·3 million unemployment would have been considered unthinkable only five or six years previously. But by 1979 such an antithesis of Keynesian electoral technique was not regarded as abnormal. In short, having presided over the abandonment of Keynesianism in 1976 at the time of the IMF crisis the same government in 1979 faced an electorate that had also ceased to regard unemployment as the ultimate regulator of prosperity.

That the issue of inflation dominated the economic issues in the campaign indicated how far, with 1·3 million unemployed, the rhetoric of Keynesian economics had declined. Ironically it was Mr Callaghan himself whose famous speech at the 1976 Labour Conference repudiated Keynesian demand management, who effectively broke the mould of post-war economic policy-making. In this context the 1978 reflation was a step backwards that ultimately hindered the government's electoral prospects. It is conjecture to speculate whether the 5 per cent pay policy without the 1978 expansionary measures would have held sufficiently to assist Labour at the polls. What is more certain is that the Conservatives were able to focus on inflation – and Labour's inability to control it – to maximum electoral advantage. Significantly in May 1979 the inflation trend was rising, whereas between 1975 and 1978 it had been falling. The Conservatives' success in identifying public disquiet over inflation, rather than over unemployment, was not the result of any aspect of 'monetarist' theory but was the outcome of the electorate's own disaffection with inflation over a number of years. Conservative propagandists thus referred to the 30 per cent level of inflation in 1975 as in previous elections Labour had referred to the mass unemployment of the 1930s associated with Conservative rule.

Of course such factors as greater electoral volatility and 'partisan dealignment' helped to enable the Conservatives to appeal to voters who would have traditionally voted Labour out of class loyalty. However the concentration on inflation, instead of unemployment, also played a significant part in the Conservatives' victory. If Labour had in 1976 been the first party to reject Keynesian economic strategy then the Conservatives in 1979 were the first party successfully to adjust to the post-Keynesian electoral strategy.

On 3 May the electorate voted to end over five years of Labour Government and to elect a Conservative Government led by Margaret Thatcher. The Conservatives gained a majority of 71 over Labour and of 44 over all opposition parties combined, a majority which contrasted to the precarious state of parliamentary arithmetic Labour had endured. The Conservatives gained 51 seats from Labour, 3 from the Liberals including Devon North, the seat of former leader Jeremy Thorpe,[19] and 7 from the Scottish National Party, giving a total of 339 seats. Labour regained 5 seats lost to the Conservatives at by-elections, won 2 seats from the SNP, 2 from the Scottish Labour Party and 1 from Plaid Cymru, giving a total of 268 seats compared with the 319 of October 1974. The Liberals declined from 14 to 11 seats, the SNP from 11 to 2 and Plaid Cymru from 3 to 2, reversing the trends of both February and October 1974 towards the smaller parties.

The overall national swing to the Conservatives was 5·2 per cent but this figure obscures regional voting variations. In England the swing was greater to the Conservatives than in Wales and Scotland, traditional Labour strongholds. (The Conservatives did capture Anglesey from Labour with a 12·5 per cent swing and Montgomery from the Liberals with a 7·5 per cent swing.) However the Conservatives did better in the south than the north of England, reinforcing electoral trends already discernible since the 1960s. As already mentioned the Conservatives did exceptionally well in affluent working-class areas but less well in constituencies with large immigrant populations such as Birmingham Sparkbrook and Brent South. Increased electoral volatility also manifested itself in a number of maverick results such as the Conservatives' capture of Lincoln, Brigg and Scunthorpe, and Loughborough and their failure to take Truro from the Liberals as a result of tactical voting by Labour supporters.

Apart from the reward of a strong parliamentary majority the 5·2 per cent swing was the largest since 1945 and the Conservatives lead over Labour of 7 per cent was the largest by one party over another since 1935. Labour's share of the poll, 36·9 per cent, was its lowest since the comprehensive defeat of 1931. Although the trend away from Labour can be traced back to the 1960s the issues in 1979 helped to weaken Labour's traditional support. As Crewe shrewdly points out 'whereas the majority of Conservative voters (temporarily swelled in 1979, moreover, by many without deep Conservative commitments) explicitly opposed Labour's proposals, a substantial majority of Labour voters (reduced in 1979 to a loyal core) actually supported the Conservative proposals'.[20]

A final point about the 1979 verdict concerns Jim Callaghan. Unlike Harold Wilson, who won four out of five general elections, Callaghan was denied the satisfaction of enjoying the personal legitimacy a general election victory confers on a party leader. However his campaign was skilful and he remained Labour's largest single electoral asset. The verdict was on his government, and particularly on its allies the unions, rather than on him personally. Unlike Edward Heath in February 1974, his conduct of the campaign did not contribute to electoral defeat. Callaghan certainly paid a heavy electoral price for his determination to uphold the 5 per cent pay policy and arguably for his decision to delay the election. Callaghan made mistakes both in policy terms and in electoral strategy terms but these mistakes were mitigated, not compounded, during the campaign itself. For all his mistakes and faults Callaghan conceded defeat with good grace and deserved a better exit than the one shown on national television of being heckled and shouted down by 'troops out' militants in his own Cardiff constituency.

CHAPTER X

Concluding Thoughts

THE LEFT'S CRITICISMS

Since the electoral defeat of the Callaghan Government the left versus right party turmoils have left Labour more ideologically divided than at any time since the late 1950s. The left,[1] under Tony Benn's articulate leadership, have criticised the 1974–9 Labour Government for missing the opportunities for radical change in a socialist direction by attempting to 'manage' an essentially capitalist economy. The left has argued that the 'transformation of wealth and power in favour of working people' was jettisoned in favour of the quiet life of the social status quo. The experience of 1974–9 has proved to many on the left that the government suffered from a lack of socialist transformation rather than a surfeit of it. Furthermore many left-wingers regarded the government's mistake not only to be the postponement of socialist change but also the abdication of socialist principles in adopting monetarist solutions and tolerating high unemployment.

Ian Mikardo thought '1974–9 was a greater disappointment than 1964–70. The rich got richer under Callaghan',[2] and Dennis Skinner, who voted 154 times against the 1974–9 government, recalled that: '1974–9 made me disappointed and angry. We had so many opportunities. I was angry that we gave the opportunity to the Tories that by cutting wages and the IMF cuts we could run the country effectively. It was a denial of the socialist creed which is based on the opposite of extending the welfare state.'[3]

Others on the left of the party now see such solutions as import control, £5 billion reflation, and a further extension of the public sector gaining in party support in contrast to the Callaghan years. Hodgson, who urges the socialist transformation advocated by the left, lays at the door of the 1974–9 government the destruction of the post-war 'Butskellite' consensus, arguing that:

166

It was the Labour government of 1974–79, not the new Right of the Conservative Party led by Margaret Thatcher, that dealt the death blow to this consensus. By the end of 1976 the Labour government had abandoned a Keynesian strategy. It had embraced monetarism with its tight controls on the money supply, the target reduction of the Public Sector Borrowing Requirement and a substantial reduction in public expenditure. Furthermore, it had made significant dents in the welfare state. The post-war Butskellite consensus was dead when the social democratic wing of the Labour Party had failed to defend a gradualist and reforming perspective and conceded its position to monetarism. It was forced to do this by the severity of Britain's economic crisis in 1974–6. These were the subterranean events that broke up the post-war political consensus, not Thatcher's victory at the polls. The destruction of the Butskellite consensus was accomplished by Callaghan, Healey and Crosland; not Thatcher, Joseph and Howe. The latter simply gained from the work that had already been done, and rode down the path that had already been cleared.[4]

Hodgson's analysis is quite correct; it is his socialist solution that is open to dispute. It is arguable that the policies of the left would have brought about a Thatcher Government well before 1979 by alienating to an even greater extent the very working-class voters that the left's strategy claims to defend.

Peter Townsend, like Hodgson, has criticised the Labour Government's record but does not examine how the left's strategy could have led to electoral success. He noted that 'in 1974–9 a long term public expenditure cut was substituted for socialist planning, traditional pay restraint was preferred to an effective social contract or a statutory incomes policy, the numbers in the population living below the state's unemployment doubled and a wealth tax deferred. That is not a record of success in establishing socialism.'[5] The key question is whether the definition of socialism advocated by the left would have either led to electoral popularity for Labour or to economic success in terms of higher living standards. Labour voters in 1979 moved right – many voting for an avowedly right-wing Conservative Government – rather than to the parties of the far left where explicit socialist solutions have always been found. For Marxists such as Coates,[6] the electoral dimension is essentially irrelevant once capitalism is overthrown and socialism established but for democratic socialists in the Labour Party the electoral constraint must be a factor which shapes policy priority formulation.

Many on the left argue that the more radical the manifesto, 1945 or February 1974 for example, the greater Labour's electoral appeal. Such an argument regards the wording of the manifesto rather than the party's image – plus other factors such as the appeal, or lack of it, of the Conservatives – as electorally crucial. The evidence, however, suggests otherwise. Rather than voting Labour because of the manifesto many working-class voters vote Labour despite it, preferring as in 1979 Conservative policies on such specific issues as law and order, and reducing taxation. Social class loyalty, rather than manifesto commitments, has been the determining factor of Labour's working-class support. However such support, in an era of high electoral volatility, a blurring of class divisions, and an inflationary economy which damages working-class living standards, can no longer be as surely relied upon. Labour's working-class electorate essentially wants economic prosperity, lower taxation, employment security and increased consumer comforts.

In 1979, unlike in 1945, most working-class voters paid tax, resented inflation and disliked industrial disruption, which often affected them directly. Moreover, unlike in 1945, many more working-class voters owned, or wanted to own, their own homes. To such a generation of voters the programme of the left would not have provided – had it been implemented in 1974–9 – the working class's own version of the good life. The left's ideological approach essentially appeals to radical, politically motivated, middle-class intellectuals rather than to the average Labour voter. Essentially the left-wing approach of a polytechnic lecturer such as Geoff Hodgson is light years away from that of a left-wing trade unionist such as Jack Jones. Jones's £6 pay policy certainly had its faults, as has been argued in this account, but the intention behind it – reducing inflation to keep a Labour Government in office – was directly in line with the unpopularity of inflation with working-class people. The left ignore this fundamental point by advocating either no solution to inflation or one that involves no sacrifices in terms of public spending.

The left/right split in the Labour Party over policy reflects the two different approaches to working-class voters. The left see the working class as desirous of radical socialist change while the

Labour right see socialism itself in more pragmatic terms – similar terms to that of the working-class electorate itself. As one of the great parties in British politics Labour has sought, from its earliest formative years, to liberate the working class from the dire poverty of late Victorian England. The welfare state, the growth of trade unionism and full-employment Keynesianism were all justified in terms of raising working-class living standards, itself seen as practical socialism. Jim Callaghan, perhaps unwittingly, typified this tradition when he told the 1979 Labour Party Conference that there were more doctors working in the NHS in 1979 than when Labour took office in 1974. To the Labour right such achievements are examples of socialism. To the left, socialism is much more; it is an ideological belief system which regards such achievements as merely means to an end not an end in themselves. In truth for the left it is the imposition of socialism itself – not its effect on the working class – that is paramount. The left's criticism of 1974–9 are criticisms not only aimed at specific policy 'failures' such as adopting monetarist economics, but also at the government's lack of an ideological approach to capitalism.

The left's criticisms of 1974–9 tend to be total and ideologically justifiable rather than the criticisms of the centre or right which tend to be specific and essentially non-ideological. Some on the 'soft left' of the party do not regard 1974–9 as an unmitigated failure at all. Joe Ashton, who served in the Whips Office, argued that:

The 1974–9 government did a magnificent job with hardly a majority. It's only now we look back at the successes of 1945–51. In 20 years people will be saying the same of 1974–9. You had to be in government to know how thin the thread was. We never revealed the wheeling and dealing to ensure a majority.[7]

Similarly Albert Booth, a 'soft left' member of the Cabinet after 1976, recalled that the government's achievements were considerable when judged against the narrow parliamentary majorities:

In retrospect I think it will be a long time before the Labour movement comes to terms with the experience of government 1974–9. The crude analysis of the Labour conference (following the election defeat) can't be the final judgement. If Clem Attlee had thought of carrying through 90 per cent of a radical manifesto he would have thought a majority of 50 would have been needed. It was a period of experiment, some of which was remarkably effective. Some of the successes were industrial democracy under another name – ACAS and the Manpower Services Commission for example.[8]

Jack Jones also based his assessment of the government's record in specific, rather than simply ideological terms. Apart from his support for incomes policy – which ideologically cut him off from the hard left – Jones was an exponent of import controls and an opponent of the IMF cuts. However, his view was that '1974–9 was a missed opportunity. So much more could have been done although there was considerable progress 1974–7 with favourable legislation. The NEB with all its limitations was a step forward.'[9] One Tribunite thought that '1974–9 achieved a great amount. It's nothing like as bad as painted – 1966–70 was the real wasted opportunity. But it's not factually true that 1974–9 was a brilliantly successful government.'[10]

The criticisms of the 'soft left', of which the above examples are but a few, though typical, are far removed from the total ideological criticism of the more extreme left. It is arguable however that it is the former group rather than the latter that is the greater practitioner of socialism in a Labour Party context of improving working-class living standards. In this sense the 'soft left' has more in common with Labour's right wing than with the left of Tony Benn. Croslandism may have died as a leading Labour Party philosophy after 1976 but Crosland's comment in relation to the anti-growth lobby, that 'my constituents in Grimsby have their own version of the environment', had, and still has, a wider implication for the Labour Party. It is the left, not the rest of the party, that is out of line with socialism, when such an approach to Labour's working-class electorate is overridden by ideological considerations. In criticising the 1974–9 government for not introducing socialism, the left are correct to point to policy betrayals given the left's policy successes in 1970–5. But in the wider context of the Labour Party's aims the left's criticisms assume the Labour Party to be a party it never was – committed to ideological objectives ahead of practical socialism. To the left the role of the state in establishing socialism becomes an end in itself rather than the well-being of individual members of the working class. The left's vision of socialism is little more than the use of state power to destroy capitalism, or in Britain's case the mixed economy. It is scarcely surprising that, as Luard points out, 'given the role of the state everywhere . . . in socialist thinking, socialism . . . comes to mean state socialism; that social ownership is taken to mean national ownership; and that the extension of social ownership means an extension of state power. Everywhere the supreme aim of socialism comes to be the socialist *state* [emphasis in original].'[11] Such a description ideally fits the ideological approach of the Labour left but does not fit the Labour Party's traditional practical socialist aspirations of raising working-class living standards.

It is arguable that there is nothing unsocialist in reducing inflation if this benefits working-class people. Similarly there was nothing unsocialist in abandoning Keynesian demand management if the end result was a higher standard of living and a more prosperous economy. The Labour left can attack the 1974–9 government as unsocialist, according to their ideological aims, but equally the Labour right can defend the government's record in socialist terms, according to their own pragmatic aims. While it is true that the Labour right cannot point to ultimate electoral victory, nor can the left point to an electorate thirsting for left-wing solutions. Labour's recovery of popularity in 1978 followed the abandonment of the traditional commitment to full employment and the rejection of the left's policy alternatives. If Labour had won an October 1978 election the left would have effectively lost, for the foreseeable future, the debate within the party. Ironically the militant trade unionism and 'direct action' advocated by the left helped to bring down the Callaghan Government, which in turn paved the way for the left to strengthen its position within the party for the strongest challenge to the right in the party's history. As one member of the Cabinet put it 'the tragedy of 1974–9 was that we lost. The unions didn't help us in any way. The government was a creature of the unions so we were let down in the end by our own people.'[12]

Apart from the debate within the Labour Party the left's criticism and solutions in relation to 1974–9 deserve further attention. Import controls were a favourite panacea, particularly at the time of the IMF crisis. The intellectual inspiration for import controls came, from the mid-1970s onwards, from the

Cambridge Economic Policy Group headed by Professor Wynne Godley, which advocated general non-discriminatory import controls rather than specific selective import controls aimed at protecting industries in trouble. Professor Godley's computer predictions of economic circumstances in 1990[13] showed the import control alternative reducing unemployment to 500 000 while conventional policies were estimated to lead to unemployment of 4 600 000.

Part of the attraction of the argument for the left is that import controls can replace traditional Keynesian demand management as a painless way of achieving full employment. Thus, as Patrick Minford rightly argues:

> Whenever unemployment rises, the pressures for protection rise with it. Imports are seen often by those whose jobs are threatened as the cause of their unemployment, and the reduction or elimination of those imports as an obvious remedy. The remedy is obvious because the interests of foreigners are not identified as having much value by comparison with those of your fellow-citizens. It is tempting and not altogether misleading to draw parallels with the search for scapegoats and the persecution of minority groups in times of political stress.[14]

Although the left have portrayed import controls as a radical solution, in reality the concept is an old one. The protectionism of the 1930s – when counter-protectionist measures led to a decline in world trade – aggravated rather than ameliorated unemployment. Import controls, seen from Professor Godley's Cambridge model, may seem temporarily attractive but in the 1970s and beyond the threat of retaliation is arguably greater to Britain's trading patterns than in the Empire preference era of the 1930s.

A further difficulty is exactly which goods would be subject to import controls and how the controls would be quantified.[15] Would foreign cars be excluded from Britain to assist BL (and presumably Chrysler)? Would foreign wine and sherry be excluded to boost fledgling British production? Would raw materials be exempt in certain industries or all of them? Even assuming there was no retaliation by other countries, such import controls would arguably reduce working-class living standards more than living standards of the better off. Black markets would favour those on higher incomes, as is the case in the Soviet-style economies. Smuggling – as in the late eighteenth and early nineteenth centuries – would be a growth industry and those convicted would presumably swell the already overburdened prison system.

If cheap Japanese cars, such as Datsun and Honda, were excluded the consumer victims would be those people who could afford only cheap cars rather than the more affluent who enjoy a greater choice of model. If cheap foreign wines were excluded, working-class people would be forced to pay more for British wine, while, one suspects, Professor Godley and his colleagues dining at Cambridge high table would have access to plentiful stocks of college French or German wine piled up before import controls were introduced. In short, the loss of consumer choice caused by general import controls would harm particularly those on lower incomes whom the left purports to defend. Nor should the above examples be considered frivolous or extreme. They all flow directly from the application of the philosophy of import controls in the same way as 'norms', 'relativities boards', 'guidelines' and 'sanctions against employers' flow directly from the application of incomes policy philosophy.

The most extreme economic application of import controls exists, of course, in the Soviet Union and other Eastern European economies, and it existed in a severe form in the corporatist Nazi and Fascist economies. In the context of state socialism import controls are consistent with breaking the power of the private, entrepreneurial sector. More than formal nationalisation, import controls give the state power over not only the citizen's production but his consumption as well. To the Labour left import controls are a matter not of economics but of ideology. To Labour voters and particularly those on low incomes, import controls are damaging to living standards, restrict consumer choice and ultimately destroy employment prospects. For a democratic socialist party such as the Labour Party, import controls would spell electoral catastrophe. The 1974–9 government deserves credit for resisting the superficially attractive simplicity of the import control panacea.

Another of the left's preferred solutions for the economic problems of the 1974–9 period was an extended, radical industrial strategy. Without repeating the arguments used in Chapter III, in relation to the failure of the government's industrial strategy, the crucial factor the left failed to appreciate was that employment and prosperity depended ultimately on customers – particularly in world markets – rather than on the government's good intentions in the distribution of public money. A more extensive industrial strategy would not have made steel, the railways, BL, Chrysler or British Airways more efficient and competitive simply by investing more public money. Investment by itself is of no merit; it is the rate of return on investment, whether public or private, that is crucial in providing employment and raising living standards. Indeed the left's industrial strategy would have been in effect the opposite of radical change; it would have entrenched and strengthened industrial fossilisation.

Finally the left's criticism of public expenditure cuts during the 1974–9 government deserves further comment. The left's political case against the cuts – that the welfare state, education, housing and so on should never be contracted by a Labour Government – is plausible enough in a socialist context. But in the context of economic reality the criticism is no more than a recipe for higher inflation. The left failed to realise the resentment felt by working people at prices that seemed to be perpetually rising – as well as failing to recognise the economic damage in more conventional ways as, for example, on export performance. The left did not believe that the success in reducing inflation from near 30 per cent levels was worth the public expenditure sacrifices. The left thus failed to appreciate that the resources on which the public services depend for finance would be hampered by a high inflation rate and stimulated by a low inflation rate. It is no coincidence that the period of economic recovery, 1976–8, occurred after the 1976 IMF cuts which restored a semblance of balance to public expenditure and to the economy generally, leading to single-figure inflation, albeit temporarily. Public expenditure cuts, rather than being an attack on living standards, as the left claimed, were a necessary precondition for inflation control without which living standards would not have recovered from 1977 onwards.

Thus, writing in September 1978 Walter Eltis correctly noted that:

> this year's increase in living standards is due to the Government's remarkable success in cutting the real size of the public sector. The Conservatives would not have been believed if they had announced in 1977 that they could cut real public spending four per cent in one year but Mr. Healey has achieved just this

through the use of cash limits and the IMF inspired cuts. Public spending was four per cent less in 1977–8 than in 1976–7, and if the Conservatives win the election they can now cut public spending further by using precisely the methods which Mr. Healey and his colleagues pioneered.

This cut in public spending has, of course, allowed the average worker in industry and commerce to buy substantially more. Hence his 6–7 per cent increase in real spending power this year when he has produced perhaps two per cent more. But this fillip can hardly be repeated year after year. The worker in industry and commerce has gained only because the public sector has shed resources. If the public sector picks them up again, then Mr. Healey is increasing real public spending six per cent this year to more than make good last year's cuts. The public sector will gain once more and the private sector will lose.[16]

Part of the left's criticisms of the cuts stemmed from a belief that inflation was acceptable as long as wages were keeping pace with prices. The left viewed cuts to reduce inflationary pressure as equivalent to cuts in the social wage and hence unsocialist. This argument simply missed the point that a high-wage, high-inflation economy, such as many in Latin America, leads to falling working-class living standards, even when public expenditure is also high. The left's failure to recognise the deleterious economic effects of inflation on other aspects of the economy thus contributed to the failure to recognise the necessity of public expenditure cuts in 1976. The left's alternative economic strategy, consequently, never centred upon inflation control because the strictly economic solution – deflating excess demand – was politically unacceptable. In regard to inflation control therefore, the 1974–9 government, while it made plenty of policy mistakes, did adopt a more realistic attitude to the threat of inflation than that proposed by the left.

THE SOURCES OF ECONOMIC POLICY FORMATION

Not even the most committed political opponent of the Labour Government could describe the whole of the 1974–9 period as an economic disaster, nor the most passionate advocate describe the government's record as impeccable. During five and half years of

Labour Government, two Prime Ministers, a major change in trade union leadership, and the trauma of the IMF crisis, policy shifted and changed on numerous occasions. The economic statistics also showed their volatility. The balance of payments deficit was a pitiful and wretched inheritance from the Heath Government but by 1979, largely thanks to North Sea oil and the post-1976 deflation, Britain was finally in surplus. The 1974–9 government deserves credit for this turnaround and arguably more credit than it received during the 1979 election campaign. Inflation, which became a major policy concern for the longest period of time in post-war policy management, stood at just below 10 per cent in May 1979 although the trend was upwards after Mr Healey's ill-judged electioneering reflation during 1978. However, the government had presided over nearly 30 per cent inflation in 1975 and it had added to the chronic inflationary problems inherited from the 1970–4 Conservative Government. The record on inflation is therefore a mixed one. On unemployment the government's record in economic terms is again mixed – given the artificial way in which many workers were kept off the unemployment register – which in political terms meant that the government felt confident enough in May 1979 to present a 1·3 million total as a good performance.

Before looking in greater detail at the picture presented by the statistics between 1974–9, it is worth analysing the sources of policy-making in view of the competing theories of where exactly in the British system of government power to affect the economy really lies.[17] The first, and perhaps the most essential point, is that the government was sufficiently in charge of policy to bear responsibility for both successes and failures. The Prime Minister in Cabinet, whatever the extraneous influences on him, essentially approved of the direction of policy. On some occasions the Prime Minister went further, specifying policy detail, for example Jim Callaghan during the last months of 1976 and again in the adoption of the 5 per cent pay policy for Stage IV. The cabinet ministers' alternative of either backing the Prime Minister or threatening resignations was often resolved in terms of reluctant acquiescence. Spending ministers continually faced this dilemma and one senior Treasury official recalled that 'the constant criticism of spending ministers was that policy was made by the PM and the Chancellor'.[18] The ministers involved, however, preferred to keep their Cabinet seats. Consequently Cabinet resignations, as opposed to Cabinet leaks, were conspicuous by their absence in the 1974–9 period. Indeed the behaviour of dissident Cabinet members, such as Tony Benn, in ultimately backing the Prime Minister's and the Cabinet's collective decision is testimony, albeit posthumously, to Dick Crossman's thesis that Britain has prime ministerial rather than Cabinet government.

Throughout 1974–9 individual cabinet ministers could do little short of resignation, which they were not prepared to do, to defy prime ministerial policy changes. Harold Wilson effectively butchered the radical industrial strategy and demoted Tony Benn from Industry to the non-job of Energy Secretary. The incomes policy U-turn introduced in July 1975 was evidence of a Wilson–Jones axis which presented the Cabinet with a *fait accompli*. The public expenditure cuts of 1976 which seriously divided the Cabinet, were imposed in accordance with prime ministerial wishes strongly backed up by the Chancellor. The collapse of the Croslandite opposition to the cuts, and subsequent support for Jim Callaghan in the face of ideological scruples, conforms almost exactly to the Crossman theory of prime ministerial power. One senior Treasury official, commenting on the flow of information, recalled that 'it was rare that economic forecasts were released to other ministers not because of the Treasury officials but because of the PM'.[19] Similarly the decision to target 5 per cent as the Stage IV norm originated with Jim Callaghan's trip to Germany and New Year, 1978, broadcast and was essentially unaltered by Cabinet discussion or TUC objections. Ironically, although 1974–9 confirms the trend towards prime ministerial government, the Prime Minister's prerogative of deciding an election date most conducive to his party was denied to Jim Callaghan. No Prime Minister can decree parliamentary arithmetic as he can decree an incomes policy norm.

The trade unions' role in policy formation between 1974 and 1979 depended more on individual union leaders than on institutional links such as those between the TUC and Labour Party. In the early Social Contract period union leaders such as Jack Jones and Hugh Scanlon eclipsed TUC General Secretary Len Murray in working out the legislative detail of the Social Contract. Similarly Jack Jones initiated and delivered the £6 pay policy which brought the Social Contract to an end and enabled the government to introduce incomes policy with ostensible TUC support. Jack Jones's influence on economic policy was therefore considerable but this is not the same as saying that the TUC's influence was considerable. Institutionally the TUC fell in behind Jones whose primary commitment was the political survival of a Labour Government – the same commitment as that of Prime Minister Wilson. It is no coincidence that union influence with the government declined after the retirement of both Jones and Scanlon and culminated in the winter of discontent. The unions demonstrated their power to destroy the 5 per cent policy once it had been imposed but not their influence to prevent its original adoption. Such an approach was arguably the antithesis of the 1974–5 Social Contract spirit of cooperation. While the unions undoubtedly possessed the industrial power to affect government economic policy Taylor is right to argue that 'the influence of the unions on Labour in the 1970s was much exaggerated'.[20]

The role and the extent of the power of the Treasury in policy formation has attracted much controversy in relation to the 1974–9 period, particularly since the publication of *Inside the Treasury* by Joel Barnett. Harold Wilson recalled that 'in the Treasury were a very arcane set of people . . . their figures weren't always accurate. There was an undue preponderance of classics graduates and numeracy wasn't regarded as essential for a long time.'[21] Most criticisms of the Treasury, however, usually focus on specific policy responsibilities. To many on the Labour left the Treasury is the principal villain of the monetarist direction of policy, a point strongly denied by Treasury Minister Robert Sheldon who recalled that 'the Treasury wasn't the villain – everyone always said nasty things about the Treasury'.[22] However, as Joel Barnett's book indicates, the Treasury constantly clashed with spending ministers so it is not difficult to imagine that the Labour left, and sometimes the party as a whole, suspected the Treasury's intentions in relation to public spending. Thus one Tribunite MP recalled that 'Joel [Barnett] became institutionalised. The leakers in the spending ministries made it easy for him. He knew all the figures including the fall-back when spending ministers came to see him.'[23] Mr Barnett has since confirmed such leaking.[24]

However, as with the influence of the unions, the influence of the Treasury was dependent largely on the individuals concerned. One senior Treasury official, who was sceptical of monetarist economics, put it that 'it's wrong to ascribe a monolithic view to the Treasury'.[25] The Treasury, particularly over public expenditure cuts in 1976, was split between hawks such as Derek Mitchell and doves such as Sir Douglas Wass. Similarly the Treasury was reluctant to adopt cash limits in 1977 because a number of senior officials were wedded to a basically Keynesian view of the economy. Denis Healey, assessing his own five and a half years at the Treasury, thus recalled that:

> We've got more effective control of public expenditure than any previous government. Joel Barnett has been the main figure here. The cash limit system, *which was resisted by the Treasury at the time* [emphasis added] has been immensely valuable. We've also – and this has been a matter of political will, rather than new machinery – made sure that the contingency reserve is not exceeded.[26]

The Permanent Secretary, Sir Douglas Wass, is correctly regarded as the most enthusiastic proponent of the Keynesian approach. Joel Barnett commented that 'Wass was the nearest to an unreconstructed Keynesian'[27] and one Treasury official summed up 'the Treasury's position as a whole being in the "unbelieving monetarist" category. Douglas Wass was an "unbelieving monetarist" '.[28]

Treasury advice, 1974–9, though influential was far from decisive with the government especially as the Treasury itself was far from united on policy methods. The one particular occasion when the Treasury did make policy – without the approval of Prime Minister Harold Wilson[29] – the result was disastrous. This concerned the 4 March 1976 selling of sterling on a falling market which unleashed the crisis which culminated in the IMF medicine. Wilson noted in his memoirs that 'it was only later that I learnt that the markets had for long heard rumours that the Treasury had been harbouring a fetish based on a belief that the real value of the £ should be $1·88. Perhaps they were right but it was *in fact contrary to what the Chancellor believed and to his words of reassurance* [emphasis added].'[30]

Similarly a further example of Treasury influence, though on this occasion with the government's approval, occurred over the 1976 July measures when the Treasury omitted at a late stage a commitment to a 12 per cent limit on monetary growth for 1976–7. The damaging effects of this omission aggravated the sterling crisis, by further undermining confidence in the pound. Overall the Treasury's record, 1974–9, is less than distinguished though not for the reasons advocated on the left. If the left wish to find a bogey figure for the emergence of monetarism as official government policy a more plausible example would be the City, which welcomed money supply targets, rather than the Treasury.[31]

As has already been noted the Labour Party in Parliament, and particularly the left, rebelled against government policy on numerous occasions between 1974 and 1979. Potentially backbench rebellions can devastate government policy and backbenchers can secure at least important concessions to prevent an embarrassing government defeat. The rebellion in 1969 over *In Place of Strife* had demonstrated the power of Labour MPs to affect key aspects of government policy.[32] During 1974–9 backbench rebels did succeed in changing some government policies – such as Rooker and Wise in 1977 and the vote against sanctions in 1978 – but the effect of a number of rebellions was mitigated by the succeeding vote of confidence. In this way Public Expenditure White Papers, which were repeatedly defeated by left-wing rebels, were made into votes of confidence so that the rebels would not be prepared to precipitate a general election. Moreover, away from the power of the division lobbies to change or influence government economic policy, the left had no success in convincing the government to adopt the alternative economic strategy. On the question of import controls even Jack Jones bemoaned that 'Dell, Healey and Shore were opposed to import controls even though there was a clear case against the Japanese. I tried and tried again to persuade them.'[33] The parliamentary left were scarcely likely to be more persuasive. With hindsight it may be argued that the government's overall success at deflecting the policy recommendation of both the parliamentary and the extra-parliamentary left contributed greatly to the left's attempts since 1979 to secure greater power over not only policy formation but also the hierarchical structure of power within the party.

Finally what can be concluded from the IMF as a policy source 1974–9? The simple answer is that the IMF came to control policy over and above the Prime Minister, Cabinet, unions, Treasury and parliamentary party. However, unlike such permanent policy influences – with which any government has to contend – the IMF conditions represented a one-off policy input. In this way the IMF medicine may be seen as a policy consequence rather than a policy source. Recourse to the IMF was ultimately not the IMF's decision but the British Government's. While it may be argued that failures in government policy led to the IMF crisis it does not follow that the existence of IMF borrowing facilities leads, necessarily, to policy catastrophe. The IMF's policy input is ultimately an example of prime ministerial power given the original Cabinet opposition. Defying the IMF may have been as rational a course as pretending that 2 + 2 equalled 5 but this does not prove that the IMF, or the laws of mathematics, were policy sources. Rather, the IMF conditions were policy outcomes of political decisions taken during 1974–6.

A similar argument can be made in relation to the EEC and NATO. Britain's membership of both organisations necessitated financial sacrifices in other areas of domestic policy, and as such affected policy, but, while such obligations were consistent with the government's political aims, they cannot be counted as direct economic policy sources. In principle the recourse to the IMF was the same even though the policy implications were extensive. The public expenditure cuts imposed by the IMF were not imposed unilaterally from outside; instead they followed directly, as consequences of government policy and Treasury mismanagement. The IMF crisis demonstrated that political ambitions cannot indefinitely defy international economic realities. The IMF loan and conditions were one policy option while hyperinflation, a collapsed pound and mass unemployment were the other. The final policy decision to choose the former was the government's not the IMF's. The lessons of 1974–9 demonstrate that, whatever influences on policy formation there were, either internal or external, the ultimate responsibility for policy direction lay with the government and, in an age of reduced collective Cabinet authority, with the Prime Minister. The IMF episode confirms, rather than refutes, the Crossman thesis.

THE OVERALL ECONOMIC RECORD

The government's record in 1974–9 was a mixed one. Whatever the policy nadirs of 1976, Mr Callaghan bequeathed to the Conservatives a more promising inheritance than that of utter disaster which Mr Wilson inherited from Mr Heath. The most valuable contribution of the 1974–9 government was arguably not in any specific policy at all but in the change of intellectual direction in the latter months of 1976 away from Keynesian economics towards what is known as monetarism. While it may rightly be objected that 1978 saw a policy reversal in this context it did not see an intellectual retreat to the simplistic Father Christmas economics of crude Keynesianism which dominated the Social Contract period. The most well-known intellectual rejection of post-war Keynesian demand management came from Jim Callaghan at the 1976 Labour Party Conference and his speech certainly marks a watershed in attitudes to the expectations and effectiveness of government stimulus to the economy. The public expenditure cuts of 1976, and the subsequent economic recovery, both intellectually and practically, demolished 'Croslandism', 'Butskellism', 'the middle way' and 'consensus politics'. The Conservative Party leadership's commitment to sound money policies was intensified and in the Labour Party the choice effectively became that of supporting the government or embracing the left's alternative socialist strategy.

The change in attitudes and ideologies after 1976 was possibly the most profound in contemporary British politics since that engendered by the 1945–51 Labour Government which laid the foundations of the modern welfare state. This is not to say that monetarism became an establishment, still less a Conservative Party, orthodoxy. After 1976 Keynesian reflationists have still advocated such policies as expansion-cum-incomes policy, occasionally in conjunction with more socialist aims. However the context into which such policy suggestions are now put is radically different from pre-1976 and many in the Labour Party are not likely to forget the lessons of 1974–6 despite a Parliament, or longer, in opposition.

In specific terms the post-1976 change of approach saw reducing inflation regarded as the prime policy objective ahead of full employment. Partly the change had been presaged by Jack Jones's fears in 1975 that inflation would destroy the Labour Government but after 1976, as many on the left regret, inflation control *officially* eclipsed reducing unemployment.[34] The 1974–9 government deserves praise for the way it reduced inflation from the near 30 per cent levels of 1975 to the single figures of 1978–9. More than any other policy success this contributed to the economic well-being of the British people when economic circumstances were generally difficult. To be sure the 1978 reflation, which led to the Thatcher Government facing 20 per cent inflation levels in 1979–80, was regrettable but understandable given the government's electoral situation. It is a price to pay – quite rightly – in a democracy, that elected politicians try to satisfy electoral demands in the short term that are in the long term economically unjustifiable. Perhaps it can be concluded from the issues of the 1979 election that the electorate's demands have shifted more in favour of price stability than politicians thought in 1978.

The 1974–9 Labour Government also deserves credit for not being blown off course by the unemployment bogey which distracted the Heath Government.[35] With the exception of the government's industrial strategy, which really only disguised unemployment through subsidised overmanning, the government did not panic when the unemployment figures crossed the politically sensitive one million barrier. The government was rightly oblivious to the politically inspired 'right to work' demonstrators.

It is not the purpose of this account to repeat familiar arguments which show that the official figures grossly overestimate the scale and nature of unemployment.[36] However it is relevant to the record of the 1974–9 Labour Government to point out that in May 1979, 94·5 per cent of the working population were employed compared to a mere 5·5 per cent who were not. This scarcely represents an economic imbalance meriting such policies as inflating the economy which penalise the 94·5 per cent. Moreover labour shortages existed in many parts of the country in 1979 with regard to postmen, milkmen, construction workers, bus and tube drivers and secretarial assistants. Demand deficiency leading to unemployment was conspicuous by its absence between 1974 and 1979. On the contrary the unemployment that did exist originated in such factors as skills mismatched, trade union restrictive practices, and the relationship between social security, taxation and the willingness to work.[37]

With regard to the industrial strategy the government's employment subsidy policy does deserve censure. The colossal subsidisation of British Leyland, Chrysler, British Steel, British Rail and a variety of 'job creation' schemes kept public expenditure higher than it otherwise would have been or else transferred resources from other areas of the public sector such as health and education. The gain in terms of jobs saved was entirely illusory if such jobs were not justified in terms of providing products which would ultimately satisfy a customer. Not only is such subsidisation a waste of scarce financial resources it is also a cheat on those whose jobs are allegedly 'saved' by bolstering the very industrial fossilisation which will ultimately create no more employment. The absence of any consideration of product range by the government or the Department of Trade and Industry is the most striking testimony to the futility of the jobs subsidisation policy.

The economically damaging aspects of such an industrial strategy cannot be explained away in terms of the political embarrassment the government would have encountered if the unemployment figures had risen further. The problems of over-manning and the subsidisation of non-jobs simply passed the political buck to the Thatcher Government and in economic terms held back the development of new industries, particularly in the service sector.

Such subsidisation was particularly ironic in view of the growth of the black economy – which is good for the economy but bad for the exchequer – and the growth of the female labour force. The latter factor highlighted that the industrial strategy of the government was essentially subsidising unionised, male, manu-facturing employment while the growth areas of the economy had to rely upon an increasingly non-unionised female labour force. As the former Director of Statistics at the Department of Employment has noted:

> The great change in the labour force has been in the number of women, particularly married women. This is almost entirely due to the tremendous increase in the proportion of married women working, particularly the proportion who return to work after having their families. The participation rates for married women in Britain are amongst the highest in the countries of the industrial West, and so far have confounded each successive forecast by rising even more than expected. This has been especially true within the last few years, when an unprecedented fall in the birth rate has made more married women available for employment, and when equal pay legisla-tion has increased the incentive to seek work.[38]

The clear fact emerges that the government was subsidising past jobs rather than present or future ones. The money spent on jobs subsidy would have been better used if spent on educational or retraining purposes which furthered, rather than held back, the deindustrialisation of the economy. As Nossiter has pointed out, such a policy is enormously beneficial in exploiting Britain's comparative advantage in world markets.[39]

Similarly the growth of Britain's black economy contrasted sharply with the mentality of jobs subsidisation to prevent unemployment. In March 1979, barely weeks from the fall of the Labour Government, Sir William Pile, the Chairman of the Board of the Inland Revenue, estimated that the black economy accounted for $7\frac{1}{2}$ per cent of the entire economy or £11 billion of income each year escaping income tax. Moonlighting, not only by the unemployed, but by those in work, had become a distinctive feature of the British economy by the late 1970s. Thus Sir Marcus Sieff the chairman of Marks and Spencer discovered that the boom in sales in alleged areas of high unemployment was attributable to the extent of moonlighting, in this particular case largely by the unemployed.[40] In view of the unofficial expanding areas of the economy, which contributed to the total GDP, the government's industrial strategy of jobs subsidisation was an attempt to avoid a kind of unemployment that was swiftly vanishing.

Whatever the loss to the Exchequer, which can be made up in other ways, the government would have been better advised to welcome the growth of the productive and profitable black economy rather than subsidise such unprofitable and declining industries as shipbuilding, railways and BL. The rechannelling of money previously used for subsidy would have enabled cuts in the PSBR, cuts in taxation, greater resources for other public sector services, or a combination of all three.

Part of the government's failure in relation to the industrial strategy was not only the political aim of minimising the official unemployment statistics but also the economic aim of increasing investment. The jobs subsidy schemes were the apotheosis of the investment mentality. Whatever can be said of BL or British Steel, lack of investment was not the problem. The real failure lay in an inadequate rate of return on investment because the investment itself was in an inadequate product range. It is a cliche to say that 'we invest to live not live to invest' but it is none the less true. The 1974–9 industrial strategy – and the more extensive policy option of the left – simply failed to recognise this aspect of reality. As with the reflationary plans of Keynesian economics, the industrial strategy's failure proved that good intentions, and extensive public investment, by themselves are not enough.

No overall assessment would be complete without a mention of the balance of payments, sterling and the IMF crisis. The government's handling of the 1976 crisis itself is open to considerable criticism, mitigated, to be sure, by the Treasury's culpability. However the balance of payments surplus bequeathed to the Thatcher Government represents a herculean transformation of which ministers could be proud even allowing for the contribution of North Sea oil. The 1964–70 Wilson Government has been repeatedly criticised for its obsession with the external balance[41] but the government's error, 1974–6, was insufficient attention to the effects of reflationary policies on the deficit which led to consequences far more serious than those of 1964–70. In the context of this early neglect, the surplus of 1979 and the overall economic stabilisation are creditable.

Finally it is appropriate to conclude with the government's record of dealing with the unions and incomes policy since the failures of the Heath Government in such matters helped to bring about the Labour Government in March 1974. The series of events which led from the Social Contract to the winter of discontent can partly be explained by the changing personnel of ministers and union leaders. It can be explained in terms of the power the trade unions possess – and were encouraged to possess by the 1974–9 government – so that government policy can be destroyed by industrial militancy. But arguably the most important lesson that arises from union–government relations in this period concerns the philosophy of compulsory incomes policy itself. The 'success' of initial stages was followed, as in previous incomes policies, by an ultimate disintegration that was damaging both in terms of individual strike action and in terms of 'consensus' politics. Once again incomes policy proved to have little positive to contribute in terms of reducing inflation and much damage to inflict in other ways, not least to the concept of the rule of law.

The 5 per cent pay norm was not the only casualty of the winter of discontent. The relationship between the government and the unions suffered in a way that would have been unthinkable only three years before. The public's dislike of blatant, rather than merely covert, trade union abuses of power reached a level previously unknown. The Labour Party itself was the final casualty as a national swing of 5·2 per cent put Mrs Thatcher into office. Despite such calamities for the government in the last months in office, the overall verdict on 1974–9 is that the record was a mixed one.

Notes and References

CHAPTER I

1. For a comprehensive analysis of the Heath Government see M. Holmes, *Political Pressure and Economic Policy: British Government, 1970–4* (London: Butterworths, 1982).
2. Interview, Sir Harold Wilson.
3. Interview, Reg Prentice.
4. Harold Wilson, *Final Term: the Labour Government, 1974–6* (London: Weidenfeld & Nicolson, Michael Joseph, 1979).
5. Barbara Castle, *The Castle Diaries, 1974–6* (London: Weidenfeld & Nicolson, 1980).
6. H. Wilson, op cit., p. 22.
7. Interview, Sir Harold Wilson.
8. For a full account of the dispute see M. Holmes, op. cit., ch. 7.
9. B. Castle, op. cit., p. 39.
10. See M. Hatfield, *The House the Left Built* (London: Gollancz, 1978) for a full account.
11. Geoff Hodgson, *Labour at the Crossroads* (Oxford: Martin Robertson, 1981) p. 96.
12. See M. Holmes, op. cit., ch. 3, for a full account of this period.
13. Quoted in David Coates, *Labour in Power? A Study of the Labour Government, 1974–9* (London: Longmans, 1980) p. 4.
14. Interview, Albert Booth.
15. B. Castle, op. cit., p. 61.
16. Interview, senior Treasury official.
17. W. Keegan and R. Pennant-Rae, *Who Runs the Economy? Control and Influence in British Economic Policy* (London: Temple-Smith, 1979) p. 31.
18. Joel Barnett, *Inside the Treasury* (London: Andre Deutsch, 1982) p. 23.
19. Interview, Robert Sheldon.
20. H. Wilson, op. cit., p. 26.
21. J. Barnett, op. cit., p. 24.
22. The threshold payments, which Labour had supported when in Opposition, led to three payments with the publications of the RPI in May 1974.
23. H. Wilson, op. cit., p. 28.
24. Samuel Brittan, *The Economic Consequences of Democracy* (London: Temple-Smith, 1977) p. 80.
25. J. Barnett, op. cit., p. 32.
26. B. Castle, op. cit., p. 50.
27. Ibid., p. 150.
28. Interview, Reg Prentice.
29. Interview, Stanley Orme.
30. Interview, Robert Sheldon. For a useful view of union-government

relations in this period see Robert Taylor, *The Fifth Estate: Britain's Unions in the Modern World* (London: Pan, 1980) ch. 4.

31. Interview, Ian Mikardo.
32. S. Brittan, op. cit., p. 77.
33. Denis Barnes and Eileen Reid, *Government and Trade Unions: The British Experience, 1964–79* (London: Heinemann, 1980) pp. 199–200.
34. H. Wilson, op. cit., p. 44.
35. D. Coates, op. cit., p. 62.
36. B. Castle, op. cit., p. 119.
37. Interview, Albert Booth.
38. Interview, Reg Prentice.
39. Interview, Ian Mikardo.
40. H. Wilson, op. cit., p. 83.
41. Interview, Robert Sheldon.
42. H. Wilson, op. cit., p. 84.
43. J. Barnett, op. cit., pp. 31–2.
44. J. Barnett, op. cit., p. 32.
45. H. Wilson, op. cit., p. 85.

CHAPTER II

1. Interview, Lord Scanlon.
2. Interview, Ian Mikardo.
3. B. Castle, op. cit., p. 224.
4. Barnes and Reid, op. cit., pp. 201–2.
5. Interview, cabinet minister.
6. D. Coates, op. cit., p. 29.
7. J. Barnett, op. cit., p. 34.
8. Interview, former Treasury official.
9. B. Castle, op. cit., pp. 352–4.
10. J. Barnett, op. cit., p. 64.
11. Interview, Treasury minister.
12. H. Wilson, op. cit., p. 112.
13. B. Castle, op. cit., p. 372.
14. Barnes and Reid, op. cit., p. 202.
15. B. Castle, op. cit., p. 336.
16. B. Castle, op. cit., pp. 283–4.
17. Interview, Jack Jones.
18. Interview, senior Treasury official.
19. Interview, Albert Booth.
20. Interview, Joel Barnett.
21. Interview, Sir H. Wilson.
22. Barnes and Reid, op. cit., p. 205.
23. See B. Castle, op. cit., pp. 410–11, for an interesting eye witness account of Mr Benn's reaction to his demotion.
24. Ibid., p. 426.
25. H. Wilson, op. cit., pp. 115–16.
26. Keegan and Pennant-Rae, op. cit., p. 159.
27. Interview, Neil Kinnock.

28. Interview, Albert Booth.
29. Interview, Stanley Orme.
30. Interview, Lord Scanlon.
31. Interview, Jeremy Bray.
32. See M. Holmes, op. cit., chs 4–7 for a full and detailed account of this policy.
33. S. Brittan and P. Lilley, *The Delusion of Incomes Policy* (London: Temple-Smith, 1977) p. 176.
34. Ibid., p. 174.
35. Ibid., p. 175.
36. Interview, Stanley Orme.

CHAPTER III

1. To continue my earlier analogy, the corresponding attitude in the Conservative Party would concern NATO, the questioning of which would incur similar displeasure.
2. Quoted in D. Coates, op. cit., pp. 86–7.
3. For a lucid and enlightening account of the development of thinking on the left, see Alan Budd, *The Politics of Economic Planning* (London: Fontana, 1978) ch. 7.
4. H. Wilson, op. cit., p. 33.
5. D. Coates, op. cit., p. 91.
6. See pp. 44–54.
7. D. Coates, op. cit., p. 98.
8. Wyn Grant, *The Political Economy of Industrial Policy* (London: Butterworths, 1982) p. 105.
9. Interview, Dennis Skinner.
10. Interview, Joe Ashton.
11. H. Wilson, op. cit., pp. 143–4.
12. Interview, Neil Kinnock.
13. B. Castle, op. cit., pp. 410–11.
14. Interview, Lord Peart.
15. Interview, Jeremy Bray.
16. J. Barnett, op. cit., p. 35.
17. Ibid., pp. 72–3.
18. H. Wilson, op. cit., p. 139.
19. B. Castle, op. cit., pp. 374–5.
20. Reported in the *Guardian* (12 Sept. 1978). Similarly in February 1978 Leyland recalled over 180 000 cars sold in America including Jaguars, Marinas and Triumph sports cars, to correct defects involving fuel leaks, throttle linkages, headlamp switches and windscreen washers and wipers.
21. The author, who has owned at various times, a Morris 1100, Austin 1300 and Marina 1·3, can speak from experience of this safety defect.
22. *Guardian* (8 Feb. 1979).
23. *Guardian* (30 Sept. 1977).
24. *Guardian* (26 Oct. 1977).
25. J. Barnett, op. cit., p. 74.
26. W. Grant, op. cit., p. 58.
27. Interview, Lord Lever.

28. Interview, Robert Sheldon.
29. Interview, Albert Booth.
30. B. Castle, op. cit., p. 545.
31. J. Barnett, op. cit., p. 73.
32. Interview, Lord Lever.
33. Interview, cabinet minister.
34. Interview, Jack Jones.
35. *Observer* (13 Aug. 1978).
36. *Guardian* (29 Sept. 1978).
37. Interview, Neil Kinnock.
38. Interview, junior minister.
39. *Guardian* (5 Dec. 1977).
40. Interview, Albert Booth.
41. Interview, Stanley Orme.
42. To Marxists like David Coates (see *Labour in Power?*, pp. 130–1, for example), the answer is simply to abolish world capitalism, although how this is to be done and what would replace it is barely discussed.
43. See M. Holmes, op. cit., pp. 40–2, for a detailed description of the Heath Government's rescue of Rolls Royce in 1971.
44. *The Times* (13 Dec. 1977).
45. See M. Holmes, op. cit., pp. 42–4 for a full account.
46. *Guardian* (28 Feb. 1979).
47. *Guardian* (1 March 1979).
48. *Guardian* (3 March 1979).
49. S. Brittan, op. cit., pp. 153–4.
50. A. Budd, op. cit., pp. 139–40.
51. W. A. P. Manser, *Britain in Balance* (Harmondsworth: Penguin Books, 1973) pp. 17–18.
52. Bernard Nossiter, *Britain: a Future that Works* (London: Andre Deutsch, 1978) pp. 92–3.
53. B. Nossiter, ibid., p. 197.

CHAPTER IV

1. B. Castle, op. cit., p. 558.
2. Samuel Brittan in *Incomes Policy*, ed. Robin Chater *et al.* (Oxford University Press, 1982) p. 174.
3. B. Castle, op. cit., p. 559.
4. *Guardian* (2 Oct. 1975).
5. B. Castle, op. cit., p. 512.
6. Interview, Treasury minister.
7. J. Barnett, op. cit., p. 79.
8. Interview, Dennis Skinner.
9. B. Castle, op. cit., pp. 548–9.
10. J. Barnett, op. cit., pp. 80–2.
11. B. Castle, op. cit., p. 682.
12. Denis Healey's abrasiveness in his speech has been widely regarded as contributing to his defeat in the subsequent leadership battle.
13. J. Barnett, op. cit., p. 84.

14. Quoted in *Callaghan: The Road to No. 10* by Peter Kellner and Christopher Hitchens (London: Cassell, 1976) pp. 167–8.
15. Interview, Reg Prentice.
16. B. Castle, op. cit., pp. 689–90.
17. Interview, Jack Jones.
18. Interview, Lord Peart.
19. H. Wilson, op. cit., p. 239.
20. Interview, Jeremy Bray.
21. B. Castle, op. cit., p. 672.
22. H. Wilson, op. cit., pp. 267–8.

CHAPTER V

1. See P. Kellner and C. Hitchens, op. cit., ch. 15, and J. Barnett, op. cit., ch. 8 for more detailed accounts of the campaign.
2. Kellner and Hitchens, op. cit.
3. *Private Eye* (2 April 1976).
4. Interview, Robert Sheldon.
5. Interview, Ian Mikardo.
6. Interview, Sir Harold Wilson.
7. Interview, Peter Jay.
8. Interview, senior Treasury official.
9. Interview, Treasury official.
10. Interview, Treasury minister.
11. Interview, cabinet minister.
12. Interview, former Treasury official.
13. Interview, Treasury official.
14. H. Wilson, op. cit., p. 227.
15. Stephen Fay and Hugo Young, *The Day the £ Nearly Died* (London: Sunday Times Publications, 1978) p. 11.
16. H. Wilson, op. cit., p. 227.
17. Interview, cabinet minister.
18. Interview, Treasury official.
19. According to Fay and Young, Harold Lever shared this view.
20. Fay and Young, op. cit., p. 11.
21. Interview, Treasury official.
22. Interview, former Treasury official.
23. Keegan and Pennant-Rae, op. cit., p. 162.
24. Quoted in Fay and Young, pp. 12–13.
25. J. Barnett, op. cit., p. 88.
26. Brittan and Lilley, op. cit., p. 25.
27. S. Brittan in *Incomes Policy*, p. 174.
28. Interview, Tribune Group MP.
29. Interview, Jeremy Bray.
30. Interview, Reg Prentice.
31. Fay and Young, op. cit., p. 14.
32. Interview, Treasury minister.
33. Interview, Treasury official.
34. Keegan and Pennant-Rae, op. cit., p. 163.

35. S. Brittan, op. cit., p. 88.
36. Interview, cabinet minister.
37. Fay and Young, op. cit., pp. 14–15.
38. See J. Barnett, op. cit., p. 89.
39. Ibid.
40. Fay and Young, op. cit., p. 16.
41. Ibid., p. 16.
42. Interview, former Treasury official.
43. Interview, Albert Booth.
44. Fay and Young, op. cit., p. 18.
45. Interview, cabinet minister.
46. Interview, former Treasury official.
47. S. Brittan, op. cit., p. 89.
48. Interview, Peter Jay.
49. Fay and Young, op. cit., p. 20.
50. Interview, cabinet minister.
51. Keegan and Pennant-Rae, op. cit., p. 167.
52. Interview, Treasury official.
53. Interview, Albert Booth.
54. Interview, Stanley Orme.
55. Fay and Young, op. cit., p. 24.
56. Interview, former Treasury official.
57. J. Barnett, op. cit., p. 97.
58. Interview, cabinet minister.
59. Interview, Robert Sheldon.
60. Fay and Young, op. cit., p. 37.
61. Interview, Neil Kinnock.
62. Fay and Young, op. cit., p. 38.
63. Interview, Lord Peart.
64. Interview, Albert Booth.
65. Interview, junior minister.
66. Interview, Reg Prentice.
67. J. Barnett, op. cit., p. 105.
68. Interview, cabinet minister.
69. Fay and Young, op. cit., pp. 40–1.
70. Interview, Stanley Orme.
71. Interview, Jeremy Bray.
72. Interview, Neil Kinnock.
73. J. Barnett, op. cit., p. 106.
74. Interview, Jack Jones.
75. Interview, cabinet minister.
76. Interview, Lord Peart.
77. Interview, Treasury minister.
78. Interview, Lord Scanlon.
79. Interview, Joel Barnett.
80. Interview, Ian Mikardo.

CHAPTER VI

1. For a full account see *The Pact: the Inside Story of the Lib-Lab Government, 1977–8,* by Alistair Michie and Simon Hoggart (London, Quartet, 1978).
2. David Steel, 'An Experiment in Power', *Observer* (8 April 1979).
3. Ibid.
4. See J. Barnett, op. cit., p. 116.
5. Interview, Neil Kinnock.
6. Interview, Stanley Orme.
7. D. Steel, op. cit.
8. J. Barnett, op. cit.
9. For a highly critical account of Jones's conduct at the conference see *Private Eye* (2 Sept. 1977) p. 19.
10. Interview, Treasury minister.
11. Cmnd. 6882 (London: HMSO, 1977).
12. Barnes and Reid, op. cit., p. 212.
13. Interview, Jack Jones.
14. Interview, Treasury official.
15. Interview, Albert Booth.
16. Interview, junior minister.
17. Interview, Robert Sheldon.
18. Interview, Lord Scanlon.
19. Interview, Jack Jones.
20. Anthony King in *Britain at the Polls, 1979,* ed. Howard R. Penniman (Washington, DC: American Enterprise Institute, 1981) p. 55.
21. *Sunday Times* (25 Sept. 1977).
22. See M. Holmes, op. cit., chs 4 and 5.
23. In October 1977 the long-term unemployed, defined as those unemployed for over one year, totalled only 324 000.
24. Interview, Jeremy Bray.
25. Interview, Joe Ashton.
26. J. Barnett, op. cit., p. 50.
27. *Guardian* (26 Sept. 1977).
28. *Guardian* (27 Sept. 1977).
29. *Guardian* (27 Oct. 1979).

CHAPTER VII

1. Interview, Lord Scanlon.
2. *Daily Telegraph* (22 Dec. 1977).
3. *Guardian* (9 Jan. 1978).
4. Cmnd. 7049 (London: HMSO, 1978).
5. J. Barnett, op. cit., p. 141.
6. Michie and Hoggart, op. cit., p. 171.
7. Interview, senior Treasury official.
8. Interview, Treasury official.
9. *Guardian* (12 April 1978).
10. Michie and Hoggart, op. cit., p. 172.
11. *Guardian* (30 Dec. 1977).

12. *Guardian* (3 Jan. 1978).
13. Interview, Treasury minister.
14. Interview, senior Treasury official.
15. Interview, Treasury official.
16. Interview, Robert Sheldon.
17. *Guardian* (5 Jan. 1978).
18. *Guardian* (15 May 1978).
19. See Barnes and Reid, pp. 212–15 for a presentation of views within the unions.
20. Mr Duffy took over formally in October 1978.
21. Interview, Robert Sheldon.
22. Interview, Jack Jones.
23. Keegan and Pennant-Rae, op. cit., p. 187.
24. Cmnd. 7293 (London: HMSO, 1978).
25. J. Barnett, op. cit., pp. 162–3.
26. Interview, Stanley Orme.
27. Ibid.
28. Interview, Joel Barnett.
29. Interview, Sir Harold Wilson.
30. Interview, cabinet minister.
31. Interview, Neil Kinnock.
32. Interview, Joe Ashton.
33. See *Britain at the Polls, 1979*, ed. Howard R. Penniman, pp. 95–101 for an excellent description of the decision to delay the election.
34. *The Times* (20 July 1978).
35. *Guardian* (7 Sept. 1978).
36. J. Barnett, op. cit., p. 154.
37. Interview, Joe Ashton.
38. Interview, Stanley Orme.
39. Interview, Robert Sheldon.
40. *Guardian* (8 Sept. 1978).
41. Interview, Joel Barnett.
42. Dick Leonard, in *Britain at the Polls, 1979*, ed. Penniman, p. 99.
43. See 'The Go Stop Prime Minister', *Sunday Times* (Sept. 1978) for a contemporary analysis of the decision to delay.
44. For the best analysis of this aspect of Callaghan's character see the *Crossman Diaries* in general and the 23 November 1964 entry in particular describing Callaghan as 'heavy and gloomy as ever . . . obviously overawed and full of self-pity'.
45. Interview, Ian Mikardo.
46. Interview, junior minister.
47. Interview, Reg Prentice.
48. Interview, Lord Scanlon.

CHAPTER VIII

1. *Guardian* (26 Sept. 1978).
2. J. Barnett, op. cit., p. 164.
3. Quoted in J. Barnett, op. cit., p. 165.

4. *Observer* (7 Jan. 1979).

5. Barnes and Reid, op. cit., p. 217.

6. See M. Holmes, op. cit., pp. 133–6.

7. *Guardian* (11 Jan. 1979).

8. J. Barnett, op. cit., p. 170.

9. Interview, Sir Harold Wilson.

10. *Guardian* (17 Jan. 1979).

11. J. Barnett, op. cit., p. 173.

12. See Robert Taylor 'NUPE: The Four-Letter Union', *Observer* (4 Feb. 1979).

13. J. Barnett, op. cit., p. 175.

14. Interview, cabinet minister.

15. Interview, Robert Sheldon.

16. Interview, Lord Peart.

17. Interview, Joe Ashton.

18. Interview, Neil Kinnock.

19. Interview, Lord Scanlon.

20. Interview, trade union leader.

21. Interview, Albert Booth.

22. Barnes and Reid, op. cit., p. 217.

23. The miners, arguably the most powerful union in Britain, settled for 9 per cent, for example.

24. The Commission was ultimately to be headed by Professor Hugh Clegg.

25. Quoted in the *Observer* (11 Feb. 1979).

26. J. Barnett, op. cit., p. 177.

27. *Guardian* (24 Feb. 1979).

28. For two excellent accounts of civil service privilege see David Porter 'Is the Civil Servant a Public Enemy?', *Guardian* (13 March 1979), and *Your Disobedient Servant* by Leslie Chapman (Harmondsworth: Penguin Books, 1979).

29. J. Barnett, op. cit., p. 178.

30. *Guardian* (7 March 1979).

31. Interview, junior minister.

32. H. Wilson, op. cit., p. 241.

33. See M. Holmes, op. cit., pp. 146–7.

34. S. Brittan, in *Incomes Policy*, p. 179.

35. Jack Jones, *The Human Face of Labour* (London: BBC Publications, 1977) p. 7.

36. Barnes and Reid, op. cit., p. 219.

37. G. Hodgson, op. cit., p. 122.

38. Interview, Albert Booth.

39. Anthony King in *Britain at the Polls, 1979*, ed. Penniman, p. 83.

CHAPTER IX

1. Dick Leonard in *Britain at the Polls, 1979*, ed. Penniman, p. 103. As well as the economy, devolution was a long running issue. Only 32·5 per cent voted in favour of the government's proposals while Parliament had stipulated a 40 per cent yes vote as necessary. In Wales there was a four to one vote against devolution.

2. Leonard, ibid., p. 103.

3. The Unionist group was committed to voting with Mrs Thatcher.

4. *Guardian* (29 March 1979).

5. Ibid.

6. Ivor Crewe in *The Times Guide to the House of Commons, May 1979* (London: Times Books, 1979).

7. *Guardian* (4 March 1979).

8. See David Butler and Dennis Kavanagh, *The British General Election of 1979* (London: Macmillan, 1979) for a comprehensive coverage of the campaign.

9. Labour Manifesto, 1979.

10. Max Beloff and Gillian Peele, *The Government of the United Kingdom: Political Authority in a Changing Society* (London: Weidenfeld & Nicolson, 1980) p. 149.

11. Interview, Albert Booth.

12. Interview, junior minister

13. See M. Holmes, op. cit., pp. 133–6 for a full assessment.

14. Conservative Manifesto, 1979.

15. Ibid.

16. William Livingston, *Britain at the Polls, 1979*, ed. Penniman, p. 122.

17. Arguably Labour won the intellectual argument in that Mrs Thatcher's Government has constantly agonised over public expenditure cuts which allowed either tax reductions or a reduction in the PSBR, but not both.

18. See M. Holmes, op. cit., pp. 6–9.

19. Mr Thorpe's trial, on charges of conspiracy and incitement to murder, was postponed because of the election in which a Liberal majority of 6721 was transformed into a Conservative majority of 8473.

20. Ivor Crewe in *Britain at the Polls, 1979*, ed. Penniman, p. 300.

CHAPTER X

1. In the course of this chapter I am taking the left to mean the extreme left or 'hard left' rather than the centre left or 'soft left'.

2. Interview, Ian Mikardo.

3. Interview, Dennis Skinner.

4. G. Hodgson, op. cit., p. 127.

5. P. Townsend in *Labour and Equality*, p. 23.

6. See particularly D. Coates, op. cit., chs 4–7.

7. Interview, Joe Ashton.

8. Interview, Albert Booth.

9. Interview, Jack Jones.

10. Interview, Neil Kinnock.

11. Evan Luard, *Socialism without the State* (London: Macmillan, 1979) p. 41.

12. Interview, Lord Peart.

13. Such computer predictions so far into the future may be treated with scepticism in the light of the failure of many economic models to predict correctly merely months ahead.

14. Patrick Minford in the *Guardian* (5 Jan. 1978).

15. Any answer to this question must be entirely subjective given the assumed downgrading of consumer choice.

16. Walter Eltis, *Sunday Times* (17 Sept. 1978).

17. For a good introductory analysis to the debate see Keegan and Pennant-Rae, op. cit.

18. Interview, former Treasury official.

19. Interview, former Treasury official.

20. R. Taylor, op. cit., p. 149.

21. Interview, Sir Harold Wilson.

22. Interview, Robert Sheldon.

23. Interview, Neil Kinnock.

24. Interview, Joel Barnett.

25. Interview, senior Treasury official.

26. Interview with Frances Cairncross, *Guardian* (15 Feb. 1979).

27. Interview, Joel Barnett.

28. Interview, Treasury official.

29. H. Wilson, op. cit., p. 227.

30. Ibid.

31. Strangely a Marxist critique of 1974–9 such as David Coates's *Labour in Power?*, only once in 300 pages mentions the City.

32. See the *Crossman Diaries*, condensed version (London: Methuen, 1979) p. 625.

33. Interview, Jack Jones.

34. Such official recognition does not mean – even if it erroneously implies – that reducing inflation and reducing unemployment are alternatives. A high inflation rate can damage job prospects as Harold Wilson rightly pointed out in 1975. See H. Wilson, op. cit., pp. 267–8.

35. See M. Holmes, op. cit., ch. 4.

36. For an excellent analysis see Robert Miller and John B. Wood, *What Price Unemployment: an Alternative Approach*, IEA, Hobart Paper 92, 1980.

37. See Frances Cairncross, *Guardian* (17 March 1979) and Peter Bauer, *Observer* (11 March 1979) for detailed descriptions of the unemployment situation in the last months of Labour Government.

38. A. R. Thatcher in *De-industrialisation*, ed. Frank Blackaby (London: Heinemann/NIESR, 1978) p. 27.

39. B. Nossiter, op. cit., pp. 191–201.

40. See the *Guardian* (28 March 1979).

41. See for example *The Labour Government's Economic Record, 1964–70*, ed. Wilfred Beckerman, ch. 1.

Select Bibliography

Denis Barnes and Eileen Reid, *Government and Trade Unions: The British Experience, 1964–79* (London: Heinemann, 1980)

Joel Barnett, *Inside the Treasury* (London: Andre Deutsch, 1982)

Max Beloff and Gillian Peele, *The Government of the United Kingdom: Political Authority in a Changing Society* (London: Weidenfeld & Nicolson, 1980)

Frank Blackaby (ed.), *De-industrialisation* (London: Heinemann/NIESR, 1978)

Samuel Brittan, *The Economic Consequences of Democracy* (London: Temple-Smith, 1977)

S. Brittan and P. Lilley, *The Delusion of Incomes Policy* (London: Temple-Smith, 1977)

Alan Budd, *The Politics of Economic Planning* (London: Fontana, 1978)

David Butler and Dennis Kavanagh, *The British General Election of 1979* (London: Macmillan, 1979)

Barbara Castle, *The Castle Diaries, 1974–6* (London: Weidenfeld & Nicolson, 1980)

Robin Chater, A. Dean and R. F. Elliott, *Incomes Policy* (Oxford University Press, 1982)

David Coates, *Labour in Power? A Study of the Labour Government, 1974–9* (London: Longmans, 1980)

Stephen Fay and Hugo Young, *The Day the £ Nearly Died* (London: Sunday Times Publications, 1978)

Wyn Grant, *The Political Economy of Industrial Policy* (London: Butterworths, 1982)

M. Hatfield, *The House the Left Built* (London: Gollancz, 1978)

Geoff Hodgson, *Labour at the Crossroads* (Oxford: Martin Robertson, 1981)

M. Holmes, *Political Pressure and Economic Policy: British Government, 1970–4* (London: Butterworths, 1982)

Jack Jones, *The Human Face of Labour* (London: BBC Publications, 1977)

W. Keegan and R. Pennant-Rae, *Who Runs the Economy? Control and Influence in British Economic Policy* (London: Temple-Smith, 1979)

Peter Kellner and Christopher Hitchens, *Callaghan: the Road to No. 10* (London: Cassell, 1976)

Evan Luard, *Socialism without the State* (London: Macmillan, 1979)

W. A. P. Manser, *Britain in Balance* (Harmondsworth: Penguin Books, 1973)

Alistair Michie and Simon Hoggart, *The Pact: the Inside Story of the Lib–Lab Government, 1977–8* (London: Quartet, 1978)

Bernard Nossiter, *Britain: a Future that Works* (London: Andre Deutsch, 1978)

Howard R. Penniman (ed.), *Britain at the Polls, 1979* (Washington, DC: American Enterprise Institute, 1981)

Robert Taylor, *The Fifth Estate: Britain's Unions in the Modern World* (London: Pan, 1980)

P. Townsend and N. Bosanquet, *Labour and Equality: a Fabian Study of Labour and Power, 1974–9* (London: Heinemann, 1980)
Harold Wilson, *Final Term: the Labour Government, 1974–6* (London: Weidenfeld & Nicolson, Michael Joseph, 1979)

INDEX